D1452808

Moving to Market:

Restructuring Transport in the Former Soviet Union

Harvard Studies in International Development

Other volumes in the series include:

Reforming Economic Systems in Developing Countries
edited by Dwight H. Perkins and Michael Roemer, 1991

Markets in Developing Countries: Parallel, Fragmented, and Black
edited by Michael Roemer and Christine Jones, 1991*

Progress with Profits: The Development of Rural Banking in Indonesia
by Richard Patten and Jay K. Rosengard, 1991*

Green Markets: The Economics of Sustainable Development
by Theodore Panayotou, 1993*

The Challenge of Reform in Indochina
edited by Borje Ljunggren, 1993

Asia and Africa: Legacies and Opportunities in Development
edited by David L. Lindauer and Michael Roemer, 1994*

Macroeconomic Policy and Adjustment in Korea, 1970–1990
by Stephan Haggard, Richard N. Cooper, Susan Collins, Choongsoo Kim, and Sung–Tae Ro, 1994

Framing Questions, Constructing Answers: Linking Research with Education Policy for Developing Countries
by Noel F. McGinn and Allison M. Borden, 1995

Industrialization and the State: The Korean Heavy and Chemical Industry Drive
by Joseph J. Stern, Ji–hong Kim, Dwight H. Perkins, and Jung–ho Yoo, 1995

*Jointly published by the International Center for Economic Growth.

Moving to Market: Restructuring Transport in the Former Soviet Union

John S. Strong
John R. Meyer

with

Clell G. Harral
Graham Smith

Harvard Institute for International Development
Harvard University

Distributed by Harvard University Press

Published by Harvard Institute for International Development
January 1996

Distributed by Harvard University Press

Editorial Management: Don Lippincott
Editorial Assistance: Sarah Newberry
Design and production: Desktop Publishing & Design Co., Boston, MA

Library of Congress Cataloging-in-Publication Data

Strong, John S.
    Moving to market: restructuring transport in the former Soviet Union / by
John S. Strong, John R. Meyer with Clell G. Harral, Graham Smith.
        p. cm. -- (Harvard studies in international development)
    Includes bibliographical references and index.
    ISBN 0-674-58814-2 (cloth)
    1. Transportation--Former Soviet republics. 2. Transportation and
state--Former republics. 3. Former Soviet republics--Economic
policy. I. Meyer, John Robert. II. Title. III. Series.
HE255 .A2S77 1995
388' .0947--dc20   95-40080
                                                     CIP

Contents

Contributors

John S. Strong
School of Business Administration
College of William and Mary
Williamsburg, Virginia

John R. Meyer
John F. Kennedy School of Government
Harvard University
Cambridge, Massachusetts

with

Clell G. Harral
and
Graham Smith
European Bank for Reconstruction and Development
London, England

Preface

Since the inception of market reforms in the new republics of the former Soviet Union in 1992, the Harvard Institute for International Development has been deeply involved in analyzing options for economic policy and in providing advice to senior policy makers. The new study by John S. Strong and John R. Meyer (with Clell G. Harral and Graham Smith of the European Bank for Reconstruction and Development) on the transport sector of Russia, Ukraine, Kazakhstan, and Belarus, represents an extremely important contribution to this analytical and advisory effort. The authors are world-renowned masters of their trade, for reasons that are evident throughout the text. Their study is a comprehensive and knowledgeable account of the key options facing these countries in transportation policy, as they strive for market reforms and improved economic efficiency.

If there is one overriding theme in the text, it is that transportation policy requires a shift from quantity to quality. As in many other sectors in transition economies, transportation problems are not really ones of physical capacity (except in some particular niches), but rather problems of organizational efficiency and responsiveness to market needs. The authors remind us of the incredible quantitative achievements of the Soviet transport system: a rail network, for example, that carried perhaps one half of the world's rail freight! The authors make clear that despite the gross tonnage-kilometers carried by the system, the quality and usefulness of transport services have fallen vastly below potential, and could become a critical bottleneck to further economic restructuring and growth unless the sector is restructured.

The authors' systematic discussions of each transport mode – air, rail, road, water – are models of clarity and rigor. Transport services vary enormously in terms of market organization, technology, administration, and in the appropriate role for government in the efficient operation of the sector. For all sectors, appropriate pricing and incentives are vital to eliminate enormous wastes (such as the inappropriate choice of transport mode, long queuing times, ineffi- cient storage facilities, insufficient means for inter-modal shipping). Also, all transport sectors still suffer from an excessive vertical integration and monopolization of transport services. For example, airports and airlines are jointly owned, while trucking conglomerates control fuel supplies, terminals, and maintenance facilities.

The authors note that different organization forms will be appro- priate for each sector in a market setting, though they stress that privatization will be necessary in most cases to overcome deep and pervasive incentive problems. They also note that intra-modal market competition will tend to be strong in road, air, and water transport. Even in rail transport (with a greater tendency towards natural monopoly), inter-modal competition, such as from trucking, may be enough to maintain competitive pricing in rail services. Thus, they strongly recommend that the government look to market competition and private ownership, rather than government regulation, in most cases. They do stress, however, that in some circumstances – such as air safety and air traffic control – the government indeed has a vital role, and one that is unfortunately unfilled in the current stressful conditions.

In sum, the authors provide history, analysis, and policy recom- mendations on a crucial yet under-examined challenge of economic reform in the republics of the former Soviet Union. The book will be of great value to economic reformers and analysts in the transition economies.

HIID and the authors are very thankful for having had the opportunity to carry out this study. The project was initially conceived by the European Bank for Reconstruction and Development, and was funded largely through a grant from the Bank to Strong and Meyer. HIID gratefully acknowledges the Bank's valuable support and collaboration on all aspects of the project. Strong's participation also was supported by sabbatical leave from The College of William and Mary, and by facilities provided by HIID, where he spent a significant portion of that leave.

Much of this report is based on four modal studies of transport in Russia, Ukraine, Kazakhstan, and Belarus. These modal studies were commissioned by the European Bank and were prepared by Travers Morgan and Booz-Allen & Hamilton (rail transport); COWIconsult and TecnEcon (road transport); Nedeco Consultants (water transport); and Aerodev Consultants Ltd. (air transport).

The authors especially would like to thank three colleagues for their contributions and extensive reviews of the manuscript. Benjamin Berman made major contributions to the air transport sections, and provided extremely detailed and thoughtful comments and suggestions throughout. José A. Gómez-Ibañez contributed many of the ideas pertaining to regulatory issues and privatization. Holland (Ho) Hunter's pioneering work on Soviet transport systems provided the authors with a great deal of information and perspective on the historical development and political economy of transport at the advent of transition. Ho's comments and ideas have shaped much of the manuscript, reflecting the insights of his distinguished career.

The authors also would like to thank Dwight Perkins for his comments on the manuscript and for his support as Director of HIID during 1993. The authors also received comments and suggestions from Paul Joskow, Merton J. Peck, K. Przelomski, John Tilton, Barry Blair, and Nils Bruzelius. Don Lippincott and Sarah Newberry of HIID's publications office provided editorial management and assistance for this volume. Excellent administrative support was provided by Paula Holmes Carr and Joanna Cavitch at Harvard, and by Carole Chappell, Phyllis Viands, Terry Trojak, and Nancy Smith at William and Mary.

The Harvard Business and Government Seminar served as a valuable discussion forum for many of the issues raised in the book. Special acknowledgments go to John White, Ray Vernon, Mike Scherer, and Bob Lawrence. The June 1993 Moscow Conference on Modernising Russia's Transport System, co-sponsored by the European Bank and by the Russian Ministry of Transport was extremely valuable in discussing policy issues and transport investment needs.

As with any project of this scope, this book represents the contributions of many persons in the transport sector in the new republics of the former Soviet Union and at the European Bank. The book is much better as a result of their efforts and assistance.

Jeffrey Sachs
December 1995

Part 1

The Soviet Legacy

1

Transport in the Soviet Union

Unleashed by the transition from a centrally planned economy, transport in the former Soviet Union experienced massive changes in the late 1980s and early 1990s.[1] These changes, in turn, were conditioned by larger or more universal forces shaping transport globally.[2]

First, economic activities have decentralized both spatially and functionally, in part because of the decreasing importance of scale economies. Second, governmental involvement has shifted from operating responsibility to an enabling, monitoring, and oversight role. Third, competition has increased both between and within transport modes. Finally, alternative mechanisms for investment in and financing of both transport operations and infrastructure have emerged.

Types of Transport Environments

These global forces have interacted with local political and economic arrangements to create distinctive transport environments. These may be broadly classified into three types: developing countries, mature market economies, and economies in transition from command structures. Each situation presents a different set of starting conditions, problems, and solutions.

Less developed environments generally have been characterized by rapid population and economic growth,[3] with accompanying shortages or underinvestment in physical transport capacity. These shortages often are exacerbated by urbanization and agglomeration pressures. These factors induce congestion and environmental externalities in some parts of the transport system, whereas other parts remain underutilized or underdeveloped. The principal needs are to expand physical capacity (particularly the extent of the network), relieve congestion, and manage the bottlenecks created by economic and population growth.

By contrast, mature market economies commonly have networks that largely are completed, and additional expansion is costly in both financial and environmental terms. The principal tasks involve managing system demands to increase effective capacity (for example, shifting traffic to off-peak periods) and to mitigate congestion and environmental consequences. These situations also are characterized by debates over the appropriate balancing of public and private transport.

The transition economies are in yet another distinctly different transport environment that requires innovative approaches to operations and institutions. For example, the former Soviet economies generally have adequate physical capacity, both in terms of channel capacity and the extent of the transport network. In some cases, pronounced overcapacity may come to exist once market-determined prices, costs, and traffic flows emerge. This situation often parallels that found after deregulation in mature market economies, in which cross-subsidies and other distortions induced by regulation led to overinvestment in specific types of transport.

The transition economies typically do suffer, though, from some specific bottlenecks, from shortfalls in quality and service, and from underdevelopment of road transport compared with other modes of transport. Outmoded technologies and underdevelopment of legal, financial and institutional structures also hinder the change to a decentralized, market-oriented transport system.

Although transition societies often have a wealth of technical and scientific expertise, this know-how has not been oriented toward determining how markets might affect the economic feasibility of particular transport technologies. Prolonged isolation from the international economy also has meant that transport in transition economies has been largely "left behind," while innovations elsewhere have not only taken root but become dominant. This disparity, of course, creates both major problems and opportunities for technological, organizational, and financial linkages across transport networks.

To exploit these opportunities, institutional reforms in property rights, bankruptcy procedures, antitrust laws, licensing, and other regulatory dimensions are needed. There also is a need for market-based tools for macroeconomic management and social safety nets, long provided under the command rubric but under extreme strain during transition. Market structures also are lacking at the microeconomic level, including effective domestic capital markets, procurement procedures, and intermediaries such as wholesalers and forwarders; those institutions serve both to balance demands and capacity while acting as a counterweight to pressures and incentives to establish monopoly power on unilateral or bilateral terms.

In sum, economies in transition face an inheritance, a macroeconomic and global context, and a set of operational and institutional issues quite distinct from developing countries or mature market economies. The historical legacy is taken up in the remainder of this chapter, before turning to macroeconomic matters in chapter 2 and the challenges faced in the wake of innovations in transport, product markets, and financing structures in chapter 3.

Transport Geography of the Former Soviet Union

Transport in the former Soviet Union was influenced heavily by physical factors of climate and geography, as well as by economic and political factors. The distances are vast and the climate is awesome. Three distinct climatic regions are encompassed – the steppe, the taiga, and the tundra. The steppe lies west of the Ural mountains and contains most of the former Soviet Union's agriculture and industry, along with about three-fourths of the population. The thickly forested taiga and the tundra lie in the extreme north, with a harsh climate that is not moderated by oceanic or wind patterns. Approximately two-thirds of the land area lies in these regions. Most energy reserves and natural resources are there as well. Almost half of the land area is subject to permafrost, which limits the growing season and makes construction of industrial infrastructure difficult at best and prohibitive at worst. Many rivers and seas are frozen for periods ranging from three to nine months each year. Even Odessa, the major Ukrainian port on the Black Sea, can be closed for a month each year.[4]

Although the republics of the former Soviet Union have a coastline of more than 37,000 kilometers, water transport is still relatively limited. The seas are peripheral to most economic activity, and they are separated from each other by major geographical barriers. For example, connections between the Black Sea ports and the Pacific coast require travel through the Mediterranean, the Suez Canal, across the Indian Ocean, and past China (or in the summer months, via the Arctic Ocean).

Although some rivers, particularly the Volga, have been important in historical development, most of the inland waterways have provided only limited, region- or commodity- specific benefits. The extent to which inland waterways can contribute to economic development is constrained by geography, because most of the major rivers run from the center to the periphery, and flow north–south rather than east–west. The main rivers do not link major production centers or markets. For example, the Siberian rivers flow north and the two main rivers of Soviet Central Asia flow into the Aral Sea; neither region is tied by inland waterways to European Russia.

Some of the features that make maritime and road transport difficult are, however, well suited for railroads. The huge land mass largely free of mountainous territory is conducive to rail development. The Caucasus and Ural mountain ranges have been crossed or skirted by rail. For the more populated regions and industrial centers, railroads have offered a low-cost means of moving heavy freight traffic. Low costs per tonne-kilometer are offset to some degree, however, by relatively long lengths of haul.

In general, the Soviet economy depended on sources of raw materials and fuel that are widely scattered from each other and from the major cities. The principal exceptions may be oil and natural gas sites in the Caucasus region, in the Volga valley, and north of the Caspian Sea.

Historical Development

The Russian transport network at the beginning of the twentieth century was shaped largely by foreign trade and investment.[5] Two main sets of rail lines were established for grain exports. The first ran from Baltic seaports into central Russia; the second ran from the Black Sea into the agricultural regions of Ukraine and southern Russia. Transport also was oriented to the export of primary materials to Europe. For example, an oil pipeline from Baku to the Black Sea was completed in 1904, and there was substantial trade in timber.[6]

Foreign direct investment also was an important factor in the Russian transport network before World War I.[7] The Ukrainian steel industry that developed in the 1870s received much financial capital from England. Similarly, the growth of the petroleum, machinery, and other manufacturing sectors was attributable largely to French, German, and other European investments.

This early dominance of foreign investment helped shape Bolshevism, which held that a more self-sufficient economy was required to prevent exploitation of the Russian economy by European powers.[8] When the Bolsheviks took power, there was a repudiation of outstanding Russian debts, and a sea change in Western participation in Soviet economic development. The First Five-Year Plan, published in 1929, was aimed at creating an economically independent industrial base. Although the industrialization did produce some periods of import growth, the Soviet economy remained remarkably autarkic throughout its existence.[9]

This policy of self-sufficiency had major effects on transport. First, the rail network was redirected from serving export markets to carrying raw materials to domestic factories. This change required many new connections, particularly in east–west directions, to open up natural resources in the country's center.

The inward-looking economic policy also isolated the easternmost parts of Soviet territory from lower-cost economic relationships with China, Japan, and Korea. Tying this eastern region with the population and economic centers of western Russia required massive investments in basic transport, principally rail. At the same time, the inward-looking approach meant that Russia participated only to a limited extent in the revolution in road transport and infrastructure that took root in Europe and North America during this period.

The Russian pattern of growth during early industrialization was to locate investment capital near the large cities and transport raw materials from the hinterland. This situation may have been based as much, or more, on political aspects as on economic considerations. The only important exceptions to this pattern were recurrent initiatives to develop natural resources in the Siberian territories, which assumed increasing importance over time, as sources nearer to population centers were successively exhausted.

Geographical integration also was important for other regions and for other reasons. Lenin wrote extensively on how the old centers of St. Petersburg, Moscow, and other cities in imperial Russia had exploited the peripheral regions. Regional economic relations were complicated further by ethnic conflicts between Russians and various minorities. These issues came to the fore with the rise of Stalin, whose base in the ethnic regions led to emphasis on economic development of the periphery and a shift from the established economic centers. Stalin, as commissar of nationalities, instituted a policy in 1923 that gave each major ethnic group a distinct geographical territory. The nation-state consisted of eleven soviet socialist republics and several dozen autonomous oblasts, or regions. Although this federal structure encouraged regions to seek central support for development, it also introduced a localist orientation that has remained a central feature of transport and other policies.

Implementation of Stalin's policies required an industrial strategy of locating factories more uniformly across the country and closer to sources of fuel and raw materials than to markets. This new pattern, with many centers located far from the old major cities, induced a huge shift in freight transport demand patterns and accompanying investment needs.

This decentralization might have produced a fine network of small-scale industries and economically diversified regions were it not for the decisive emphasis placed by the Soviets on the rapid development of heavy industries. These heavy industrial sectors were subject to substantial economies of scale, or at least were thought to be, which encouraged development of a few large plants. These facilities often were integrated vertically as well, perhaps at least partially as a response to coordination problems in a nonmarket economy.

Transport in the Economy of the Former Soviet Union

These development patterns and industrial policies have had major effects on transport. Compared with Western market economies, the Soviet economy uses inordinate amounts of freight transport and relatively little passenger transport. Goods transport represented 9.1 percent of gross domestic product (GDP) in 1990, compared with 6 to 7 percent in Western Europe and the United States. This difference is even greater if one compares the physical amount of transport. Soviet transport in tonne-kilometers per unit of GDP in the late 1980s was ten to fifteen times that of Western Europe, almost six times that of the United States, four and one-half times that of China, and approximately five times that of the countries of Eastern and Central Europe.[1] Although part of any difference was due to distance and geographical conditions, the Soviet transport intensity also was the result of industrial structures, the dominance of rail transport, and the incentives provided by pricing inputs (especially fuel) far below world prices.

Industrial raw materials, especially fuel, dominated traffic flows. This emphasis led to a transport sector oriented toward low-value, high-bulk commodities, with underdevelopment of transport for other types of goods. The orientation toward industrial goods rather than consumer and agricultural goods meant that feeder networks for the farm sector, consumer goods, and light industry were developed only to a minor degree. The emphasis on heavy industry over agriculture and consumer goods was aided by Russia's rather modest rate of population growth, which placed fewer demands on transport resources than in other countries with more rapid growth.[11] Primary emphasis was given to freight rather than passenger transport (with many examples of passenger trains being held on sidings while freight cars passed by).

The emphasis on heavy industry and the reliance on rail also worked against the development of highways and truck transport. Although road transport has superior economic characteristics for short deliveries of high-value goods, these demands have not been a prominent feature of Soviet economic development. Thus, the freight task is dominated overwhelmingly by rail, especially when large volumes of crude oil and natural gas transported by pipeline are excluded. Specifically, rail accounted for roughly one-half of all tonne-kilometers of freight traffic in 1990 and pipelines just less than 40 percent. Road transport totaled only 7 percent of tonne-kilometers but handled 61 percent of all tonnage. Obviously, the truck was a very short haul mode in the Soviet Union. Although this rail-oriented system might have been expected given the geography and climate of the Soviet Union, the transport structure also owes much to the policy choices made by government officials in the first half of the twentieth century.

This same pattern of government influences can be seen in passenger travel. Per capita annual travel in the former Soviet Union was very low, only half that in Western Europe. This lack of mobility was due in part to shortages or nonavailability of rail or air services and to the lack of automobiles and the insufficiency of public transport for local trips. Although the metropolitan subway systems and buses in major cities were well-developed, severe shortages of vehicles existed for suburban transport.

While by Western standards passenger travel was low in the Soviet Union, air transport carried a remarkably large share of what travel there was. Aeroflot accounted for approximately 22 percent of total intercity passenger miles in 1990. This rate was roughly the same as in the United States and Canada, which had by far the highest reliance on air travel of all the Western nations. This relatively high use of air travel in the Soviet Union reflected vast continental distances between many cities (as in Canada and the United States). However, government pricing policies also played a role. Artificially low fuel prices favored energy-intensive air travel. Air travel in the Soviet Union also may have benefited, as in many other parts of the world, from defense-justified (or rationalized) subsidies. Subsidized air travel also was seen as an economical way of weaving outlying locales into the national fabric.[12]

Sellers' markets that allocated goods by queues rather than by prices resulted from these industrial and transport policies. Also, severe capacity bottlenecks restrained economic growth and in some cases resulted in losses, as agricultural products spoiled and factories were unable to operate. Productivity gains, which helped meet needs in earlier years, apparently slowed dramatically in the 1980s.[13] These pressures on the transport system might have reached acute proportions were it not for the general economic downturn after 1988 that accompanied the breakup of the Soviet Union. Even so, several rail mainlines and pipelines remained at or near physical limits in the early 1990s. Deferred maintenance problems were apparent, especially in rail rolling stock, urban streets, and rural roads.

The impact of autarkic policies and a command economy was strikingly apparent in outdated technology. Two of the major driving forces of technological change in market economies – emphasis on service quality and the substitution of capital for increasingly expensive labor – were absent in the command economy. "Just-in-time" inventory management and other logistics innovations were unimagined. Computerization and containerization were only beginning to take root in the early 1990s. There was little intermodal transport.

Another impeding factor to transport development was the economic organization of transport. Each transport sector generally was organized as a giant and vertically integrated spatial monopoly. The rail, aviation, and maritime sectors were run by single authorities that controlled operations for the entire Soviet Union. Roads and inland waterways were managed by separate authorities for extensive geographical areas in each republic. These authorities not only operated transport services, but were vertically integrated into a host of supporting activities, each with its own monopoly. Thus, the aviation authorities operated airlines as well as airports and air traffic control. Similarly, road transport authorities operated vehicle servicing and repair facilities. Prices were controlled rigidly by the State Committee on Prices (Goskomtsen) and did not change for decades in some cases. There was no pressure and little economic incentive to modernize services or respond to customer needs.

Transport and the Economic Environment of the Early 1990s

In most countries gross domestic product (GDP) and transport activity are correlated highly, with an elasticity of approximately one (expressed in tonne-kilometers) or, in more advanced economies, slightly less than one (0.7 to 0.8) as light industries and the service sectors grow disproportionately. Thus, in most economies, transport can be expected to grow at about the same pace or a little more slowly than the overall economy. In the Soviet Union, transport growth was more rapid than GDP during the 1960s and 1970s, before slowing down in the 1980s. The rapid growth of Soviet freight transport demand was due principally to energy investments and the expansion of the pipeline system. Nonenergy freight transport grew more slowly than GDP during the period.[14]

Total volumes of freight traffic grew until 1988, peaking at more than 13 billion metric tonnes and approximately 8.2 trillion tonne-kilometers per year. Consistent with the overall economic downturn, freight transport activity declined by approximately 35 percent from 1988 to 1992.[15]

Determining the future impact of macroeconomic developments and associated structural reforms on the transport sector is difficult. The effects will occur through two mechanisms: the direct effects of economic policies with respect to transport regulation, organization, and operations; and the indirect effects through shifts in production, consumption, and trade, with subsequent modifications of derived transport demands.

Many forecasters think that it will be 2005 or so before the former Soviet economies recover to 1988 production levels. The production and associated transport of primary products is likely to fall further and recover more slowly than other sectors, given the effects of moving toward market prices for energy. Some primary sectors are unlikely ever to regain 1988 levels, given high or market-determined energy and transport costs. If the transition to a market-determined system continues, there will be large shifts in mode choice, de-emphasizing rail and air, and to a lesser extent water, while increasing the role of road transport. Forecasters expect road transport to reach between 22 and 41 percent of nonenergy freight transport, compared with an estimated 13 percent in 1992.

Consequently, those transport sectors involving carriage of primary products should need little in terms of network capacity expansion for years to come.[16] If market-determined, transport investment is likely to be focused on quality improvement and modernization, rather than on total capacity growth. Any shift toward consumer goods would increase requirements for road transport and for intermodal operations. Geographically, market factors, in lieu of politics, would reduce the trading intensity with the former eastern European countries, lessen the dominance of east–west traffic flows, and increase trade and transport requirements between Russia and the Pacific Rim.

Summary

The transport system in the former Soviet Union was conditioned by a harsh climate and vast geographical area. Soviet resource geography and the existing pattern of industrial location necessitated huge movements of grain, fuel, and raw materials over long distances. Public policies toward heavy industry and economic development helped produce a transport system with a very high freight intensity per unit of GDP. The Soviet system also was characterized by low human mobility with little attention to passenger travel. Within sectors, rail was dominant, in part due to the operating environment, but also due to policy choices concerning industrial structure and the associated emphasis on unit costs rather than value of service. Prices and tariffs were maintained at artificially low levels, abetted by energy costs far below world prices.

Perhaps the most important historical inheritance from the former Soviet Union was an economic organization characterized by large monopolies, controlled prices, and administrative directives. This structure produced a transport system marked by a low rate of technological innovation, chronic shortages, and rationing by queues and other nonprice mechanisms. This inherited institutional structure means that any transition to a market-based transport system will require accompanying regulatory and organizational change as a sine qua non of reform. In emphasizing structural, institutional, and organizational changes, the transport situation in the transition economies represents a distinct type of transport environment, with needs clearly different both from the less developed countries and the mature market economies.

Notes

1 To better understand these phenomena, sectoral analyses of rail, road, water, and air transport were commissioned by the European Bank for Reconstruction and Development (EBRD) in 1991. These four reports, which are available from the EBRD, are: Travers Morgan/Booz-Allen and Hamilton, *Railway Sector Survey of Russia, Belarus, Ukraine, and Kazakhstan*; COWIconsult/TecnEcon, *Roads and Road Transport Study*; Nedeco Consultants, *Waterborne Transport Survey*; Aerodevco Consultants Ltd., *Aviation Surveys of Russia, Belarus, Ukraine, and Kazakhstan*.

2 For an extensive survey, see C. Winston, "Economic Deregulation: Days of Reckoning for Microeconomists," *Journal of Economic Literature*, XXXI, 3, (September 1993): pp. 1263–1289.

3 There are, however, many cases of slow growth or actual declines in economic activity, most notably in sub-Saharan Africa.

4 The Black Sea is located at about the same latitude as the Great Lakes in North America, which, along with the separation of the population and resource locations, suggests that Canada and Alaska may be useful comparisons for understanding the physical aspects of Soviet transport.

5 Much of this section draws from H. Hunter, *Soviet Transport Experience* (Washington: Brookings Institution, 1968), chaps. I,II.

6 See M. Falkus, *Industrialization of Russia 1700–1914* (London: Macmillan, 1972).

7 See R. Munting, *The Economic Development of the USSR* (London: Croom Helm, 1982); A. Nove, *An Economic History of the USSR* (London: Penguin, 1969); A. Bergson, *Planning and Performance in Socialist Economies* (London: Unwin Hyman, 1989); A. Nove, *The Soviet Economic System* (London: Routledge, 1986).

8 For a discussion of the New Economic Policy, see A. Smith, *Russia and the World Economy* (London: Routledge, 1993), chap. 2.

9   Smith, *Russia and the World Economy*, chap. 2; see also J. Hough, "The Soviet Attitude toward Integration in the World Economy," in G. Bertsch and S. Elliot-Gower, eds., *The Impact of Governments on East-West Economic Relations* (London: Macmillan, 1991).

10   GDP measured at purchasing power parity. *World Bank Development Report 1991* (Washington: World Bank, 1991).

11   Soviet cities did not experience the rapid growth of urban areas that characterized many other countries in the first half of the twentieth century. Although urban migration was high, severe housing shortages and low birth rates kept population growth to modest levels. World War II also had a tragic demographic impact. Eason estimated that the effects of military and civilian casualties, lower birth rates, and higher child mortality reduced the Soviet Union's population by 45 million persons. See W. W. Eason, "The Soviet Population Today," *Foreign Affairs*, 37 (July 1959): 598–606. Areal redistributions both during and after the war resulted in a population more dispersed by the 1960s than it was at the time of the 1917 Revolution. See R. W. Davies, M. Harrison, and S. G. Wheatcroft, eds., *The Economic Transformation of the Soviet Union*, 1913–1945, (New York: Cambridge University Press, 1994).

12   This perspective is common in vast continental or archipelagic countries, like Canada, the United States, China, and Indonesia.

13   See S. Fischer, "Russia and the Soviet Union: Then and Now," Working Paper 4077, (Cambridge, MA: National Bureau of Economic Research, May 1992); and W. Easterly and S. Fischer, "The Soviet Economic Decline", Policy Research Working Paper 1284, (Washington, DC: World Bank, 1994).

14   For a more extensive discussion, see H. Hunter, P. Dunn, V. Kontorovich, and J. Szyrmer, "Soviet Transport Trends, 1950–1990," *Soviet Economy*, 1, 3 (July–September 1985): 195–231.

15   World Bank, *Sector Report: Russian Federation Transport Sector Strategy* (Washington, DC: World Bank, May 1993). The figures cited are for the CIS, not solely the Russian Federation. Total cumulative output decline for 1991–1992 alone was 26 percent in the former Soviet Union. See European Bank for Reconstruction and Development, *EBRD Economic Review: Annual Economic Outlook*, (London: European Bank, September 1993): 97.

16   This point mainly applies to transport other than pipelines. Additional fixed capital investment in pipeline renovation and upgrading might quickly pay for itself through reduced losses and spillage, especially if moves toward market-based world energy prices are implemented; this also would reduce some primary demands on the rail system.

2

The Macroeconomic Context

An assessment of the prospects for industrial and transport reforms in the former Soviet Union inevitably focuses on the importance of what Dutta has described as a "macroeconomic core for microeconomic optimization."[1] In particular, the study of the restructuring of transport activities must begin with a discussion of macroeconomic matters that condition the development of market institutions at the microeconomic level.

The Inherited Macroeconomic Structure

In the Soviet command planning system, the State Planning Commission (Gosplan) received instructions from the Politburo of the Communist Party about objectives such as economic growth and allocation of resources among consumption, investment, and defense sectors. These objectives were drawn together or coordinated as part of integrated "materials balancing plans." Given the strong import substitution and autarkic policies pursued by the Soviet Union, internal production was the dominant source of supply. The economy suffered endemic supply shortages, not only because imports were proscribed but also because of the magnitude of the material balancing task, the crudity of the material balancing practices and the suppression of the price mechanism in resource allocation.[2] By 1981, the annual master plan and the associated ministerial plans projected requirements for only approximately 35,000 products, although Soviet economists estimated that there were approximately 24 million required items in industrial production alone.[3] Only first-round effects (i.e., only the product and the direct inputs needed to produce that product) were forecast. The resources needed, in turn, to produce those direct inputs commonly were not included in the plans, except in an aggregate way. When these secondary and tertiary requirements inevitably resulted in excess demand, shortages were met by taking resources from the consumer sector. Reduction of industrial production targets simply was not considered; this reflected the rigidities built into the system. Autarky, as noted, precluded a major role for imports as a balancing or buffer mechanism.

Shortages also produced heightened administrative pressures to raise productivity. The resource allocation process was characterized by a great deal of administrative bargaining.[4] Annual plans were almost always late; failure to fulfill targets by one enterprise could have severe repercussions on others. Moreover, managerial incentives were geared almost completely to meeting targets specified in physical terms. Given the interrelated structures and the endemic shortages, managers responded by hoarding both labor and materials while underreporting capacity so that targets (and bonuses) could be achieved. Aganbegyan estimated that the value of the goods hoarded by enterprise managers was almost 75 percent of national income, about three times higher than comparable inventory levels prevailing in Western economies.[5]

Because of these command and coordination problems, the government in the early 1970s established production and industrial associations as intermediate levels of control between the ministries and individual enterprises.[6] These structures were aimed at achieving decentralization from the ministries to broad sectoral levels of industry. The ministries resisted these initiatives, and the establishment of new associations apparently was halted in 1979. The association structures persisted, however, after the Soviet breakup and have produced a particularly difficult legacy in the transport sector (e.g., Aeroflot is the Aviation Production and Commercial Association).

Despite reform efforts in the early 1980s, the ministries retained vast power within their sectors, controlling relations between associations and enterprises. Perhaps even more importantly for transport, the ministries also were the primary connection between producing enterprises and distribution activity. As a result, many of the marketing, distribution, and commercial functions carried out at the firm level in market economies were conspicuously absent at the enterprise or even the association level in the Soviet Union.

Macroeconomic Performance During the 1980s and Early 1990s

Economic reform in the Soviet Union in the mid-1980s was slower than political and social change.[7] This pattern resulted from a combination of factors. Perhaps the most important was that senior Soviet officials, having experienced failed efforts at economic reform since the 1960s, were largely convinced that political and social reforms were necessary preconditions for economic restructuring. Gorbachev was forced to rely on the Communist Party–controlled bureaucracy to formulate proposals and decrees. Almost by definition, this process was biased toward gradualist measures and in continuing gaps between decrees and their subsequent implementation.

Gorbachev's initial reform program called for combining a continuing (but more efficient) state sector for large-scale industry with an increased role for the private sector in services, agriculture, and smaller industries. During 1985 and 1986 a set of "superministries" was created to improve coordination among the heavy industrial ministries and to thereby reinforce the central planning process. The superministry structure replaced the industrial associations and was intended to strengthen direct links between ministries and enterprises. At the same time, production associations were augmented, especially through increased vertical integration. The result was a three-tier structure of ministries, production associations, and enterprises that produced little change in the performance of heavy industries.

In response, starting in 1987 the government changed course and undertook a program aimed at decentralization, with accompanying changes to the systems of banking, foreign trade, taxation, and prices. The overall goal was to lessen enterprise and association subordination to ministerial authority and to substitute performance-based contractual relationships. The central planning system was to be replaced gradually by a system of state orders for enterprise output. These orders would be accompanied by guarantees concerning prices, inputs, and deliveries.

Beyond the state orders, enterprises were to be free to produce, sell, or barter. Enterprises were to become more autonomous and responsive to financial and price signals, in particular to cover costs from their revenues. Managers also were given more control over capital investment decisions, and to finance this investment from internal funds and bank loans rather than ministerial grants. Many of the associations were transformed into joint stock companies, made possible by legislation passed in December 1990. These organizations supported individual enterprises at first, but came under strain as member enterprises learned how to operate independently and other supporting institutional structures began to emerge. This milieu of historically integrated associations and increasingly autonomous enterprises set the stage for the privatization and restructuring debates of the early 1990s.

However, many of the reform elements were introduced without needed complementary policies or, even worse, were combined into packages of mutually contradictory proposals. The result was a disintegration of control over basic structures such as the money supply, the budget, domestic supply and demand, and the trade balance. The liberalizations also changed relative prices and thus made it more difficult to mobilize and coordinate resources. In the absence of effective institutions to provide information, the transfer of labor and natural resources to growing sectors was impeded.[8]

Thus, attempts to introduce new methods into the old system simply generated new inconsistencies. In particular, central controls were weakened but had not been supplanted by market forces, so that the system often was operating with even more distortions or imperfections than before. As noted by the European Bank:

> It was a paradoxical consequence of the liberal reforms undertaken in the 1980s that, in undermining centralized economic control, they brought about a systemic weakening of the economy's institutional apparatus, not the strengthening intended ... the decentralized system that began to develop in the 1980s could work only poorly until a range of necessary market and financial institutions were put in place.[9]

The net effect of these changes was to exacerbate the country's economic problems. The economic disintegration of 1990 and 1991 involved an accelerated decline in output, with severe inflationary pressures. In 1990, the budget deficit was estimated at 150 billion roubles, about 14 percent of official gross national product (GNP), while cash in circulation increased almost fivefold and outstanding credit doubled.[10] According to official statistics, national income fell

15 percent in 1990, with even larger declines in the heavy industrial and agricultural sectors.[11]

The 1992 Macroeconomic Reforms

By 1992 the economies of the former Soviet Union found themselves both in a growth crisis and in severe macroeconomic disequilibrium, manifested in a large budget deficit, high inflation, and balance of payments difficulties.

Price liberalization absorbed a substantial amount of liquidity by converting repressed inflation into actual inflation. Monetary policy was complicated by the absence of financial instruments and capital markets to fund government borrowing. Budget deficits could only be financed by expanding the money supply. Moreover, the Russian central bank (Gosbank), which had become responsible for money control in the rouble zone, had no power to prevent the central banks of the other republics from issuing rouble credits.

The budget deficit worsened as government revenue sources shifted from enterprise surpluses and consumption turnover taxes to a new system based on personal and enterprise taxes. This shift adversely affected revenues, because the necessary regulatory and collection authorities had not been established. As a result, import duties and export taxes were required to play a much larger role as sources of government revenue. This requirement created a further incentive to keep price controls on domestic production to enhance export incentives and to keep the relative prices of imported goods higher than they otherwise would have been.

Macroeconomic stability also was threatened by the rapid growth of inter-enterprise credits, which the Russian central bank estimated had reached 1.4 trillion roubles (25 percent of GNP) by April 1992.[12] These credits largely resulted from the failure or inability of large state-owned enterprises to pay their suppliers.[13] This problem was in part an inheritance from the centralized system, in which enterprises simply passed on their output to the next stage of production according to plan directions, with no need to assess the solvency of the downstream customer.

All these problems were aggravated by banking reforms that replaced the Soviet unitary banking structure with five specialized state-owned banks that were under the general supervision of Gosbank. The banks were organized functionally, specializing in investment, housing, savings, agriculture, and foreign trade. In addition, many cooperative and commercial banks began operation in late 1988. These banks came to be major sources of credit expansion.

Excess liquidity of state enterprises traditionally had been absorbed into government general accounts as enterprise tax revenues. The fiscal and organizational changes generated by the Gorbachev reforms, however, redirected this liquidity into nongovernmental bank deposits. Demand for credit principally came from cash-strapped state enterprises that could not obtain credit through traditional channels. In the absence of bankruptcy and liquidation procedures, which were not widely available under the inherited Soviet legal code, commercial banks stimulated and facilitated inter-enterprise credits because there was little perceived default risk and, arguably, few other acceptable locales for placing loans.

This growth in inter-enterprise credits resulted in a spiraling trend of interrelated receivables and payables. This trend increased the velocity of the money supply and resulted in an effective subsidy to industries that received an interest-free credit during a period of high inflation. Virtually all enterprises with liquidity problems seemingly managed to find a relatively easy source of credit, despite the prevalence of negative real interest rates.

Viable enterprises became caught up in the "debt chains," so that it was difficult to assess enterprise viability by looking at short-run cash positions. There was an accompanying fear that a large bankruptcy could induce a sequence of failures, with concomitant production and social problems.

In total, these processes led to large net job losses and accompanying social welfare pressures.[14] These dislocations also produced pressures for policies to expand credits, increase the budget deficit, raise aggregate demand, and prop up otherwise failing enterprises[15], perpetuating what Kornai calls "unemployment on the job."[16]

Finding a Way Out

The strategy for the reform or transition of socialist economies usually contains five related elements.[17] First, prices should be set by market forces rather than administrative fiat. Second, prices must be reasonably stable. Third, both industrial and agricultural outputs must be available for purchase and sale, rather than allocated by administrative mechanisms. Fourth, there should be competition among enterprises. Fifth, enterprise managers should be oriented toward the market, with freedom to increase profits by reducing costs or increasing sales, but not by lobbying for additional public subsidies.

In addition to this list, there are at least three more elements that might be deemed essential to a successful transition. There should be a reasonably rational and operative taxation program applicable to emerging private sector activity. A social safety net should be re-established, independent of place of employment, to help reduce the costs of labor market adjustments as redundant jobs are shed.[18] Finally, currency should be convertible.[19] This requirement goes beyond the valuable role that a convertible rouble would provide in providing benchmark prices for inputs and products. Convertibility also would help to break down the plethora of bilateral administered trade agreements, which codified many implicit or explicit exchange rates that varied by country or commodity. Thus, convertibility helps "get the prices right" while assisting in moving toward a multilateral and price-based trade policy. In addition, enhanced trade is likely to contribute to economic growth through upgrading of technology (as discussed in chapter 3).

Programs fashioned from these building blocks usually have embodied a combination of rapid macroeconomic stabilization with more gradual structural adjustment in trade reform and corporatization or privatization. How "gradual" these processes can or should be remains open to debate.[20] The phased approaches that have been employed in other countries, including Eastern Europe, may not be possible in the former Soviet Union. Gradualist policies may only be possible when the old system is still functioning to some extent in parallel with the reforms.

Price Liberalization

Clearly, the transition to a market economy requires prices that reflect both costs of production and consumers' willingness to pay. Getting prices right also is central to other reforms; privatization, for example, is much more difficult when current prices and profits provide little guide to the future performance and value of enterprises.

Price liberalization and realignment should be distinguished from the general price inflation that ravaged the economies of the new republics in their early years. The nominal price increases of the early

1990s were more the result of general inflation than realignments of real relative prices. In fact, the general inflation increased pressures on the government to restrain price adjustments on subsidized goods and services. This restraint occurred despite Russia's announced intention to decontrol approximately 90 percent of retail prices and 80 percent of wholesale prices in January 1992. All remaining subsidies and price controls were scheduled to be removed by the end of 1993. By that time, energy prices were supposed to be at world levels, based on market-determined exchange rates.[21]

Not surprisingly, given the subsequent political and economic turmoil, the goals simply were not achieved. Although Russian price decontrol led to a wide range of unprecedented initial "step" adjustments, many prices still did not move to world levels. For some items, such as foodstuffs, remaining price controls served as a partial substitute for the social safety net; this also was true for many energy and transport prices. In other sectors, such as utilities, price constraints remained in place as a substitute for regulatory oversight, because these sectors appeared to retain substantial monopoly power. Finally, some commodities, such as many energy products, remained under partial control as the outcome of a trade-off between providing organizations with the correct price incentives and the dangers of imposing a prematurely fatal financial shock on firms that might be viable if given time to adjust to new factor and product prices.

Taxation of the Private Sector

One of the most severe problems of transition is the strain on central government budgets. The rapid and relatively uncontrolled growth of the "transparent" private sector and the "semilegal" private sector have grave consequences for government revenues. In the absence or relative ineffectiveness of reporting and collection mechanisms in the early 1990s, tax revenues fell sharply. The public policy dilemma is that although consistent tax collection is a hallmark of fairness and fiscal responsibility, any "excessive" enforcement is likely to inhibit the development of the private sector.

The establishment of a tax-based government revenue structure depends on the establishment of legal structures and constitutional protections. The transition to a new legal and institutional structure thus requires a carrot-and-stick approach. In the business sector, this requires a fairly extensive framework, including company, banking, accounting, and bankruptcy acts, with particular emphasis on mechanisms for enforcing contracts between private parties and between private parties and the state. Such reforms also should enhance the growth of the private sector. For example, established legal principles make it easier for small and medium-sized firms to gain access to credit and capital markets. This access, in turn, creates new opportunities for private sector initiatives and reduces the incentives for banks to lend only to state-owned enterprises, with all the problems of inefficiency and loss of monetary control that such a policy entailed in the early 1990s.

The basic need is for an institutional transition from an operating role for the state to new responsibilities as monitor and enabler; in essence, defining and enforcing rules, principles, and protections but limiting the extent of direct involvement, particularly in the management of production. As noted by the European Bank:

> The key reform is a broader one ... In view of the imperfections of their bureaucracies, it is especially important that the countries ... reduce radically the extent of their public sector involvement in the private sector ... while finding ways to perform more efficiently than now the core functions of the public sector.[22]

Social Welfare Responsibilities

The introduction of market mechanisms places tremendous pressures on state-owned enterprises, which have inherited enormous social responsibilities that range from education to housing to health care for employees and their families. Soviet railroads particularly have been prone to assume such responsibilities, perhaps because there was often no other alternative supplier for such geographically remote enterprises. With the transition to a market economy, these responsibilities have become increasingly burdensome at the enterprise level, and in the absence of an effective social safety net this responsibility has not been shifted to government. In part, this situation reflects the collapse of the public budget and its inability to absorb these social costs.

Several major problems result from the Soviet social policy inheritance.[23] To start, the level and character of benefits must be modified and redirected. For example, the legal framework and regulations for social insurance take no account of unemployment.[24] The systems in place in 1992 emphasized pension programs, with unemployment programs and funding quite small in comparison. Moreover, many of the programs are tied to group, such as age or employment category, rather than to income level or actual unemployment.

A second problem is that the provider and associated financing mechanisms for these services must change. In most western countries, social insurance or pension contributions are shared between worker and employer. Such sharing provides both political and financial signals about worker responsibility; the government establishes the general institutional framework, but financing is through earnings and contributions. For economies in transition, however, the problem can be more difficult and have important incentive effects. The benefits of rapid adjustment fall largely to the enterprise, because redundant workers are shed and efficiency is increased. The general point, as noted by Barr, is that " ... public expenditure on the social safety net should be viewed alongside the resulting direct and indirect saving to the enterprises."[25]

Finally, because many of these social welfare activities were long treated as ancillary to the production task, considerable administrative and operating inefficiencies exist. The market may have an important role to play in wringing these out of the system. For example, privatization or contracting out services such as day care and health clinics may be feasible, desirable, and more efficient than retaining such services within the enterprise.

Trade and Currency Convertibility

Under the Soviet system, foreign trade was conducted by large state trading organizations. The long-term overvaluation of the rouble inhibited exports, whereas imports played only a moderate role in balancing macroeconomic fluctuations. Imports also played a small role in technology transfer or technology generation; Soviet technology was driven largely by internal research and development.[26] Furthermore, the planned economy was incapable of generating sufficient domestic innovation or the volume of exports needed to sustain the required level of technology imports to maintain economic growth.[27] For example, the attempt in 1989 to boost imports of machinery and equipment was undone by severe balance of payments pressures that contributed to the breakdown of the monetary system.

The absence of external convertibility has meant that foreign trade must be conducted in convertible currencies or through bilateral arrangements. In the Soviet Union, foreign investors had little incentive to produce for the domestic market, because rouble earnings could not be converted to pay for imported capital or inputs, nor for repatriation of profits. Even if they held legal permits to import equipment, domestic producers were unable to do so because they lacked hard currency for payment. The result was a complicated patchwork of multiple exchange rates, import-export licenses and quotas, and limitations on foreign currency reserves.

Summary

Attempts to change enterprise structure and behavior in the transition economies were made in a restricted environment for both production and consumption. In 1992 and 1993, the governments of the former Soviet Union had neither the legal instruments nor the financial capability to impose hard budget constraints on enterprises or to expose them to greater competition. The tight monetary and fiscal policy applied to the consumer sector did not reach the enterprises, moreover, because of the soft budget constraint that maintained access to easy credit and thereby contributed to accelerating inflation. Under these circumstances, enterprise managers continued to restrict output and to increase prices where possible. The continuing slow supply responses to changes in demand resulted in the production of the wrong goods, often of inferior quality, as well as in declining output and employment.

The macroeconomic instability of the early 1990s clearly made institutional and organizational restructurings much more difficult. Perhaps more importantly, delay of organizational reform raises the key microeconomic question of whether the distortions created by highly monopolistic, protected, and integrated industrial sectors will be so important that they inhibit the effectiveness of reforms. This inhibition may be a particular issue in transport, which not only represents a large share of economic activity in itself, but also is central to the development of a commercially oriented infrastructure for the rest of the economy. "Getting the macroeconomics right" is required to provide signals for supply, demand, and investment. It also influences the speed and success of enterprise restructuring. Since the demand for transport services is derived from other activities, general economic reform will play a key role in shaping transport restructuring.

Notes

1   M. Dutta, "Economic Regionalization in Western Europe: Macroeconomic Core, Microeconomic Optimization," *American Economic Review*, 82, 2 (May 1992): 67–73.

2   The basic features of the system are discussed in J. Kornai, *The Socialist System* (Oxford: Oxford University Press, 1992).

3   G. Schroeder, "Soviet Economic Reform Decrees," United States Congress Joint Economic Committee (Washington, DC: Government Printing Office, 1982): 67; see also G. Schroeder, "The Soviet Industrial Enterprise in the 1980s," in I. Jeffries, ed., *Industrial Reform in Socialist Countries: from Restructuring to Revolution* (Aldershot, UK: Edward Elgar, 1992).

4   There are a variety of views as to whether the Soviet economy could more accurately be described as centrally planned or centrally managed, with substantial adjustments and negotiations. See EBRD, *EBRD Economic Review: Annual Economic Outlook* (London: EBRD, September 1993): 98–101.

5   A. Aganbegyan, *Moving the Mountain: Inside the Perestroika Revolution* (London: Bantam Press, 1989): 43.

6   This section draws heavily from P. Joskow, R. Schmalensee, and N. Tsukanova, "Competition Policy in Russia during and after Privatization," *Brookings Papers on Economic Activity: Microeconomics 1994* (Washington,DC: Brookings Institution, 1994): 301–381.

7   This section draws heavily from EBRD, *EBRD Economic Review: Annual Economic Outlook*; A. Smith, *Russia and the World Economy* (London: Routledge, 1993), chaps. 6–10; I. Jeffries, *Socialist Economies and the Transition to the Market* (London: Routledge, 1993) chaps. 1–3; I. Jeffries, *Industrial Reform in Socialist Countries: from Restructuring to Revolution* (Aldershot, UK: Edward Elgar, 1992); A. Aslund, *The Post-Soviet Economy: Soviet and Western Perspectives* (London: Printer, 1992); Commission of the European Communities, Directorate-General for Economic and Financial Affairs, *Stabilization, Liberalization, and Devolution: Assessment of the Economic Situation and Reform Process in the Soviet Union*, 45 (Brussels: European Commission, 1990); A. Shleifer and R. Vishny, "Reversing the Soviet Economic Collapse," *Brookings Papers on Economic Activity*, 2 (Washington, DC: Brookings Institution, 1991); E. Hewett, *Reforming the*

Soviet Economy (Washington: Brookings Institution, 1988); S. Fischer and A. Gelb, "Issues in Socialist Economy Reform" PRE Working Paper 565 (Washington, DC: World Bank, December 1990).

8 The lack of information, adjustment mechanisms, and a social safety net certainly affected economic performance. J. Flemming points out, however, that the behavioral responses to relative price changes limited economic restructuring. At enterprises with *rising* relative prices, the response usually was to push up wages to the maximum. In contrast, the reaction to *decreased* relative prices was to resist wage cuts, as it was believed that the impact would be felt principally through a reduced rate of new hires. This response would be particularly expected if the conditions were expected to be temporary. See EBRD, *EBRD Economic Review: Annual Economic Outlook*, 99–100.

9 EBRD, *EBRD Economic Review: Annual Economic Outlook*, P. 100.

10 International Monetary Fund (IMF), World Bank, OECD, and EBRD, *A Study of the Soviet Economy*, 3 volumes; Vol. 1 (Paris: OECD, 1991): 53–59, 121–132.

11 IMF, World Bank, OECD, and EBRD, *A Study of the Soviet Economy*, 3 volumes; Vol. 1 (Paris: OECD, 1991): 53–59, 121–132.

12 B. Ickes and R. Ryterman, "The Inter-Enterprise Arrears Crisis in Russia," *Post Soviet Affairs* (formerly *Soviet Economy*) (October–December 1992); EBRD, *Annual Economic Outlook*, 42–46.

13 The rise of inter-enterprise credits has been attributed by Kornai to the "soft budget constraint." With such credits widely available, a firm's spending is not constrained by its financial situation. The consequences of such an environment are toleration of inefficiency, postponement of adjustments to demand changes, and misallocation of investment funds. The key issue is how the creditor reacts to this situation. In an environment of soft budget constraints, the creditor is likely to tolerate the default and encourage the transformation of these "defaults" into a rise in inter-enterprise credits. See J. Kornai, "The Soft Budget Constraint," *Kyklos*, 39, 1986, 3–30; J. Kornai, *The Socialist System: The Political Economy of Communism* (Oxford: Oxford University Press, 1992); J. Kornai, "The Postsocialist Transition and the State: Reflections in the Light of Hungarian Fiscal Problems," *American Economic Review*, 82, 2 (May 1992): 1–21.

14 See N. Barr, "Income Transfers and the Social Safety Net in Russia," *Studies of Economies in Transition,* 4 (Washington, DC: World Bank, 1992).

15 Major unresolved issues include how to protect firms which have long-run viability from short-run bankruptcy due to liquidity problems, while still managing to close nonviable enterprises.

16 J. Kornai, "The Postsocialist Transition and the State: Reflections in the Light of Hungarian Fiscal Problems," *American Economic Review*, 82, 2 (May 1992), 1–21.

17 For full discussions of policy reform proposals in Eastern Europe and the CIS, see D. Lipton and J. Sachs, "Creating a Market in Eastern Europe: The Case of Poland," *Brookings Papers on Economic Activity, 1* (Washington, DC: Brookings Institution, 1990); J. Kornai, *The Socialist System: The Political Economy of Communism* (Oxford: Oxford University Press, 1992); A. Aslund, *The Post Soviet-Economy: Soviet and Western Perspectives*. See also D. Perkins, "Reforming the Economic Systems of Vietnam and Laos," in *The Challenge of Reform in Indochina*, B. Ljunggren, ed. (Cambridge, MA: Harvard Institute for International Development, 1993). For an earlier treatment, see D. Perkins, "Reforming China's Economic System," *Journal of Economic Literature*, XXVI, 2 (June 1988): 601–645.

18 See T. Boeri and M. Keese, "Labour Markets and the Transition in Central and Eastern Europe," *OECD Economic Studies*, 18 (1992): 133–63.

19 See B. Granville, *Price and Currency Reform in Russia and the CIS* (London: Royal Institute of International Affairs, 1992).

20 See L. Balcerowicz and A. Gelb, "Macropolicies in Transition to a Market Economy: A Three-Year Perspective," paper presented at the World Bank Annual Bank Conference on Development Economics (Washington, DC: World Bank, April 1994); J. Sachs, "Russia's Struggle with Stabilization: Conceptual Issues and Evidence," paper presented at the World Bank Annual Bank Conference on Development Economics (Washington, DC: World Bank, April 1994).

21 Details of this program were published in a document called "Memorandum on the Economic Policy of the Russian Federation," approved by the Russian government on 27 February 1992. This document formed the basis for Russia's early 1992 letter of intent to the IMF.

22 EBRD, *EBRD Economic Review: Annual Economic Outlook*, 9.

23 See N. Barr, "Income Transfers and the Social Safety Net in Russia".

24 N. Barr, "Income Transfers and the Social Safety Net in Russia," 16.

25 N. Barr, "Income Transfers and the Social Safety Net in Russia," 32.

26 Western restrictions on export of advanced technologies to the Soviet Union also were a significant factor. See M. Goldman and R. Vernon, "U.S. Economic Policies toward the Soviet Union," and R. Vernon, "The Fragile Foundations of East-West Trade," both in R. Vernon, ed., *Exploring the Global Economy: Emerging Issues in Trade and Investment* (Lanham, MD: University Press of America, 1985), 177–199 (Goldman and Vernon) and 199–212 (Vernon).

27 See A. Smith, *Russia and the World Economy*, chaps. 4, 7.

3

Technological, Financial and Institutional Lags: Consequences for Transport

Like many industries, transport has undergone major global changes in technology, organization, and financing during the postwar period. In the West, changes in patterns of population and economic growth have resulted in a decentralization of markets, which has been followed by an even more marked decentralization of production. These shifts also have induced major changes in the organization and control of economic activities.[1] These adjustments and innovations have yet to take root in the new republics, but are likely to do so in the transition to a market economy.

Four changes in technology, organization, and financing have been particularly important. First, a new scope and variety of technologies and production sharing arrangements has arisen. Investment projects face a variety of suppliers and of supplying relationships, such as joint ventures or coproduction agreements. Difficult decisions often must be made about technical integration of different suppliers into network activities or complex systems.[2] These systems must be managed at the outset, because initial decisions about such matters as investments and joint ventures may tie or constrain subsequent investments and performance.

Second, the postwar period has been marked by an almost continuous rethinking of which services should be publicly provided, operated, and financed. The result is a blurring of boundaries and increasing integration of the public and private sectors. Privatization, corporatization, and other organizational changes have created opportunities for new types of financing and for old types to be used in new ways.[3]

Third, financial markets have experienced a wave of innovations in such areas as risk management and control. These innovations have resulted in an unprecedented role for private financing of investments and activities long the domain of governments or multilateral financial institutions. As noted by Jeffrey Sachs:

> Now, once a governmnt is creditworthy, it looks to private capital markets rather than to the IMF [International Monetary Fund] for its cues … The traditional project-financing role of the World Bank is rapidly becoming passé … world capital markets are mobilizing project finance of a kind that was unthinkable a few years ago. The markets are channeling tens of billions of dollars into roads, ports, telecoms, and power generators – and thereby supplanting the long-standing role of the Bank itself.[4]

This private capital often has better defined and segmented risk through security structures, contingent contracts, and organizational forms.[5]

Other major innovations have been concerned with control and incentive structures, in particular the design of mechanisms so that "agents" behave more in the interest of their "principals." Incentive conflicts may arise in many situations, such as motivating managers to act in the interest of shareholders, or state enterprises to act in the public interest.[6] Overall, the changes in organization, investments, and financing all might be viewed as attempts to better manage risks, improve incentives, and increase economic efficiency. Unfortunately, while the new organizational and financial tools may be well suited to systems undergoing rapid change (such as transport), they also contain powerful incentives for opportunism and for striking "deals" that may benefit particular interests to the detriment of the larger society.

As the modal surveys in part II suggest, these changes in product, process, and financial markets apparently did not shape the transport sector in the Soviet Union. To a considerable degree, developments elsewhere have simply "passed by" the former Soviet Union. Transport markets in the new CIS republics also have been much less dynamic. In particular, a history and continuation of energy prices held well below international levels has produced a transport sector lacking many of the efficiency and operating innovations found elsewhere. As a result, much of the transport equipment in service is ill-suited for a market economy and for global energy costs and environmental requirements. In addition, the closed economy of the Soviet Union precluded joint ventures or production alliances, so that many technological advances in transport equipment were not embodied in Soviet transport technology. The concentration on "captive" trade with Eastern Europe extended the emphasis on domestic markets, while underpriced raw materials and energy supported expansion of manufacturing beyond efficient scale. Although technically trained skilled workers were available,[7] their efforts were not directed toward the goals of energy conservation and increased productivity, compared to enterprises elsewhere.[8] Finally, and critically, developments in financial markets that supported and encouraged many of the innovations in transport elsewhere were absent in the former Soviet Union.

Evolution of Product and Service Markets

For most of the twentieth century, industrial growth was thought to be related to access to natural resources and to the existence of large domestic markets. These factors gave rise, in turn, to economies of scale, and were reflected in dominant industry and export positions for firms in those markets.

Another contributor to development, especially in technology and capital-intensive sectors, was massive public and private investment in research, development, and science made after 1945. This investment also was related to the rise of indigenous technological communities, which represent a type of collective learning that generated and diffused new technologies, first for production and later (in the West) for consumer goods. Several innovations took advantage of the mass distribution and marketing opportunities presented by improved transport and communications. Another prominent feature was the rising importance of production, sales, and service organizations. For example, the need for long-term service networks for durable goods spurred further organizational innovations, including franchises and third-party networks not tied to the original seller.

This cumulative technological learning, whatever its source, was long defined by national borders. It now appears to have diffused across political boundaries. Six factors explain much of this trend. First, increased international trade eroded the advantages of large national market size and low domestic raw material costs. Second, technology has become more generally accessible, if requisite skills are available and requisite commercial and infrastructure investments are made. Third, there has been an increase in research and development activity in locations that previously had little such activity; this helps establish internal competence to exploit technologies from abroad and to create new technologies. Fourth, a decline apparently has occurred in the importance of spillovers from military research and development into civilian technology.[9] Fifth, many of the process and technology innovations in market economies have reduced minimum efficient scale and further eroded the cost advantages of large-scale production. Sixth, internationalization of financial markets increasingly has facilitated foreign direct and intermediated investments of the type well suited for facilitating technology transfer.

The result of these trends is that the period since the 1960s has seen a striking change in international product markets. A substantial narrowing has occurred among the mature market economies in per capita income and in productivity, both in the aggregate and across a broad spectrum of industries.[10] Evidence on this convergence at the aggregate and sectoral levels for Organization for Economic Cooperation and Development (OECD) countries is presented in Tables 3-1 through 3-5.[11] The increased globalization of trade is shown in table 3-1. Although the overall shares have shifted only moderately, the composition has changed markedly: the share of manufacturing exports by non-OECD countries almost doubled, while non-OECD shares in both agriculture and natural resources fell sharply.

For the OECD countries taken as a whole, production processes and structures apparently have become more alike since the 1960s. This convergence can be measured by the coefficient of variation, defined as the ratio of the standard deviation of the performance measure divided by its mean. In other words, the coefficient of variation measures how far apart individual country values are relative to a common standard. Table 3-2 shows that in all three subclasses of manufacturing and for transport equipment, the variation in labor productivity narrowed between 1963 and 1986, and that

Table 3-1   **Percentage Share of World Exports, 1963 and 1985**

	1963	1985
Total world exports		
Germany	11.3	11.6
Japan	4.2	11.2
United States	17.7	13.0
Other OECD	44.0	43.7
Non-OECD	22.9	20.5
World manufacturing exports		
Germany	16.7	14.3
Japan	6.4	15.0
United States	19.7	13.3
Other OECD	49.6	42.8
Non-OECD	7.6	14.5
World agricultural exports		
Germany	1.5	5.2
Japan	1.3	1.2
United States	16.4	16.0
Other OECD	38.8	47.4
Non-OECD	41.9	30.3
World mineral and energy deposits		
Germany	6.2	3.0
Japan	0.1	0.3
United States	9.6	6.6
Other OECD	27.2	46.2
Non-OECD	56.9	43.9

Source: United Nations World Trade Data. World totals are sum of exports of countries reporting to United Nations Statistical Office.

the average productivity level rose relative to the productivity level in the United States. Table 3-3 shows similar results for total factor productivity (TFP), which represents the ratio of outputs relative to all inputs. The convergence in productivity is due in part to a narrowing of capital-labor ratios, as shown in table 3-4. For all

Table 3-2   Average Measures of Productivity Convergence[1] for Heavy,
Medium, and Light Industries of 13 Industrial Countries,
1963 and 1986

	Coefficient of Variation		Average of Productivity in 12 Countries Relative to U.S. Productivity	
	1963	1986	1963	1986
All manufacturing	0.36	0.24	0.47	0.60
Heavy industries[2]	0.50	0.34	0.42	0.53
Medium industries[3]	0.33	0.20	0.59	0.66
Light industries[4]	0.46	0.39	0.42	0.50
Transport equipment	0.26	0.23	0.71	0.71

[1] Value added per work hour.
[2] Chemicals, iron and steel, nonferrous metals.
[3] Paper, printing, rubber, plastics, pottery and glass, metal and nonmetal products not elsewhere classified, machinery, transport equipment.
[4] Textiles, clothing, leather, footwear, wood products, electrical goods.

Source for Tables 3-2–3-5: D. Dollar and E. Wolff, *Competitiveness, Convergence, and International Specialization* (Cambridge, Ma.: MIT Press, 1993), chap. 4.

Table 3-3   Indices of Total Factor Productivity (TFP), OECD Countries,
1967 and 1985

	Coefficient of Variation		Average TFP[1] Relative to U.S. TFP	
	1967	1985	1967	1985
All manufacturing[2]	0.34	0.26	0.66	0.73
Heavy industries	0.45	0.24	0.70	0.87
Medium industries	0.32	0.23	0.66	0.71
Light industries	0.33	0.22	0.60	0.72
Transport equipment	0.26	0.23	0.71	0.71

[1] TFP equals Y / [aL + (1 minus a)K] where y equals value added; L equals unemployment; K equals gross capital stock; and a equals wage share of total costs.
[2] Definitions as in table 3-2.

Table 3-4   Measures of Convergence in Capital-Labor Ratios, OECD
Countries, 1963 and 1985

	Coefficient of Variation		Average Capital-Labor Ratio Relative to U.S. Capital-Labor Ratio	
	1963	1985	1963	1985
All manufacturing[1]	0.39	0.30	0.75	1.00
Heavy industries	0.47	0.36	0.59	0.68
Medium industries	0.39	0.25	0.74	0.99
Light industries	0.35	0.33	0.85	1.20
Transport Equipment	0.29	0.18	0.78	0.88

[1] Definitions as in table 3-2.

Table 3-5   Productivity of Transport and Communication Service
Sector, OECD Countries, 1970 and 1985

	Coefficient of Variation		Average Relative to U.S. Productivity	
	1970	1985	1970	1985
Labor productivity	0.26	0.19	0.60	0.65
TFP	0.24	0.16	0.67	0.74
Capital-labor ratios	0.47	0.33	0.40	0.51

manufacturing subclasses and for transport equipment, the variation
in capital intensity declined.

For the OECD countries taken as a whole, production processes
and structures apparently have become more alike since the 1960s.
Many of the same trends characterize transport and communications
services as well, as shown in table 3-5. Convergence in labor
productivity, TFP, and capital-labor ratios is again apparent. This
convergence has had major effects on the nature of competition.
When coupled with rising trade volumes, transport equipment has
become an international product characterized by substantial local
production and, in some products, assembly operations from im-

ported parts. There also is some evidence of a learning process by which countries "graduate" from kit production to expanded domestic production.

With different institutional and incentive structures, the Soviet transport sector developed quite differently. This difference is somewhat surprising, because along some dimensions, the Soviet Union shared the same features as the United States – a large domestic market, production activities dominated by economies of scale, a large natural resource base, and massive research and development expenditures. The Soviet Union also had a strong technical and operational "community," which in many ways remains one of the principal economic assets of the new republics.[12] However, the concentration of Soviet research activity on national security led to many transport products and services being produced only by defense-oriented enterprises. For example, in 1990, 14 percent of the tractors, 25 percent of the rail freight cars, 11 percent of the passenger cars, 53 percent of the motorcycles, and 43 percent of the bicycles produced in the Soviet Union were made by defense enterprises.[13]

The dominance of sellers' markets in the Soviet Union also meant that innovations in marketing, distribution, and service networks were largely absent. This absence was critical, since many of these innovations were essential in shifting transport toward increased emphasis on timeliness, service, and other aspects of quality. Shortfalls in these qualities were at the heart of many of the problems facing transport in the transition economies in the early 1990s (as described in part II).

Table 3-6 compares data for production of a variety of types of transport equipment in Eastern Europe and the former Soviet Union with that in the rest of the world. Although such data always are subject to reporting and definitional differences, several features are striking. First is the remarkable consistency of production in the command economies, with little of the variations experienced in the rest of the world due to energy shocks or cyclical effects. Another aspect of table 3-6 is the extremely low level of most road transport equipment production in Eastern Europe and the former Soviet Union relative to the rest of the world. Also, there is some evidence of technology differences, possibly even lags, in the command economies, as shown by the greater ratio of diesel locomotives in the rest

Table 3-6   **Production of Transport Equipment Eastern Europe (EE)/
Former Soviet Union (FSU) compared with Rest of
World (ROW)**

	1970	1975	1980	1986	1987	1989
Trailers and semitrailers (thousands)						
EE/FSU	201	257	271	264	264	280
ROW	278	305	481	451	475	499
Trucks (thousands)						
EE/FSU	717	890	1,061	1,109	1,128	1,062
ROW	5,391	6,201	8,113	10,833	11,304	11,976
Cars (thousands)						
EE/FSU	996	1,924	2,313	2,320	2,368	2,279
ROW	24,885	23,130	28,633	29,218	30,111	32,638
Electric Locomotives (no.)						
EE/FSU	1,259	1,194	1,029	1,070	1,150	976
ROW	658	527	629	650	637	675
Diesel Locomotives (no.)						
EE/FSU	2,741	2,561	2,212	2,034	1,928	1,902
ROW	2,062	2,749	2,842	1,827	1,998	2,018
Merchant Ships (thousands of gross tonnes launched)						
EE/FSU	1,066	1,163	1,331	1,015	763	413
ROW	9,094	10,795	7,778	11,992	5,544	5,655

Source: United Nations, *Yearbook of Industrial Statistics*, various years.

of the world compared with the continuing role of electric locomotives in Eastern Europe and the former Soviet Union.

In sum, many of the changes in product markets, transport equipment production, and organizational changes that have marked transport elsewhere are much less evident in Eastern Europe and the former Soviet Union. These changes in transport in market economies, moreover, have come hand-in-hand with innovations in financing, as described in the next section.

Innovations in Financial Markets

The range of new organizational structures that have emerged in market economies, from licensing to joint ventures, would not have occurred without new financial tools for risk management and monitoring. The growth of financial derivative securities such as options, futures, and forward contracts has allowed transport equipment and other manufacturers to better manage and share both currency and business risks. Indeed, project finance and other limited or nonrecourse financial strategies have come to be prerequisites for much direct investment.

Many basic differences can be identified between traditional government or sovereign loans and the wide array of market-based financing structures.[14] During the past several decades, traditional financing has been provided to developing countries almost exclusively as public general obligation debt, usually with a lower interest rate and substantial control by the borrower. There has been little risk sharing between the lenders and the borrowers and little incentive for lender involvement in selecting and monitoring projects. In contrast to sovereign loans, market-based financing often involves transfers of capital combined with technology, know-how, and goods – factors that can greatly influence the expected rate of return both for the investor and the borrower. Links between projects and providers of capital are more explicit, with greater attention to risk sharing, monitoring, and management.

These changes, in turn, increase the incentives for the lender or investor to ensure that the project is a success. However, the closer ties between project and financing also may introduce strong incentives for the foreign partner and the project organization to collude, in an attempt to socialize the risks while privatizing the benefits. This collusion may be particularly true in quasi-public organizational structures, such as public enterprise or corporatized forms of joint ventures. In these situations, the links to the government or to the sovereign may be implicit; e.g., if project failure has substantial public consequences, it may require that government bail out the investment. The result may be an incentive to overinvest by both the government enterprise and the foreign partner, especially in the absence of clearly defined legal obligations or effective monitoring by the government in its sovereign role or as shareholder or regulator of the state enterprise.

To the extent that national or foreign donor interests affect financial flows, risk arises that technical assistance and bilateral aid could be channeled to favored projects and participants, even if they are not economically or financially justified.[15] This risk is particularly problematic in transport, in which long-lived investments, network considerations and externalities commonly are present. In the transition economies, with their need to "catch up," the lack of financial and investment "infrastructure" may induce opportunism and rent-seeking behavior on the part of both Western suppliers and government and enterprise managers and officials.[16]

In the command economies, incentive and default issues were not a major concern of enterprises, financial institutions, or even ministries, because all risk was borne by the state. Very little effort was made to assess creditworthiness or economic viability. Project designers were supposed to apply a "recoupment formula" comparing capital outlays with long-term gross project revenues, but these formulas often were overruled and the state budget routinely was used to cover losses. When the transition to a market economy began, these agency issues came to the fore: issues that were seemingly irrelevant under the old system were often at the root of difficulties in making markets work.[17] The enterprises themselves had little experience in monitoring and evaluating product and input markets. These roles might be filled by financial market intermediaries in market-oriented developing economies, but in the new CIS republics these intermediaries are perhaps even less developed than the enterprises themselves in monitoring and risk management functions. In contrast to many established institutions and activities that are in need of transformation or reform, institutions for monitoring and risk management had to be created *de novo*.

Market economies have developed a variety of mechanisms for monitoring and controlling such activities. These mechanisms emphasize the role of financial claims in creating incentives for improving and sustaining performance. Much of this area involves the "bundling" of financial claims so that particular classes of claimants do not have incentives to maximize the value of their own claims at the expense of other claims or the activity as a whole.[18] A financing structure in which participants hold a portfolio of different claims also increases the incentive to provide additional funding if necessary. These "blended" financial claims tend to reduce both incentive and monitoring problems.[19] In this context, transition economies need an activist-relationship investor, involved in a complete range of debt, equity, and contingent-financing claims and sharing in both the upside and downside of projects.

In an unstable transition situation, debt may be the main form of external investment, and even that may require additional monitoring and security through carefully tailored security structures or even sovereign guarantees. As risk is reduced, other sources and types of capital investment are likely to be forthcoming, so that many escrow and collateral structures or sovereign guarantees might be thought of as elements of "seed" capital. As time passes, the mobilizing and credit enhancement roles played by such vehicles actually might become detrimental. This situation could occur, for example, if in the early stages of an activity there was little economic value to capture, but once viability was achieved, the incentives to appropriate the profits or assets increased. In short, sovereign guarantees may be subject to both short-run and long-run opportunism.

Implications for Multilateral Financial Institutions

In a world of linked projects and financing, multilateral institutions (in conjunction with borrowing country governments) may be required to initiate and support institutional reforms and to help design investment structures that reduce opportunities for rent seeking. Many of the new forms of organization should be designed to transform foreign direct investment into what might be called "foreign participatory investment." The extent of participation may depend on the ability of multilateral institutions to create packages of financing that include technical assistance, institutional reform, short- and long-term debt finance, and equity capital. These components are likely to come from different sources, ranging from bilateral aid to equity-oriented country mutual funds.

A second approach is for the multilateral institution to serve as a type of venture capitalist.[20] Many new transport enterprises, for example, require relatively small amounts of capital. Given the high costs of evaluating and processing individual loans through multilateral board structures, it may be better and more flexible to put such projects in a portfolio structure, in which a pool of capital is approved for investments of designated size and type. These activities are likely to require a range of financial, operational, and governance assistance – all features of successful venture capital structures. Any such role would represent a major change from the traditions of conventional sovereign lending and should be structured to compensate for the greater risks; such compensation might not occur through higher interest rates per se, but through equity or security structures that enable the multilateral institution to share in the gains from successful projects or enterprises. To this end, options, warrants, or other contingent repayment schemes would allow the institution to share in the upside potential as it otherwise assumes a substantial amount of the downside risk. Such a participatory stake, however, could create a potential conflict of interest or moral hazard problem for the multilateral institution if it wants to continue to serve as an advisor on policy matters to the host government.

These opportunities represent a major change for multilateral institutions and for governments (everywhere, but especially in the former Soviet Union, given its history): a shift from a direct, primary provider role to a marshaling, managing, and monitoring function. Whether this transition can be achieved by these organizations remains an open question – but much hinges on their success. In transition economies, the required tasks are well suited for private capital and for smaller-scale investments. In these situations, extensive sovereign lending, especially with negative pledge clauses, may inhibit needed flows of private capital.

This problem is likely to be particularly acute if institutional and contracting structures and behaviors are not in place to provide adequate security provision for private capital. As discussed in the World Bank's *1994 World Development Report*, a need exists for developing a proper legal and institutional environment; creating transitional support structures so that private finance may supplant public funds at an appropriate time; and finding ways to manage situations in which the private investor has difficulty in obtaining the proper share of project surplus. The main lessons, though, are that as investors, governments, and direct project participants work together, more extensive and expansive roles can be played by non-sovereign finance. As the *World Development Report* states:

> New safeguards and conventions are evolving to deal with project risks and complexities. A convergence is occurring on
> … contractual forms, franchising, and the role of government

as policy maker and risk bearer. Equally important, incentive and penalty mechanisms to ensure private performance also are becoming clearer.[21]

As a result, if projects are designed to secure and manage revenues and to cover costs, the marshaling of private funds for transport projects is likely to occur. This link further reinforces the need for governments and multilateral organizations to shift from a providing to an enabling role.

Consequences for CIS Transport

Many of the new organizational and financial forms that have emerged are oriented toward technology transfer through affiliation rather than through outright sale or stand-alone production. In this sense, they are good for modernization tasks. The CIS transition economies appear well suited for such undertakings, given their production capabilities, long-term market size, and growth potential, and existing technology and human resource base.

The challenge is to modernize using as much of the existing resource base as possible. The associated task is to create incentives for enterprises to perform old activities in new ways. For example, there may be opportunities to promote the new activities and privatization of small transport initiatives like trucking and warehousing by having the existing public enterprises shift from being owner-operators of physical assets to being lessors.[22] Or, as with some restructuring activities in the West, the need is to redefine how activities are performed and to shift the roles from public provision to a hybrid form of public ownership with contracts to private groups. The new organizational and financial structures have as their *sine qua non* the need to restructure the overly integrated transport enterprises inherited from the Soviet Union.

Furthermore, given the vigorous competition among potential foreign suppliers in the transport sector, the opportunity exists for establishing (or even requiring) organizational structures that combine technical, managerial, and financial commitments. Similarly, multilateral institutions and other suppliers of capital could use international competitive tendering to reduce costs and to evaluate alternative organizational designs aimed at instituting needed technical and institutional reforms.

Summary

The new financial structures create opportunities, just as the innovations in organizations and product markets do. As described in chapters 4–7, transport in the former Soviet Union does not require capacity-building sector loans or long-term sovereign financing. Instead, the transition economies need to draw on a variety of sources and types of private investment capital, mixing them with technical assistance funding and "seed" money from development institutions. This strategy moves beyond commercial bank and foreign direct investment into a world of "competitive finance" with many sources. At the same time, innovations in product and financial markets should be brought together in structures that maximize the likelihood of an efficient and well-functioning transport sector.

Appendix A

Taxonomy of Organizational and Financial Innovations[23]

Foreign Direct Investment

Foreign direct investment (FDI), the transfer of savings from one country to an investment in another without financial intermediation, requires that a country have investment opportunities that are judged profitable by world standards and that its total financing needs exceed domestic savings.[24] In the early 1990s, the high rates of inflation in the former Soviet Union almost eliminated the large pool of domestic savings and thereby increased the importance of foreign capital. Moreover, the institutional structure of the Soviet financial system was not oriented toward intermediation of private savings and investment.

FDI is a particularly effective way of advancing economic development, because FDI can be a mechanism for transferring technology or managerial and marketing know-how, especially when channeled through joint ventures with enterprises in the host country. The host-country venture partners can be either public or private enterprises.

Direct investment often involves considerable equity commitment, accompanied by management participation. Hybrid or strip financings, combining both equity and debt from specific sources, are also quite common with direct investment. Among other advantages, such hybrid financing balances the incentives so that uniquely "hard" debt and equity viewpoints are attenuated.

FDI is not limited, of course, to continuing enterprises. Indeed, a growing portion of FDI is on a project basis for infrastructure development or for specific import sales of equipment. When done on a project-by-project basis, FDI is much less likely to involve meaningful equity participation. Indeed, these project involvements tend to be characterized by considerable leverage financed (or guaranteed) by third parties, with early payout or repatriation of any foreign equity.

Host governments almost inevitably have an indirect responsibility for or involvement with FDI by setting rules on such things as profit repatriation or currency hedging or guarantees. FDI of any kind, moreover, whether a joint venture or not, necessitates settling legal issues and property rights. Joint ventures also can be subject to very complex rules about the extent to which an FDI source can assume a majority ownership or control position. A government's role in aiding, abetting, and yet preventing abuses from FDI also can be complex, because a government commonly is involved in conflicting roles, such as simultaneously being a regulator and an entrepreneur.

As an alternative to direct investment, an intermediary can assemble savings from various sources and then put those savings to work in particular projects or activities. Intermediated savings also are associated commonly with guarantees of principal and rates of return. Classic examples of financial intermediaries are commercial banks, multilateral financial institutions, and insurance companies. Institutional investors, such as pension or insurance funds, tend to have longer investment horizons and somewhat more competence in monitoring and managing projects than commercial banks. In recent years, too, mutual funds have emerged as important sources of intermediation and, unlike insurance companies and banks, customarily assume less responsibility for risk and generally do not guarantee returns.

Joint Ventures

A joint venture involves the sharing of assets, risks, and profits, and participation in the equity of a particular enterprise or project by more than one group. Sometimes it is useful to organize a joint venture for a specific project, whereas in other cases the venture may represent an affiliation for a variety of business activities. The distribution of equity shares may be based on each partner's financial contribution or on other capital contributions such as technology or access to markets.

Joint ventures organized around technology transfer often contain a "fade-out" agreement. This structure generally involves initial equity or financial participation by the foreign investor of more than 50 percent, often 100 percent. The terms of the agreement require ownership to be transferred to one or more local parties, either in the public or private sector. The rate of transfer usually is tied to the volume of production, sales, or profits. Once the fade-out is completed, the foreign investor may retain minority participation, or no equity whatsoever. In some cases, production agreements are transformed into marketing or export contracts. In virtually all cases, the foreign investor position is transformed into a different product market organizational form, such as licensing, franchising, or management of contracts.

Production-Sharing Contracts

First developed for use in extractive industries, production-sharing contracts call for the foreign company to undertake production in conjunction with a local public or private company. This agreement is for a specified period of time in return for a predetermined share of the physical output, once the foreign firm has recovered its costs. The production "split" is specified in advance; in addition, differential tax rates on the foreign company's share of output may narrow the effective difference between shares. This type of structure has been used often in motor vehicle joint ventures, and in some aircraft production.

Risk service contracts are similar to production-sharing contracts, with the key distinction that the foreign company's share of output is paid in currency rather than in physical production. Alternatively, the foreign company may be permitted to buy output at world prices. This structure may be useful when future domestic demand levels are subject to great uncertainty. If domestic demand is high, the foreign partner in essence becomes a captive seller rather than an exporter.

Licensing Agreements

Licensing agreements are contracts in which a foreign licensor provides access to technological know-how in return for some claim of value. This claim may take the form of an initial lump-sum fee, a percentage of sales, a payout based on production, royalties, shares of equity, or goods bought at a discount, as in countertrade. Agreements also may provide for access to any technological improvements or adaptations the licensee may make.

The license gains access to technology, trademarks, copyrights, patents, or some combination, for a specified or unspecified period. Licensing agreements also may call for the training of local personnel by the licensor, or, in the case of technical assistance agreements, by the supplier.

A licensing agreement is not a "technology sale" in most cases. The licensee usually is given carefully defined access to the technology or knowledge. In addition, the licensor generally has a significant long-term stake in the application of the technology, so the licensor is more of an investor than a supplier. In both licensing agreements and joint ventures, suspicions related to defense and security issues must be overcome, because many transport and infrastructure technologies and products have actual or potential military uses.

Franchising

Franchising is a particular type of licensing or technical-assistance agreement. The franchisor usually provides the local partner with a package including some form of product or service identification or tie-in. Commonly, these franchises also provide technical, financial, and management assistance. In turn, the franchisee contributes some capital, pays royalties, and complies with requirements negotiated with the foreign firm, such as after-market service conditions or parts supply for distributor franchises. Franchises may be valuable in establishing intermediate industries, such as road construction, vehicle servicing, and parts and components production. Financing needs are likely to be related to leasing of capital equipment and working capital finance. Multinational institutions may play an indirect role through capitalization of such leasing operations.

Management Contracts

Management contracts require a foreign firm to manage a local project or enterprise. The contract also may require training of local personnel and eventual transfer of management responsibility to local personnel after a certain period. This feature has been used often in the petroleum sector. Under management contracts, the local activity may benefit from such intangibles as the managing firm's international reputation, worldwide procurement capabilities, knowledge of international product and financial markets, and access to funds.

One difference between a licensing agreement and a management contract is that the former commonly relies on an already functioning enterprise in the host country, whereas in the latter the managing company often builds the local operation from the start.

Concessions

Under build-operate-transfer (BOT) and build-own-operate-transfer (BOOT) turnkey contracts, the contractor is responsible for setting up a complete production operation or service or infrastructure project. The specific responsibilities may vary from project to project, but they often cover feasibility studies, provision of technology and expertise, design and engineering services, supply of plant and equipment, and construction of civil works. Under turnkey projects, the contractor's responsibility normally is fulfilled when the project is fully operational. In BOT projects, the contracts call for operation and maintenance for a specified period, but ownership is retained by the principal, usually a public entity.

BOT contractors are often engineering firms with assets and profits that are based on their ability to manage systems integration and to mobilize large-scale projects. These projects generally are one- or few-of-a-kind and have geographical or industrial idiosyncracies. In some ways, BOT structures are short-term franchises, and BOOT structures are franchises that contain a provision conveying property rights. These contracts do not necessarily involve a single contractor. The principal contractors generally subcontract portions of the project, and the technologies supplied generally include some that are licensed or embodied in machinery, equipment, or services supplied by other firms, often in exchange (at least partially) for an equity participation in the project.

International Subcontracting

The international subcontracting structure normally involves a foreign contractor that places orders with a local subcontractor to produce components or to assemble finished products with the inputs it provides. The final product usually is sold by the foreign company, sometimes in third-country markets. The growing importance of international subcontracting has been closely related to tariff regulations and to the proliferation of free-trade export-processing zones in developing countries.

Project Finance

There are two principal ways in which debt finance can be raised by a commercial entity: through conventional borrowing, under which the lenders have full recourse to the borrower for repayment of principal and interest; and project finance, under which the lenders have no (or limited) recourse to the sponsors-owners beyond the asset itself. Project finance lenders look initially to the cash flows of the project for repayment and servicing of the loan, and to the assets of the project entity as collateral. Through security packages and risk distribution mechanisms, the recourse of lenders with regard to certain risks may be shifted subsequently to guarantors, sponsors, and other parties.

Maturities and sources of finance generally are matched to the specific requirements of a project. The principal medium- and long-term sources of finance are private investors (ordinary and preferred shareholders), commercial banks, investment banks, bond markets, risk capital pools, export credit agencies, multilateral and bilateral agencies, lessors, and suppliers and buyers. The EBRD has developed limited-recourse project finance techniques for application in the transition economies. Short-term finance includes trade credits, supplier and buyer credits, working capital loans, and commercial paper.

Project risks can be classified by their nature and their timing in the project cycle. General commercial risks include cost overruns caused by increasing input costs, rising financing costs, and general inflation; delays in construction; declining demand for outputs in the absence of long-term purchase contracts; and *force majeure* risks. Political risks include expropriation or increased government interference through increased regulation, price controls, higher taxes, and restrictions on the export of the project outputs and the import of project inputs. In the former Soviet Union, currency convertibility and transferability risks are additional major factors.

The challenge of structuring limited-recourse project finance is to devise effective financing and security packages. Risk-spreading mechanisms allow project risks to be distributed among sponsors, lenders, governments, and interested third parties so that an acceptable allocation results. Some degree of recourse for project lenders also normally is incorporated. Governments, parent companies of controlled subsidiaries, foreign and domestic investors in joint ventures, and other owners-sponsors of projects may provide guarantees of some form and extent for the indebtedness of the project enterprise. These guarantees commonly are required by lenders when the project company has inadequate capital or a poor operating record.

Guarantees also may be provided by interested third parties. Parties interested in selling equipment or supplies or in leasing a plant or equipment to a project may be willing to extend guarantees. Suppliers may be motivated to extend guarantees by the prospect of an assured market for their product once the project facility is operating. Sponsors often provide completion guarantees to protect the lenders, because the periods of greatest risk commonly are the construction and commissioning phases of a project. Guarantors undertake to complete the project within a certain period of time and to extend financial resources to cover all cost overruns, irrespective of cause. In this sense, completion guarantees can provide "full recourse" for the lenders during the construction and startup phases of a project.

Lenders typically bear the commercial risks during the operating phase of the project. However, they may demand protection against factors that are beyond the control of the project participants and that could affect the project's ability to generate earnings to service its debt. Often an indirect guarantee is used to ensure a minimum stream of project revenues. The most common guarantees of this type are take-or-pay contracts and volume agreements. Under a take-or-pay contract, users of project output, sponsors, or third parties agree to make periodic payments in return for a given portion of the project's output. The obligation to make payments is unconditional, regardless of whether the product or service actually is delivered. Volume agreements are found commonly in pipeline projects or in railroad contracting. They stipulate that the users ship a minimum volume at periodic intervals and pay for the use of the pipeline or rail assets, irrespective of whether the stipulated amount of the product is shipped or not.

Other risk-spreading methods commonly used include forward-purchase agreements and production payments. In typical forward-purchase (sometimes called "advance payment") financing, the lender makes a loan against future output that has not yet been delivered or produced. When the project begins operating, the lenders have the right to take quantities equivalent in value to the scheduled debt service on the loans. Production payment structures involve the purchase by the lenders of a portion of the future production of a project in exchange for equity principal. They differ from forward-purchase agreements in that the stream of future payments depends on actual production rather than on a fixed schedule of payments.

Strategies to Strengthen Project Finance Opportunities

Commercial banks often view project finance as a private under-taking, and government counterguarantees introduce a sovereign element to the package. Moreover, banks may be reluctant to participate in project financing on a BOT or BOOT basis, because of the usually extensive involvement of government in these projects, either directly through off-take contracts, or indirectly through the provision of services, pricing regulations, issuance of consents, and so on. In the banks' view, the line between commercial and political risks in this context may be difficult to discern. Participation of a multilateral financial institution can mitigate these risks greatly because of the importance of the overall government – multilateral institution relationship.[25]

In some cases, lenders or investors may be unwilling to accept certain commercial risks (such as product price and off-take risks). Credit enhancement support for these risks – through guarantees, direct funding of contingency facilities, or other mechanisms – may be critical for success. In foreign-exchange-generating projects, offshore trust accounts normally are required. Foreign-exchange earnings of the project are deposited into these accounts, and debt service payments are made from the proceeds. Alternatively, the escrow proceeds could be used to set up a sinking fund for defeasance of project debt. This mechanism would thus ensure that certain foreign exchange payment obligations of the project company would be met from resources outside its control, thereby reducing currency convertibility and transfer risk.

Cofinancing

Cofinancing operations typically describe a financing arrangement in which different types of risk are shared between creditors. "Official" cofinancing usually constitutes a risk-sharing transaction between an international financial institution and another financial entity; it is intended to mobilize additional flows of funds to developing countries from both official and private sources.[26] Cofinancing provides borrowing countries with more resources on better terms through risk mitigation. It substitutes multilateral development institution risk for that of the ultimate users (or borrowers) of funds.[27] Commercial banks and official export credit agencies are the traditional cofinanciers. Bilateral export credit cofinancing may play an even larger role in the future, given constraints on official aid and demands for tied supplier financing.

Other types of cofinancing also have grown in importance. In umbrella, or standby, financing, the multilateral organization initially finances an entire project but cancels a portion of its loan when cofinancing becomes available. In channel financing, cofinanciers prefer an indirect financial relationship with a developing country by processing their funds through the multilateral bank. This mode is feasible only if cofinanciers accept the bank's guidelines and procedures on recruitment of consultants, procurement, loan disbursement, and project supervision. This form of cofinancing often is used when bilateral sources provide grant funds for technical assistance operations.[28]

Notes

1   An overview of many of these new organizational forms is presented in the appendix to this chapter.

2   National governments may have to play a coordinating role so that the integrity and connectivity of networks are maintained. The economic aspects of networks, including issues of connectivity, exclusion, and externalities, are discussed in M. Katz and C. Shapiro, "Network Externalities, Competition, and Compatibility," *American Economic Review* 75 (June 1985): 424–440; M. Katz and C. Shapiro, "Systems Competition and Network Effects," *Journal of Economic Perspectives* 8, 2 (Spring 1994): 93–115; S. J. Liebowitz and S. E. Margolis, "Network Externalities: An Uncommon Tragedy," *Journal of Economic Perspectives* 8, 2 (Spring 1994): 133–150.

3   These issues are taken up in detail in chap. 8–10.

4   J. Sachs, "Beyond Bretton Woods: A New Blueprint," *The Economist* 333, 7883 (October 1, 1994): 24.

5   This is not to say that such concerns were not addressed previously. Many transoceanic voyages in the 1600s had contingent payout structures; the construction of the Suez Canal in the 1870s was achieved through a limited recourse concession structure.

6   Shleifer and Vishny provide evidence that extreme levels of corruption characterize situations in which weak governments cannot control agencies or enterprises. See A. Shleifer and R. Vishny, "Corruption," *Quarterly Journal of Economics* CVIII, 3 (August 1993): 599–618.

7   The globalization of product markets has led to common terms and reference points, methods of measurement, and standards of technical performance. With such standards, approaches to solving problems and to managing technology have further enhanced commonality. Convergence has been most rapid in those countries with modern educational systems, strong scientific and engineering communities, and sophisticated industrial enterprises. Given the latent strengths in many of these areas in the former Soviet Union, incorporation of more modern technologies, operating practices, and customer orientation might be achieved more readily than in other situations.

8   Transport manufacturers in the West had incentives to develop products that best met the worldwide capital and energy costs. In contrast, autarkic policy led to these incentives being almost completely absent in the former Soviet Union.

9 The economic context of Western military spending and technology also has been changing over the past decades. Military technology does not appear to provide the civilian technology applications or advantages that characterized the early postwar period. In fact, many of the central military technologies in electronics, materials, and communications had their roots in civilian development. Because the commercial market for many technologies such as computers, electronics, and aircraft grew to exceed the military market. Moreover, in many instances, the performance demanded by the commercial application was actually higher than for the military. This development was apparently quite different in the former Soviet Union, in part because the defense sector was a primary producer of many goods and services used by the citizenry.

10 The most complete work on this subject has been done by D. Dollar and E. Wolff, *Competitiveness, Convergence, and International Specialization* (Cambridge, MA: MIT Press, 1993); see also M. Abramowitz, "Catching Up, Forging Ahead, and Falling Behind," *Journal of Economic History* 46 (June 1986): 385–406; W. Baumol, "Productivity Growth, Convergence, and Welfare: What the Long-Run Data Show," *American Economic Review* 78 (December 1986): 1072–1085; E. Leamer, *Sources of International Comparative Advantage* (Cambridge, MA: MIT Press, 1984); R. Nelson and G. Wright, "The Rise and Fall of American Technological Leadership," *Journal of Economic Literature*, XXX, 4 (December 1992): 1931–1964.

11 The members of the OECD are principally the developed market economies of the world.

12 Compared with Western economies, the technical human resources in the former Soviet Union are much more specialized. Stalin moved engineering training from the Ministry of Education to the various industry ministries in the 1930s. The many specialties in Soviet engineering education reflect the continual narrowing and redivision of traditional engineering training as practiced in the West. For example, mechanical engineering was broken down into specialties in agricultural machinery, machine tools, casting equipment, automobiles, tractors, and aircraft engines, among others. Graham explains that this subdivision is characteristic of virtually every field of engineering, so transfer of these technical skills is much more difficult than it is for Western economies. See L. Graham, *The Ghost of the Executed Engineer: Technology and the Fall of the Soviet Union* (Cambridge, MA: Harvard University Press, 1993), especially chap. 4, "Technocracy, Soviet Style."

13 J. Cooper, *The Soviet Defense Industry* (London: Royal Institute of International Affairs, 1991). The defense enterprise classification was quite broad, and defense production was much applied to nondefense uses.

14 See S. Claessens, "Alternative Forms of External Finance: A Survey," *World Bank Research Observer*, 8, 1 (January 1993): 91–117.

15 An OECD study found that the tying of bilateral aid to specific procurement terms can increase project costs by as much as 20 to 30 percent. See "The Tying of Aid," *OECD Report 41-91-02-1* (March 1991).

16 A distinction might be made between "rentier investors" and "entrepreneurial investors." A rentier investor assumes few risks or operational responsibilities and does little to enhance the project's ability to produce an economic surplus. The entrepreneurial investor is more likely to assume additional risk, commit resources to solve unforeseen operational problems, or supply improved technologies. The entrepreneurial investor is more akin to a venture capitalist in the private sector. The rentier versus entrepreneur distinction is especially relevant in certain manufacturing industries, such as motor vehicle and truck assembly. In these cases, relatively large multinational companies may supply technologies or components to projects, joint ventures, or enterprises that are unable to compete on world markets, often because the technology is somewhat outmoded or where the maximum output attainable is below minimum efficient scale of production. These endeavors can be part of a divestment strategy for "mature" products or technologies. The profits then are used to finance the development of newer products, often for the home market. Conflict also may arise in defining the geographic market. Often this conflict arises over whether the project will produce for export or solely for the domestic market. This conflict is most likely when the foreign firm supplies the product or competing products internationally. Also, the foreign firm and the domestic partner may side against the host government or multilateral institution: this is likely to occur in trying to protect host country market shares to generate monopoly rents if possible. The result may be a need for government or multilateral institutions to protect consumer interests.

17 In fact, these problems were not irrelevant previously, as suggested by the production and control problems continually encountered, although enterprises typically behaved as if they were.

18 McKinnon argues that because of the problems of moral hazard and ineffective monitoring, all enterprises in transitional economies should be financed solely through retained earnings or equity investment. See R. McKinnon, *The Order of Economic Liberalization: Financial Control in the Transition to a Market Economy* (Baltimore: Johns Hopkins University Press, 1991). This requirement appears a bit stringent; in many cases, the monitoring of debt capital is easier than equity capital, because payout structures and the like are contractual rather than contingent. Also, debt finance is commonly a substitute for traditional equity investment in situations with large risk; in effect, debt serves an equity role, so that where the residual claimant role begins often is quite blurred. This substitution has happened in Western economies in much of the "junk bond" and high-yield debt markets, which have risk characteristics much like equity.

19 In the former Soviet Union, opportunities exist to structure a mix of debt and equity investments. The debt claim guards against the stripping of enterprise assets, either through incentives to monitor the liquidity of the enterprise or

by collateral protection that helps to preserve the asset base. Equity should provide a longer-term perspective, however.

20 See U.S. General Accounting Office, "Enterprise Funds: Evolving Models for Private Sector Development in Central and Eastern Europe," Report NSIAD-94-77 (Washington D.C: General Accounting Office, March 1994).

21 "World Development Report 1994," draft, p. 5.15, paragraph 5.31.

22 This shift may be particularly well suited not only to trucking but also to inland waterway and port activities as well.

23 For a more extensive review of these structures, see J. Badaracco, "Changing Forms of the Corporation," chap. 4 in The U.S. Business Corporation: An Institution in Transition (Cambridge, MA: Ballinger, 1988); C. A. Bartlett and S. Ghoshal, *Managing Across Borders: The Transnational Solution* (Boston: Harvard Business School Press, 1989).

24 For capital to flow across borders, the risk-adjusted real rate of return in the country receiving the capital must be higher than it is in the country providing the capital. One reason for any such higher rate of return could be differences in the factors determining the rate of return on capital; that is, the recipient country might have a more abundant labor supply, more natural resources, lower initial physical capital stock, or lower initial human capital stock than does the source country.

25 Moreover, specific security structures may be used to reduce these risks as well. For example, the EBRD offers participating banks an opportunity to provide funds under EBRD's own lender of record umbrella structure, which ensures transferability, although not exchange rate risks.

26 This arrangement gives the multilateral institution senior status as a financial claimant. Moreover, both the World Bank and the EBRD agreements contain "negative pledge clauses" that restrict a country's ability to pledge assets or particular revenue streams from projects.

27 For example, the "extended creditor status" of the International Finance Corporation has drawn many banks in cofinancing operations. Normally there is a single loan agreement between the IFC and the borrower for the full amount of the finance to be provided by IFC and the commercial banks. The IFC loan is divided into two portions. The first is the loan for IFC's own account (A-loan) and the second (B-loan) is funded by the participating commercial banks, on agreed terms and conditions. A separate Participation Agreement is signed between IFC and each participating commercial bank. The commercial bank's relationship with the borrower is therefore indirect, through IFC, which acts as the sole lender of record and loan administrator. For regulatory purposes, the main advantage of cofinancing with IFC is that it requires no loan provisioning.

28 EBRD is pioneering Export Credit Loan Arrangement Technique (ECLAT) by which bilateral export credit finance is subjected to EBRD requirements for international competitive tendering.

Part II

Transport in the Former Soviet Union at the Advent of Transition

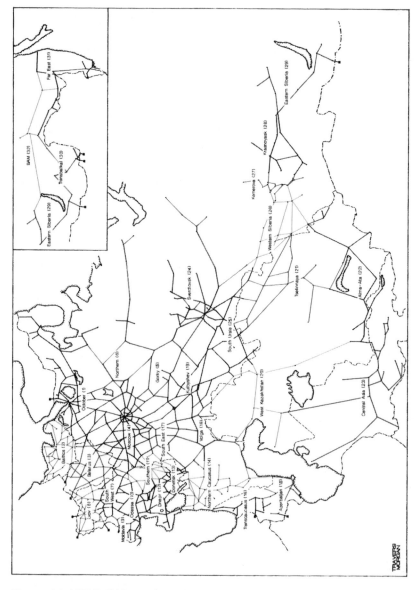

Figure 4-1: MPS Rail Network, 1989   source: Travers Morgan.

4

Railways[1]

Rail transport was one of the most integrated enterprises in the former Soviet Union, and by many measures, the largest of its kind in the world. It also was a major unifying factor in economic and social activity. The Soviet "breakup," with its contemporaneous incidence of rapid cost inflation and economic downturn, confronted rail managers and policymakers with an unprecedented challenge.

1991 and Before

Until the end of 1991, the Soviet Union's Ministry of Railways (MPS) had responsibility for 32 railway administrations in 15 Soviet republics. These railway administrations were largely autonomous operational units, but were subject to common technical, management, and financial standards. In addition, MPS was responsible for the allocation of investment funds and revenues and for interrailway train planning. With the dissolution of the Soviet Union, railway ownership was transferred to the newly independent republics, as listed in table 4-1.[2]

In 1989 these railways carried approximately 4,000 million tonne-kilometers of freight and 411 million passenger-kilometers. These amounts represented more than 2.5 times the total freight carried by all 16 class I railways in the United States and approximately twice as many passenger-kilometers as in the United Kingdom, France, Germany, and Italy combined. Passenger services can be further subdivided into long distance trains, principally overnight locomotive-hauled sleepers, and commuter (suburban) and regional services, as shown in table 4-2. As might be expected, the long-distance trains accounted for most passenger miles and the commuter and regional services dominated the passenger number statistics. Rail

Table 4-1 Railways by Republic

Republic	Soviet MPS No.[1]	Railway Russian Name	Railway English Name	Route Length (km)	Divisions	Administrative Center
Russia	1	Oktyabrskaya	October	10,186	10	St. Petersburg
	4	Moskovskaya	Moscow	9,360	13	Moscow
	5	Gorkovskaya	Gorki	5,672	6	Nizhni
	6	Severnaya	Northern	6,027	8	Novgorod
	14	Severo-Kavkazskaya	North Caucasus	6,486	9	Yaroslavl
	17	Yugo-Vostochnaya	South East	3,648	5	Rostov-on-Don
	18	Privolzhskaya	Volga	4,098	4	Voronezh
	19	Kuibishevskaya	Kuibyshev	4,835	6	Saratov
	24	Sverdlovskaya	Sverdlovsk	7,070	8	Samara
	25	Yuzhno-Ukralskaya	South Urals	4,937	7	Ekaterinburg
	26	Zapadno-Sibirskaya	West Siberia	4,181	5	Chelyabinsk
	27	Kemerovskaya	Kemerovo	1,916	3	Novosibirsk
	28	Krasnoyarskaya	Krasnoyarsk	3,167	3	Kemerovo
	29	Vostchno-Sibirskaya	East Siberia	2,665	4	Krasnoyarsk
	30	Zabaikalskaya	Trans Baikal	3,436	5	Irkutsk
	31	Dalnevostochnaya	Far East	4,432	5	Chita
	32	Baikalo-Amurskaya	Baikat Amur (BAM)	3,853	3	Khabarovsk Tinda
		Subtotal		85,969	104	
Ukraine	7	Yugo-Zapadnaya	South West	4,681	5	Kiev
	8	Lvovskaya	Lvov	4,521	4	Lvov
	10	Odesskaya	Odessa	4,242	4	Odessa
	11	Yuzhnaya	Southern	3,715	5	Kharkov
	12	Pridneprovskava	Dnepr	3,254	4	Dnepropetrovsk
	13	Donetskaya	Donetsk	2,903	6	Donetsk
		Subtotal		23,316	28	
Belarus	3	Belarusskaya	Belarus	5,507	6	Minsk
Kazakhstan	20	Zapadno-Kazakhstanskaya	West Kazakhstan	3,817	4	Aktyubinsk
	21	Tselinnaya	Tselinnaya	5,750	5	Tselinograd
	22	Alma-Atinskaya	Alma-Ata	4,581	6	Alma-Ata
		Subtotal		14,148	15	
Baltic States[2]	2	Pribaltiyskaya	Baltic	6,278	6	Riga
Moldavia	9	Moldavskaya	Moldavia	1,328	1	Kishinev
Georgia	15	Azerbaidzhanskaya	Azerbaijan	2,137	3	Baku
	16	Zakavkazskaya	Trans-Caucasus	2,346	3	Tbilisi
		Subtotal		4,483	6	
Uzbekistan	23	Sredne-Aziatskaya	Central Asian	6,330	5	Tashkent
		Total		147,359	171	

[1] Soviet MPS Railway numbering scheme (official railway reporting number).
[2] Baltic States are not members of the CIS; neither are Moldavia or Georgia.

Source for all tables to follow: Booz-Allen and Hamilton and Travers Morgan, *Railway Sector Survey of the Independent States of Russia, Belarus, Ukraine, and Kazakhstan* (London: European Bank for Reconstruction and Development, December 1992).

passenger traffic grew steadily at approximately a 2 to 2.5 percent annual rate up until the late 1980s, when it stabilized and then receded a bit. Nevertheless, rail was the dominant passenger mode in the Soviet Union, with a 42 percent market share (measured by passenger-kilometers). Bus travel, however, dominated short-distance travel, and accounted for just less than 60 percent of all passengers traveling in 1990 even though the bus share of passenger-kilometers was only 27 percent.

The 10 main freight traffic categories of the Soviet MPS are listed in table 4-3. Although the average length of haul is nearly 1,000 kilometers, a substantial portion (approximately 40 percent) had a haul length of less than 300 kilometers; the median haul length was only approximately 400 kilometers. Only a few commodities, most

Table 4-2 Passenger Activity by Category, Soviet MPS 1990 (32 railways)

	Passengers (MM)	Passenger-Kilometers (billion)	Average Trip (km)
Long-distance	432	294	681
Suburban/regional	3,841	123	32
Total	4,273	417	98

Table 4-3 Freight Activity by Category, Soviet MPS 1990 (32 railways)

Traffic Group	Tonnes (MM)	Tonne-km (billion)	Average Haul (km)
Coal and coke	772	686	888
Oil products	393	431	1,096
Ores	318	243	763
Iron and steel	193	294	1,520
Forest products	141	262	1,860
Construction materials	1,025	510	498
Cement	108	71	654
Fertilizers	138	162	1,176
Grains and products	150	185	1,235
Other	618	873	1,413
Total freight	3,856	3,717	964

notably construction materials, had hauls significantly shorter than the average. About half of all freight wagons had destinations outside the railway of origination. Table 4-4 shows the estimated distribution of overall traffic flows by distance.

In addition to the principal rail systems, there are also roughly 151,000 kilometers of "industrial" railway lines in Russia, Ukraine, Belarus, and Kazakhstan. The rail administrations in each republic normally exchange traffic with these industrial railways. For purely internal movements the industrial railways have their own wagons, often built to heavy-haul specifications. The scope and scale of the industrial railway operations by industry are summarized in table 4-5. An estimated 95 percent of the MPS traffic originated on the industrial network and 83 percent terminated there; thus, the industrial railways performed most high-cost terminal operations.

Total Soviet railway employment in 1990 was approximately 3.05 million. Railroads in the U.S. employed just over 250,000 in the same year. However, just over 1 million of Soviet rail employees were classified as nonoperational staff.[3] The railway industry, like other former Soviet industries, provided many social services for its employees. These services included health care, child care, education services, housing, vacation assistance, food supplements, and other such activities. This provision was in keeping with the Soviet system, under which employees earned low overall money wages,

Table 4-4 Freight Trip-Length Distribution, Soviet MPS 1990
              (32 railways)

Distance (km)	Tonnes (%)	Tonne-km (%)
0-100	17.4	0.9
100-300	22.2	4.5
300-500	13.0	5.4
500-700	8.0	4.9
700-1,000	8.1	6.9
1,000-2,000	16.5	24.2
2,000-3,000	7.0	17.3
3,000-5,000	6.0	23.7
5,000+	1.8	12.2
Total	100.0	100.0

but paid little in taxes while receiving basic social services from their employer.

The Soviet railways as a whole made significant operating profits (generally approximately 20 to 30 percent above expenditure, excluding some capital items). Although the Soviet financial accounting procedures did not treat interest charges as expenses, the profit margin was such that the MPS probably also would have been profitable had these been included. It was only in January 1992, under pressure from cost inflation not recouped in increased revenues, that the first monthly loss since the 1940s was recorded.

Freight operations made a higher return than passenger operations but both were apparently profitable. Within passenger operations, suburban passenger services ran at a loss but long-distance services were profitable. Since 1990, and especially since January 1992, both

Table 4-5 Industrial Rail Networks, Soviet MPS 1990

	Network Length (thousands km)	Tonnes (MM)[1]		Tonne-km (billion)
		External	Internal	
Iron and steel	18.6	1,288	2,014	21.5
Coal	11.9	820	888	17.6
Construction materials	5.1	375	376	5.0
Nonferrous metals	5.2	200	255	5.6
Energy	4.9	398	35	2.2
MPPXT	7.3	467	—	3.2
Chemicals	2.4	80	—	0.4
Fertilizer	2.7	239	—	1.2
Oil	1.4	256	29	1.9
Heavy construction	1.7	125	—	0.6
Transport construction	1.2	57	—	0.3
Timber	20.2	153	29	2.6
Heavy industry	1.2	57	—	0.3
Food processing	3.9	125	—	0.6
MPS	25.4	2,038	—	13.9
Other	38.4	1,082	—	7.4
Total	151.5	7,760	3,626	84.3

[1] Divided into that which transfers to and from MPS ("external") and that wholly within the individual network ("internal").

freight (in particular) and passenger tariffs have increased rapidly. Nevertheless, passenger fare increases lagged behind inflation so that in 1992, there was a cross-subsidy from freight to all passenger services. Rail fares also lagged behind airfares in adjusting to inflation, so a major modal shift from air to rail was induced in 1992 and 1993.

Management and Institutional Structures

A typical Soviet management structure involved a head of railway, who was responsible for overall management, relations with the government and other railways, and coordination of divisions. Deputies for operations, engineering, supplies, safety, finance, personnel, and economics reported to the head of railway.

Many marketing activities familiar in Western railways, for both freight and passenger services, were absent or minimal. Responsibility for interacting with customers resided within the economics department, and there were service planning and tariff officers within the freight branch – activities that a marketing department would carry out in a Western railway.

The personnel and social branch had a wide scope of responsibilities that included extensive medical, educational, and housing services in addition to standard Western personnel functions. The railway accounting systems provided very specific identification of these social costs, and labor statistics made a clear distinction between operational and social development personnel (although these distinctions might not always correspond to normal usage in the West).

Operating Responsibilities

Geographical divisions were the principal operating units of each railway. These divisions were responsible for train operations in their area (subject to the centrally coordinated train plan), plus train control, rolling stock and infrastructure maintenance, and social services. They had full cost and revenue accounting functions, local balance sheets, and profit and loss accounts. The management structure of a division was a microcosm of the railway management itself.

The apparent degree of autonomy in the divisions, however, should be seen in the context of a command economy in which railway objectives were defined externally in physical output terms and were relatively constant from year to year. Thus, the range of matters over which divisional management exercised real commercial management discretion in the Western sense was very limited.

Railway Administration in the Successor Republics

The Russian MPS is the Russian Federation successor to the Soviet Railways (SZD) and retains many of its former functions and characteristics. In the move toward a market economy, the Russian MPS appears to be pursuing policies that will give more management responsibility to individual railways, many of whom are pressing for such independence. In addition to the MPS, the Russian government in 1992 established a Ministry of Transport that has an overall coordinating role for rail, road, waterways, and air transport, particularly to pursue policies of demonopolization.

Belarus has pursued a policy of preserving an integrated railway operation, because approximately 80 percent of Belarussian freight traffic is to or from other railways or is transit traffic. The Belarus government, however, has raised rates independently for local traffic.

In Ukraine the six Soviet-era railways have been placed within the responsibility of the State Administration of Railways of Ukraine. These six railways are to continue as individual enterprises, although profits may be reallocated among railways as they were under the Soviet MPS. While supporting continued measures to integrate interrepublic services, Ukraine railways have pursued independent policies for internal traffic, which represents 77 percent of the Ukrainian rail-freight task.

Kazakhstan's three railways fall under the authority of the new republic's Ministry of Transport, which has responsibility for coordinating transport across all modes. The first minister was the former head of the Alma-Ata railway.

In February 1992 the republics of the CIS agreed to set up a Railway Transportation Council consisting of the administrative heads of railways in each republic. The council coordinates interrepublic operations, including fleet planning, documentation, interrailway accounting, unified safety standards, research priorities, and passenger and freight tariffs (both interrepublic and with other countries).

Rail Operations

The former Soviet MPS was responsible for producing the train plan for the entire railway system. The priorities for train dispatch were (broadly): first, commuter rail and trains that brought milk and fresh foodstuffs to the cities; second, international passenger trains; third, intercity freight trains; fourth, domestic long-distance passenger trains; fifth, local freight distribution movements; and finally, regional passenger and local freight trains.

The train demands and test schedules were processed using linear programming methods and information systems that, within the priorities established, attempted to minimize wagon hours for a given target throughput. Three related (but not fully integrated) rail freight management information systems were in force in the former Soviet Union in 1992: a freight transportation management information system (TMIS); a checkpoint freight train passing system; and a waybill data collection system. These systems were implemented by regional computer centers that were connected to approximately 2,500 freight yards, principal rail stations, maintenance depots, dispatchers, and divisional and regional headquarters. Unfortunately, as a consequence of several inadequacies not normally encountered in the west, the systems inherited from the Soviet MPS are inadequate to support the transport services required by a market economy.

Freight trains typically are hauled with single or two-unit locomotives by a two-man crew and without a caboose or a brake van. The standard features of train operations in the four republics are listed in table 4-6. Wagons are reclassified in hump yards many times between origin and destination. Each time a wagon is humped it is prone to impact loss and damage, compounded by the absence of automatic retarders in many yards. Also, rail yard masters often were evaluated based on railcars humped per day, so that incentives

Table 4-6 **Standard Freight Operating Specification**[1]

Republic	Target Speed (km/h)	Actual Speed (km/h)	Train Length (wagons)	Gross Trailing Weight (tonnes)
Russia	45	35	55	3,112
Belarus	60	50	57	2,873
Ukraine	43	33	54	3,172
Kazakhstan	45	36	57	3,313

[1] The standard length for sidings, departure, receival marshaling roads is 850 m. Several years ago the railways began to extend sidings to 1050 m, but this currently covers only 4% of route length in Russia and 11% in Kazakhstan.

encouraged yard activities rather than decreased connecting time. In addition, there is the potential for theft while wagons are standing in terminals. Fortunately, wagons moved through intermediate yards quite quickly.

With the high traffic levels of the mid- to late 1980s, the train plans inevitably tended to standardize long-distance freight trains, attaching a maximum load of mixed freight wagons scheduled at constant speed. Running shorter unit trains or specialized express trains would have reduced the achievable ratio of volume to capacity. There have been attempts to operate long-distance unit trains that bypass intermediate yards, charging premium tariffs. Many "carousel" block trains carrying single bulk commodities run in heavy industrial areas. It has proved difficult, however, to maintain the local operating discipline necessary to sustain these movements reliably.

Intermodal Operations

Rail intermodal operations are quite limited compared to Western railroads. Domestic containers are moved in general service freight trains, normally mixed with other traffic. Most domestic container terminals were built in the late 1960s or early 1970s. Most containers are small and do not meet ISO container standards. These containers limit efficiency for international freight transfer but may be well suited for connections with the existing truck fleet. These small containers also may serve well as a transitional technology because of labor costs and limited shipments of new consumer-oriented enterprises.

The usual intermodal terminal trackage design puts heavy demands on shunter or switching services. The tracks usually are connected only at one end. The design of dedicated craneways for different-sized containers makes it necessary to classify wagons before placing them for discharge; conversely, containers are not block-loaded when placed upon wagons.

Railway personnel pack and unpack less than 5 percent of all containers; freight-forwarding enterprises handle the rest. There are 150 freight-forwarder off-station container yards that perform this service for 3- and 5-tonne containers, and 40 similar yards that pack and unpack ISO 20-foot containers. Freight forwarding enterprises in the former Soviet Union, though, are not comparable to Western private intermodal companies offering door-to-door service; rather, they are state enterprises with responsibilities that often do not extend beyond operating the road trucks that serve one terminal and performing loading and unloading tasks between road and rail.

Euro-Asia Landbridge

Historically, the trans-Siberian landbridge service was controlled by the Soviet Ministry of Foreign Economic Relations and experienced limited success at best. A new Trans-Siberian Express Service (TSES) was set up as a joint venture company in March 1992 by Sea-Land Services of the United States and the Russian MPS. The MPS contributed 3,400 flat-wagons as their equity contribution. Sea-Land contributed logistics management technology and management skills. TSES negotiates transit rights and pricing with each railway along the route.

Containers are held at Vostochny until a trainload (30 to 50 wagons) of containers can be operated to a single destination. Train accumulation time ranges from 3 to 7 days. The load imbalance in the early 1990s was four container loads westbound for every load eastbound. The wagons are assembled into 3 to 5 unit trains each week handling 20- and 40-foot ISO containers from Vostochny on the Pacific Coast destined to Brest (60 percent), Chop (15 percent), and Luzhaika, Finland (15 percent). The remainder move to Tallinn, Estonia for transit to Scandinavia and Germany by ship. The total rail transit time to central Germany was marginally less than the transit time by a conference sea carrier, but port-to-port time was about the same by sea or land.

Trans-Siberia landbridge traffic volumes in 1992 were 30 percent below those experienced in 1989. Along with recession, the primary reasons for this decline were lack of consistent and timely service, and enroute theft from containers. One possibility for improving service would be to combine international domestic and transit containers in more frequent unit trains from Vostochny and Vladivostok to reduce delays and pilferage.

Passenger Operations

The railways of the new republics inherited an extensive network of long-distance passenger services from their Soviet predecessors. With few exceptions these services are based on overnight passenger trains scheduled to leave in the late evening and arrive early in the morning on the next or later days. Trains are heavy and long, typically consisting of fifteen to twenty coaches.

The standard service is known as a "fast" train. These trains operate on all trunk routes. They call only at major stations and have an average operating speed of approximately 55 to 60 kilometers per hour. The only faster service is the Moscow to St. Petersburg "express" train running during the daytime once a week in each direction. This train has an average speed of 130 kilometers per hour, completing the 650-kilometer journey in five hours.

Long-distance passenger trains have a locomotive crew of two persons. The onboard crew is headed by a chief conductor who is responsible for overall train safety as well as supervision of conductors. There are two conductors per coach for very long journeys and one per coach for day services. Comfort and amenities are basic at best. Noise levels are high, heating is not well regulated, lighting is usually dim, toilets and washbasins are spartan and catering service is very limited. Schedule reliability, however, is quite high.

All major cities have extensive suburban rail services. Many of these services extend well into hinterland areas, so it is possible to travel between many major cities by using a combination of the so-called suburban services which serve each city. As in Western countries, demands are heavily peaked. More unusually, there are more commuters in the summer than in the winter, because of travel to and from country cottages (dachas).

A regional service is provided to minor stations on main lines and to the many hundreds of stations on branch lines. In many areas, particularly in eastern Russia, rail provides the only practical means of passenger transport. There are a large number of manned stations throughout the network. For example, the Belorussian Railway has 472 manned stations (one every 11 kilometers); the October Railway (Moscow-Leningrad) has 600 manned stations (one every 17 kilometers).

Suburban and regional services are of major economic and social importance, and therefore are politically sensitive. They face several severe problems. Rolling stock is aging and expensive to operate; major reinvestment is required. Many routes appear inordinately long, incurring high operating expenses without commensurate traffic volume. Equally important are financial problems. Cost recovery from users must be improved or other financing mechanisms must be developed that are more closely related to local transport priorities and capacity.

Productivity and Pay Incentives

A high proportion of rail labor pay in the former Soviet Union is made up of bonuses related to meeting production targets. In most activities performance is measured either in physical outputs or in terms of outputs valued at official administered prices.

This incentive structure creates several problems. First, cost and profit consciousness is not a key focus of the decisions of most managers. Cost variances against budget are monitored closely, but only for a specific plan in which input sources, input prices, outputs and output prices have been predetermined.

Second, the close relationship between rewards and output targets requires some precision on the measurement of output. Inevitably this creates an emphasis on "quantity" of service, which can be readily measured, with insufficient attention to quality. In market economies, quality incentives arise through customer choice of vendor and willingness to pay. These mechanisms were largely absent in the Soviet Union.

A third and related problem of the established incentives was to discourage change and innovation. Unless directly related to exceeding an output target, the rewards of innovation are uncertain but the risks are onerous. Linking the rewards of innovation with output, rather than commercial performance, also tends to undervalue innovations that make more economical use of resources as compared with innovations to expand capacity. Finally, the lack of proper accounting for interest on the capital used by the railways (as with other enterprises) provides incentives to undervalue capital and distort investment decisions.

Rail and Right-of-Way Assets

Rail in the former Soviet Union was generally in good condition. However, the lack of comprehensive rail preservation practices and high tonnages resulted in a rerailing cycle that is considerably shorter than that of most Western railways. Indeed, a severe backlog developed during the 1980s in re-laying track. By the end of 1991, 3,000 kilometers needed re-laying; this backlog likely doubled in 1992.

Track ballast conditions varied considerably across the country, with ballast a major problem over much of the main-line network. Track with fouled and inferior quality ballast can be heavily respon-

sible for reduced life of track components. The railways do not have modern high-capacity ballast cleaning machines that can help prolong the life of major track structure components.

Power Supply and Catenary Systems

Approximately 40 percent of route-kilometers are electrified; 65 percent of the tonne-kilometers are moved by electric traction. Three different electric traction schemes are in use in the former Soviet Union, dominated by older 3,000-volt direct current (3kV-DC) systems and newer 25,000-volt alternating current (25kV-AC) systems. In addition, 10,000-volt AC is used on some industrial railways but not on the "common carrier" network. Table 4-7 lists the distribution of electrified common carrier routes in each republic by type.

The condition of both the DC and AC overhead systems is good. There is no evidence of significant deferred maintenance either in the catenary systems or within AC substations. However, about onefourth of the DC sub-stations have outdated internal switchgear and related equipment for which parts are no longer readily available. DC systems, although used in many countries for metro and commuter operations, are rarely used elsewhere for long-distance freight and passenger lines, mainly because they are more expensive to install and maintain and require more substations. However, the cost of conversion of the 24,000 kilometers of the existing DC system to AC would be prohibitive compared with the benefits to be gained. Although not as efficient as modern high-voltage AC systems, the railways continue to invest in some 3kV-DC system extensions (perhaps quite properly) to complete connections between DC systems or to extend coverage of existing systems.

Table 4-7 **Route-km of Electrification**

Republic	Type 3-kV-DC	Type 25-kV-AC	Total
Russia	18,710	19,072	37,782
Belarus	26	843	869
Ukraine	4,769	3,852	8,621
Kazakhstan	0	3,269	3,269
Total	23,505	27,036	50,541

During the 1960s and 1970s, approximately 2,000 route-kilometers of railway were electrified each year across the entire Soviet MPS network. By 1980, most of the busiest lines had been electrified; thereafter, only 600 to 700 kilometers were added annually.

Signaling and Train Control Systems

Approximately 82 percent of total route distance is controlled with continuous automatic signals. Three main types of signaling are employed: automatic block signaling;[4] centralized traffic control;[5] and two-track semaphore.[6] In addition to these systems there are more than 32,000 route-kilometers of "semi-automatic block," a manual system that allows one train at a time to occupy the track between stations or crossing loops.

Many interlockings are controlled locally by control centers, which are essentially signal boxes that control a few kilometers of track. In 1992, there were 5,896 of these centers in Russia, 454 in Belarus, 1,668 in Ukraine and 828 in Kazakhstan. In contrast, the trend in Western railways has been to consolidate system control into a small number of well-equipped control centers. Such modern control systems can readily control up to 1,000 kilometers of track with substantial savings in labor. Broadly speaking, the approximately 8,000 control centers in the former Soviet Union probably could be reduced to about 200.

Maintenance of signaling and other train control equipment on the railways is carried out according to comprehensive and stringent standards. Detailed testing of equipment occurs more frequently than on North American and European railways. The system did not exhibit any obvious signs of deferred maintenance.

Yard Facilities

As table 4-8 shows, there were few automatically operated hump yards in 1990. Most hump yards were operated manually using some

Table 4-8 **Marshaling Hump Yards by Republic, 1990**

Type	Russia	Belarus	Ukraine	Kazakhstan	Total
Manual with route selection	63	3	23	5	94
Automatic (computerized)	4	1	2	1	8
Point machines	2,504	148	920	224	3,796
Retarders	2,907	107	1,148	205	4,367

hydraulic but mainly pneumatic retarders. Some were equipped with automatic route selection. No speed control or in-motion weighing devices appear to have been used. Classification track entrance and coupling speeds were in the hands of the retarder operator. This arrangement often can lead to excessive impacts to wagons or wagons stopping short of their planned coupling (causing time and capacity penalties).

Telephone and Communication Systems

The Soviet railways operated more than 1 million telephone lines, one of the largest private telephone networks in the world. Approximately 60 percent of these telephones were installed in stations and offices. Another 30 percent were installed in the homes of active and retired railway employees, for whom service was provided at no charge. The remaining 10 percent of the telephones were used to provide commercial services in areas where it was inconvenient for other telephone networks to operate.

Although no traffic data are available, the Russian MPS estimates that its telecommunications network is operating at about one-third above practical capacity. The average traffic load over the network is reported to be 0.2 erlangs/line with an average call holding time of 10 minutes. This rate suggests a network that handles one-third of the call originations of typical Western networks, but with calls lasting three times as long. The free use of the network may be one reason for this, but it is likely that very long call setup times are also a contributing factor.

The Soviet railways also operated one of the largest private radio systems in the world, mainly designed for locomotive cab communications. The cab operators are able to communicate directly with dispatchers and track maintenance workers. A network of 14,000 base stations has been created, but heavy radio congestion exists in many locations.

Locomotives and Rolling Stock

The locomotive fleet of the Soviet MPS was the largest of any railway in the world. In 1990, the fleet totaled approximately 36,600 locomotives containing an estimated 62,000 individual units. In most cases, locomotives are in fact two units semipermanently coupled together. Most trains operate with one such dual unit. The 1990 active fleet (excluding shunting locomotives, those in overhaul and out of service, and reserves) is listed in table 4-9.

Locomotives appeared in good condition, given the age of the fleet and intensity of use. Maintenance schedules represent considerably more maintenance input than would be expected on Western railways, particularly for electric units. For the former Soviet Union as a whole, total out-of-service rates are approximately 10 percent, similar to Western railways. The electric locomotives are robust and fit for their purpose, although out-of-date in design and control technology. Nearly three-fourths of the MPS's diesel-electric fleet was powered by two-cycle, in-line, opposed piston engines. These units are difficult to maintain. They also have a tendency to burn relatively large quantities of lubricating oil during sustained operation, creating heavy emissions. Even the Soviet four-cycle units, though, smoke excessively and are not very fuel efficient. Fuel has been cheap relative to world prices, so no special effort has been made to minimize fuel consumption. Traction control, low-idle and auxiliary power control systems, and modern diesel design technologies could reduce fuel consumption by some 25 percent or more, as well as reduce air pollution and lubricant consumption.

The average age of the locomotive fleet at the end of 1992 was approximately 18 years for diesel locomotives and 17 years for electrics. However, assuming that the oldest 25 percent of locomotives will not be required because of reduced traffic resulting from the transition, the average age of the active locomotive fleet is probably 14 years. Russian MPS statistics indicate that in January 1992 about 20

Table 4-9 **Broad-Gauge Active Freight and Passenger Locomotive Fleet by Republic, 1990**

| | Freight | | Passenger | | |
	Electric	Diesel	Electric	Diesel	Total
Russia	7,339	3,706	1,881	1,195	14,121
Ukraine	1,232	1,121	441	442	3,236
Belarus	43	318	35	104	500
Kazakhstan	383	1,035	58	224	1,700
Other CIS and Baltic countries	408	935	130	230	1,703
Total	9,405	7,115	2,545	2,195	21,260

percent of diesel locomotives were older than 20 years and about 7 percent of electric locomotives were older than 30 years.

Passenger Equipment

Total passenger rolling stock ownership as of 1991 is listed in table 4-10. The average age of carriages is approximately 18.5 years. The Soviet SZD treated carriages as fully depreciated after 28 years; these vehicles comprise 13 percent of the fleet. Multiple unit (MU) equipment is used both for suburban services and local services in rural areas. The average age of MU rolling stock appeared to be 15 to 18 years for both diesel and electric MUs in 1991. Long distance passenger equipment has wheel drive generator equipment for on-board power. Much of this equipment also has coal-fired boiler heating. Very few carriages are air-conditioned; many wagons are heated electrically.

Freight Wagons

The broad-gauge wagon or freight-car fleet of the former Soviet SZD consisted of approximately 1.8 million units (table 4-11) with an average age of 16 years. The fleet was generally in good condition. The SZD wagon fleet was carried predominantly on conventional three piece bogies with a total of four axles per wagon. Each four-axle wagon had a gross weight not to exceed 90 tonnes to achieve a

Table 4-10 **Passenger Equipment, Soviet MPS, 1991 (32 railways)**

Type	In Service	Repair/Cleaning	Total
Hauled equipment			
Passenger	34,850	15,300	50,150
Dining/rest	6,540	2,020	8,560
Suburban	2,830	2,830	2,830
Other	1,300	1,300	1,300
Subtotal	45,520	17,320	62,840
Multiple-unit equipment			
Electric	18,760	970	19,730
Diesel	3,240	270	3,510
Subtotal	22,000	1,240	23,240
Total	67,520	18,560	86,080

Table 4-11   Soviet MPS Broad-guage Wagon Fleet[1]

	Russia	Belarus	Ukraine	Kazakhstan	Other[2]	Total MPS
Box cars	197.4	9.0	55.8	24.9	45.3	332.4
Container flats	18.6	0.7	3.4	1.8	3.0	27.5
Platform flats	155.5	5.4	28.2	17.0	26.3	232.4
Gondolas	363.7	8.5	129.1	45.3	38.0	584.7
Cement hoppers	49.0	4.7	12.0	4.6	8.8	80.0
Grain hoppers	35.9	1.2	11.7	5.1	7.8	61.7
Refrigerators	26.7	1.3	8.3	2.2	11.6	50.1
Refrigeratorazs (Mech)	3.9	0.3	2.4	0.1	2.2	8.9
Tank cars	172.8	8.3	41.2	18.2	35.4	275.9
Specialized	19.3	1.2	5.9	1.5	3.8	31.7
Subtotal active	1,043.4	40.7	298.1	120.6	182.1	1,685.7
Reserve	92.6	3.2	32.7	7.5	11.9	147.1
Total	1,136.0	43.9	330.7	128.1	193.9	1,832.8

[1] Fleet numbers based on average wagons on-line 1987-1990.
[2] Other CIS countries, Georgia, and Baltic countries.

standard loading of 22.5 tonnes per axle. Typical tare weights of wagons ranged from 28 to 32 tonnes, yielding a payload of between 58 and 62 tonnes.

Maintenance Facilities

Table 4-12 summarizes workshop and depot information in the four republics in 1991. Most railway workshops and depots were old and many had been converted from steam engine work. Each large depot and major workshop contained a traction motor re-manufacturing unit, blacksmith shops, foundries, and wheel and air brake shops.

The existing shops generally are designed poorly. Tracks are often too close to permit the use of mobile material-handling equipment. Lighting can be poor and overhead material-handling equipment often is limited in capacity. Very few modern machine tools appear to be available. Some of the shop machinery dates from the 1940s, and much of it was built in the 1950s and 1960s. There are often two or three machines on hand to do the work of one modern machine working part time. In general, one more modern shop might suffice for a whole region.

Table 4-12 Workshops and Depots, 1991

	Russia	Belarus	Ukraine	Kazakhstan	Total
Workshops					
Locomotives	14	1	9	0	24
EMU/DMU	2	0	1	0	3
Carriages	2	0	1	0	3
Wagons	11	2	9	2	23
Total	29	3	19	2	53
Depots					
Locomotives	280	16	77	48	421
Carriages	47	2	14	4	67
Wagons	56	9	31	12	108
Total	383	27	122	64	596

Although most major workshops and many large depots have extensive manufacturing capabilities, major manufacturing has been performed in the main by other ministries. For example, the Ministry of Heavy Machine Building has been responsible for diesel locomotives, engines, some track machines, wagons, and other major components; the Ministry of Metallurgy has managed rails and other steel structures; the Ministry of Forestry and Paper has handled wooden sleeper tie manufacture, with sleeper treatment plants operated by the railways; and the Ministry of Electrotechnical Instruments and Computers has been responsible for electric locomotives, computers, and some instruments.

In addition, the railways purchased equipment and various other railway materials from Eastern Europe. East Germany produced compartmented sleeping cars, thyristors, and other components; Czechoslovakia made passenger locomotives and EMU equipment; Hungary manufactured EMU and DMU equipment; Finland produced some wagons; and the Baltic states made some passenger equipment. The dissolution of the Soviet Union disrupted much of the previous manufacturing and sourcing of component parts. In the early 1990s, supply from outside each republic was tenuous at best and often depended on barter because of the lack of foreign exchange. In many cases, final production stopped because critical components could not be procured.

Additional disruptions arose from political uncertainty. Many manufacturing facilities became nearly independent entities – not necessarily private but also not receiving state backing or much direction. Because of these supply problems, the railways in the early 1990s performed more rebuilding and placed fewer new orders to outside vendors than they did previously. Many functions were delayed or stopped for lack of appropriate materials. In addition, many railway facilities began to manufacture critical components that were not otherwise in ready supply. Although this may be a feasible short-term solution, it is unlikely to prove economically sound in the long term.

Safety and Environmental Issues

Accident rates on the new republics' railroads appear to be low relative to traffic levels and significantly below the rate of major railways in the United States and Western Europe. The main safety priority is to improve the track structure to reduce train derailments and spillage of hazardous materials.

The railways' largest environmental exposure is from air and water pollution. The railways annually use 1 billion cubic meters of water. Approximately 160 million cubic meters of sewage is discharged into open waters. Of this amount, about 10 percent is untreated and another 70 percent is treated inadequately. In addition, many pollutants are discharged in raw form from various railway installations. These include chemical preservatives used at sleeper treatment works as well as diesel fuel and oil from locomotive depots.

In December 1991, the Supreme Soviet passed a bill, "On the Protection of the Natural Environment," tailored to address environmental issues in a market economy. This bill, along with presidential decrees and the adoption of former USSR regulations regarding environmental conditions, forms the basic body of regulations affecting the Russian railways' relationship to the environment. Collectively the regulations are based on a "pay-for-pollution" principle. In 1991, the Soviet SZD approved an environmental program for the railways for the period 1991 to 1995. The program acknowledged the need for changes in attitude and culture in meeting environmental standards.

A system of maximum permissible discharges establishes standards (for air, water and solids) for particular pollutants and enterprises. Discharges below these levels are taxed at one basic rate, while discharges above these levels are charged at rates that are five to six times the basic rate. Concealing or misreporting discharges attracts the maximum penalty rate. In addition, differential coefficients related to the current condition of the environment have been developed for different air and water basins and these coefficients are applied to basic rates to determine pollution payments. The coefficients range from 1.0 for far-eastern areas to 2.0 for air emissions in the Urals, and 2.0 for solid waste disposal in the Central Chernozem region, to 2.9 for discharges into the Kuban river in the Krasnodar (North Caucasus) territory.

Financial Considerations

Tariffs

Until 1990, freight and passenger tariffs were set on a uniform basis throughout the Soviet Union.[7] Since 1991, separate tariff structures have been applied to intrarepublic and interrepublic traffic, as individual countries have adjusted their own tariffs at different times. Freight tariffs are based on distance traveled and wagon-type used, with tonnage minimums specified by commodity. Separate rates apply for railway-owned and industry-owned wagons and for container traffic and small lots. Seven major wagon types are differentiated (together with many specialized multi-axle vehicles). Cargo is classified according to the Unified Statistical-Tariff Freight Classification (UTSFC), which lists 11 branches of the economy (agricultural products, timber and paper, ores, fuel and energy, minerals and construction materials, metals, metal products, chemicals, food products, manufacturers, others) subdivided into 69 groups and 245 subgroups.

The tariffs charged after 1990 were constructed using a series of formulas. These consist of a loading/unloading charge, expressed as a rate per wagon (consisting of a constant term and a second term variable with the tonnage loaded), and a line-haul fee per wagon-kilometer, again varying with the load carried. For general wagons there is also a steeply rising charge for loads between 64 and 80 tonnes. Table 4-13 summarizes traffic volumes and yield by commodity group in 1990.

Table 4-14 summarizes passenger yields. Long-distance passenger fares are structured on a zone basis, with a range of "steps" increasing from 10-kilometer increments for trips under 200 kilometers to 400-kilometer steps for trips more than 6,700 kilometers. The basic fare is the "common" fare, with percentage mark-ups applied for superior classes of service. Special fares are charged for the express trains running between St. Petersburg and Moscow. The fare structure has a strong taper, with long distance unit prices much lower. For example, the fare per kilometer for a 12,000 kilometer trip is approximately 25 percent of the per kilometer tariff for a 100 kilometer journey.

Commuter and suburban fares also are structured on a zonal basis, with zones of approximately 10 kilometers. Most commuter-fare structures contain 16 zones, with adjustments for any journeys in excess of 160 kilometers. There are large discounts for periodic tickets; a monthly ticket is equivalent to about eight single trip tickets; an annual ticket equates to about ten monthly tickets. This level of discount would be considered excessive on most Western commuter railways.

Table 4-13   Soviet MPS: Average Yield by Commodity, 1990

Product	Tonnes (MM)	Tonne-km (billions)	Revenue (MM R)[1]	% Total Revenue	Average Yield (Kp/ntkm)[2]
Coal and coke	772	686	1,880	9	0.27
Oil products	393	431	2,705	13	0.63
Ores	318	243	996	5	0.41
Iron and steel	194	294	1,119	6	0.38
Forest products	141	262	1,178	6	0.45
Construction materials	1,025	510	3,029	15	0.59
Cement	108	71	396	2	0.56
Fertilizers	138	162	704	3	0.43
Grains and products	150	185	777	4	0.42
Other	618	873	7,414	37	0.85
Total	3,857	3,717	20,198	100	0.54

[1] Million roubles.
[2] Kopecks per net tonne-kilometer.

Accounting Systems

The railways employ accounting systems much like those used on Western public-sector rail systems. Balance sheets and income statements are prepared at every organizational level to a standard format, with varying degrees of computerization depending on the railway. Each railway also has a series of management accounts to compare actual and budget (or "plan") expenditure with revenues. Financial accountability descends to a comparatively low level and is linked closely to the bonus system. While the monitoring of expenditure at a relatively detailed level is little different from Western practice, the procedure of calculating a "profit" for operating units such as locomotive depots and stations, based on standard prices for work performed, would generally be regarded as rather advanced in the West.

Table 4-14   Soviet MPS: Average Yield by Passenger Type, 1990

Tariff	Passenger (MM)	Passenger-km (billion)	Revenue (MM R)[1]	% Total Revenue	Average Yield (Kps/passenger-km)[2]
Suburban					
Free	33.2	1.1			
General	10.8	0.5	7.7	2	1.45
Kilometer	0.3	0.0	0.2	—	0.96
Zone	116.5	5.2	49.6	13	0.96
Periodical	207.5	5.7	6.2	2	0.11
Subtotal	368.3	12.5	63.7	17	0.51
Long-distance					
Free	0.4	0.1	—	—	—
Other	22.5	6.7	105.0	28	1.58
Direct					
Free	1.4	0.7	—	—	—
Other	22.1	24.5	207.7	55	0.85
Subtotal	46.4	32.0	312.7	83	0.98
Total	414.7	44.5	376.4	100	0.85

[1] Million roubles.
[2] Kopecks per passenger-kilometer.

Financial Performance

Some republic railways clearly will have much greater difficulty operating on a purely commercial basis. Not surprisingly, the lowest costs are in railways with the highest traffic density. The highest costs are in the smaller railways, particularly where the terrain is also more demanding. Previous procedures for allocating costs among different operations clearly masked a substantial degree of cross-subsidy between railways and between republics. Undoing these cross-subsidies could be a critical issue in any future commercialization of the railways.

The Soviet MPS undertook an annual analysis of costs to allocate them between passenger and freight traffic. This assessment was done in a manner similar to that of most Western railways. The analysis separately allocated around 300 cost items and carried down to the division level. Table 4-15 lists the consolidated results in 1990.

No specific results are readily available at a more disaggregated level (e.g., for commuter services). In 1990, at a system-wide level, permitting service-specific costs to be estimated, the suburban services only recovered 55 percent of costs, while the long-distance services recovered 134 percent (table 4-16). After 1990, the cost recovery in both these sectors declined significantly as fares lagged behind inflation.

Financial Planning and Budgeting

Under the Soviet system, budgets were established at several levels of detail, depending on the time horizon of the plan. The most important of these was the annual plan, which was developed in a top-down fashion. There were several components to the annual plan. Virtually all line items were displayed on an actual and plan basis. Plans were established for railroad work, ancillary activities, and non-transport-related activities. Budgets were developed in terms of both physical and monetary inputs and outputs where appropriate. Annual plans included revenue and expenditure budgets by operating unit and by cost item. Plans also were developed for social development activities, such as housing and health, and for subsidiary industrial activities.

Previously, the decision to invest in new capacity generally was not made by the railway enterprise, but rather through centralized planning agencies. The building of a new rail line would result from

Table 4-15 Financial Results by Sector, Soviet MPS, 1990 (32 railways)

	Cost (MM R)	Traffic Volume[1] (billion ntkm, pax-km)	Unit Cost (Kps/unit)
Expenditure			
Freight			
Electric	7,814	2,367	0.33
Diesel	6,934	1,350	0.51
Total	14,748	3,717	0.40
Passengers			
Electric	1,385	189	0.73
Diesel	1,171	109	1.07
EMU[2]	713	106	0.67
DMU[3]	203	13	1.60
Total	3,472	417	0.83
Total Expenditure	18,221	4,551	0.40
Revenue			
Freight	21,275	3,717	0.57
Passengers	3,703	417	0.89
Total Revenue	24,978	4,134	0.60
Cost recovery (%)			
Freight	144		
Passengers	107		
Freight loading/unloading	283	844	3.36

[1] Passenger-kilometers for passenger activity; net tonne-kilometers for freight.
[2] EMU are multiple elecric units.
[3] DMU are multiple diesel units.

a decision that some existing or proposed facility required service, and that rail was the most economical mode.

Financial Outlook

Any transition to market prices will have differential impacts on the various rail operations and their costs. Under a median forecast of future economic activity for the year 2000, rail demand will be approximately 75 to 80 percent of the 1990 task. Analysis by Travers Morgan/Booz-Allen and Hamilton indicates that this 20 to 25 percent decline will result in reductions in total operating cost of approxi-

Table 4-16   Estimated Financial Results by Subsector, Soviet MPS, 1990 (R MM)

	Cost (MM R)	Revenue (MM R)	Cost Recovery (%)	Unit Cost (Kp)
Freight	14,828	21,275	143	4.00
Passengers				
Suburban	1,086	601	55	0.88
Long-distance	2,307	3,102	134	0.79
Subtotal	3,393	3,703	109	0.81
Total	18,221	24,978	137	0.40[1]

[1] Per equivalent unit.

mately 17 percent, and an increase in unit cost of 5 to 6 percent. Although these changes are large in historical terms, they are manageable. If labor productivity remains constant, increases of around 43 percent over 1990 tariffs would be required to break even; if a 3 percent annual productivity increase is achieved, tariff increases of only 33 percent will be needed. If existing capital is regarded as a sunk cost, then interest charges should be levied only on new investment, and the required increase in tariffs might be reduced to approximately 22 percent.[8]

Segmentation of transport needs, costs, and revenues of different transport markets is vital to commercial management and economic efficiency. Fortunately, the data and accounting systems required to do so are generally available within the railways' established accounting practices. Nevertheless, existing management accounts routinely do not address all the questions that managements would ask in a market economy. For example, these accounts do not measure the financial performance of individual freight or passenger market segments, because answers to such questions were not required previously. However, the systems provide the building blocks to undertake such analyses, and the skills are in place to undertake these tasks in the future.

Institutional Issues

In the Soviet system, railway performance was judged not on how well it responded to its market, but on how well it did what it was told. A program of corporatization, or privatization (possibly with accompanying regulation), should be encouraged to move the railways toward a more commercial orientation. In practice, this will require separation and valuation of assets and financial accounting records; establishment of interrailway terms for shared traffic; contracting with the government for noncommercial responsibilities; and establishment of new board, management, and employee governance structures. As different demands evolve on each railway, so too will different management structures. For example, a railway that handles mostly bulk materials for a few major customers is likely to emphasize operations, whereas a railway that faces emerging road transport competition may emphasize commercial and marketing activity.

Private-sector involvement may be less viable in direct railway operations than in ancillary activities, such as equipment repair and manufacturing, freight forwarding, communications, and terminals. Indeed, activities that can be separated operationally should be spun off, unless there are strong mitigating factors to the contrary. Many of these spinoffs could require substantial up-front investments and thus may necessitate joint ventures with external institutions.

Unlike other modes, the separation of infrastructure provision from operations is unlikely to lead to important efficiency gains in the republic railways. The Western experience with such structures is quite limited, with few conclusive results. Given these uncertainties, and the overarching need to stabilize and restructure production during the transition, any separation of right-of-way from rail operations seems best postponed. In lieu of such separation, promotion of competition between railroads might be encouraged by granting track access rights on a contractual basis for both intrarailway and interrailway traffic. Such access could reduce the power of spatial monopolies and allow industrial enterprises to seek competitive bids for their traffic in at least some situations. Such track rights also might be used by freight forwarders, intermodal operators, bulk users with specialized rolling stock, and other railways.

Summary

Railroads in the former Soviet Union were responsible for an exceptional share (by Western standards) of total transportation activity. They met these needs efficiently, especially after allowing for the aged character of much of their available equipment and technology. The railways achieved this efficiency by managing and using their facilities very intensively, recording in many categories the highest usage densities observable on railroads anywhere. Bottlenecks bedeviled the system and often were met by further degrading an already low level of rail service.

The sharp economic downturn of the early 1990s greatly changed these conditions. Few physical bottlenecks bedeviled rail operations, where once they were commonplace. The problem became not so much finding new capacity as better maintaining or upgrading that which was already in place.

In the future, the railways of the new republics will probably have to make a transition to a new market environment. This transition will require the development of many new skills as well as continued use of many old skills, particularly in containing costs and conducting operations efficiently. Fortunately, many of the requisite support systems and capabilities exist, even though they are in need of modernization and refurbishing. All in all, Soviet railways were probably closer to best Western practice at the advent of transition than any of the other transport modes of the former Soviet Union.

The railways still face an immense challenge to modernize and focus their operations so as to better serve shippers and travelers. The challenge, though, is mainly managerial and structural. Physical capacity is generally adequate. The railways do not require a massive infusion of capital to develop entirely new facilities. Rather, they need highly targeted and specific investments to improve the quality and productivity of existing operations, particularly in rolling stock and maintenance. Management also badly needs modern communications and information systems to help it better focus on key decisions. Better focus also could be achieved by spinning off into separate enterprises all those activities not directly concerned with the transport function, including many maintenance functions.

Notes

1   This chapter was largely based on Travers Morgan/Booz-Allen and Hamilton, "Railway Sector Survey of the Independent States of Russia, Belarus, Ukraine, and Kazakhstan" (London: European Bank for Reconstruction and Development, 1993). To the extent possible, the original presentation of that report has been preserved.

2 Subsequently, two additional railways have been created in Russia for the Sakhalin narrow-gauge system (previously part of the Far East Railway) and the isolated Kaliningrad system (previously part of the Baltic Railway).

3 Soviet nonoperational staff also included conductors and loading personnel who would be categorized as operational staff in Western railroads.

4 Most automatic block signaling ABS systems in use in the four republics provide two-block, three-aspect color-light wayside signal protection for following train movements on the same track. In some high-density areas, a three-block, four-aspect system is used that allows a closer spacing, at safe braking distances, for following train movements. Most four-aspect signaling is in the commuter areas around major cities.

5 The main system is two-block, three-aspect but there is also some three-block, four-aspect with wayside and in-cab signaling.

6 This very old train control system is still in use on approximately 11,000 kilometers of lightly trafficked lines.

7 It was possible to apply local freight rates in special circumstances and commuter-rate guidelines differed among cities.

8 All percentages expressed after adjusting for inflation.

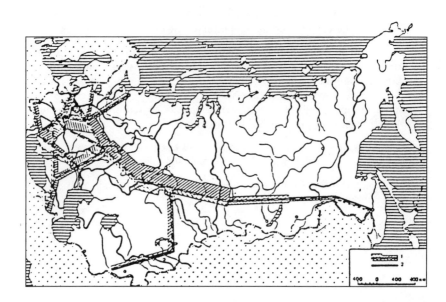

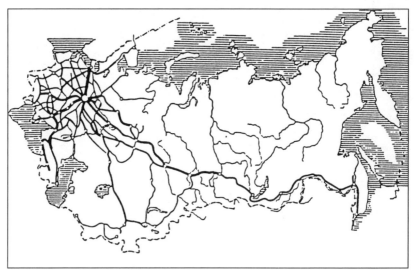

Figure 5-1: Principal Road Transport Routes

Main goods traffic and main passenger traffic routes in the

Soviet Union

source: A.T. Kruscev and I.V. Inkol'skij (edit.): Ekonomiceskaja geografija SSSR. Used
with permission of cowiConsult/TecnEcon and EBRD.

5

Road Transport[1]

The long-standing Soviet policy of channeling transport investment mainly into rail meant a narrowly defined role for road transport in the Soviet Union. This role was exceptionally small by the standards of modern market economies. In 1988, for example, car transport had approximately a 20 percent market share of passenger-kilometers in the Soviet Union, compared with 70 to 80 percent in the United States. Similarly, traffic volumes on non-urban roads were low, due principally to the low level of car ownership (58 cars per 1,000 population compared with 574 per 1,000 in the United States). Congestion problems thus were rare in the Soviet Union. Few capacity problems existed; those that did generally involved city traffic or approach roads to major cities.

In total, traffic on the road network is expected to grow between 2 and 5 percent annually through the year 2015; this implies a much more optimistic outlook than for other modes. In the late 1980s, there were approximately 14 million cars in Russia, Ukraine, Belarus, and Kazakhstan, with the geographical pattern of ownership following that of the population. Forecasts project that the car fleet will be between 10 and 50 percent greater in 2007 compared with 1988. The higher estimates are linked to more optimistic forecasts about economic recovery and subsequent growth.

Given the modest volumes of intercity passenger car traffic, truck traffic has composed a much larger share of total traffic on main roads in the former Soviet Union than in Western countries. On main roads in Russia, Ukraine, Belarus, and Kazakhstan, cars accounted in the early 1990s for only about 30 to 40 percent of traffic, buses approximately 10 percent, and trucks between 50 and 60 percent. Data were unavailable for traffic volumes in the early 1990s. The general view of the national road authorities has been that no substantial decline in road traffic occurred in the early 1990s, but that volumes (in tonne-kilometers) fell 5 percent in Ukraine and Belarus, 12 percent in Kazakhstan, and were constant in Russia.

If road transport becomes more market oriented, automobile traffic will take a much larger share. Future traffic growth will depend largely on patterns in car ownership and on any modal shifts away from rail and to intermodal operations. A change in transport demand from low-value bulk products to higher-value products shipped in small consignments likely will occur as well. Thus, some growth opportunities could be the result of the development of new transport markets rather than shifts from rail to road.

The Road System

Figure 5-1 shows the main road network in each of the four countries and table 5-1 lists the densities of public road systems. Road densities are very low compared with Western Europe (where there are typically around 1,000 kilometers of road per 1,000 square kilometers of land surface). This difference has led to the widespread assumption that there is a severe lack of roads in the former Soviet Union. The road statistics in the former Soviet Union are, however, not directly comparable with those of Western Europe, because the public roads in the former Soviet Union account for much less than half of the total road network.

In addition, there is less of a need for a dense road network in the former Soviet Union than in Western Europe, even in the event of

Table 5-1 Density of Population and Public Road Network by Republic, January 1991

	Russia	Kazakhstan	Ukraine	Belarus
Area (1,000 km²)	17,075.0	2,717.0	604.0	208.0
Population (MM)	148.0	16.7	51.8	10.2
Length of public road (km)	455,500.0	86,814.0	167,804.0	49,000.0
Population density (pop per km²)	8.7	6.1	85.9	49.4
Public road density (km/1,000 km²)	25.3	32.0	277.8	235.6

Source: Goskomstat SSSR: *Demograficeskis ezegodnik SSSR*. Moscow, 1990, pp. 7–13; road authorities.

traffic increases in the future. First, population densities in western Europe are much higher than in the former Soviet Union. Even Ukraine, the most densely populated of the major new republics, has a population density far below that of Western Europe. Second, large areas in Russia and Kazakhstan are uninhabited and therefore almost without roads. Third, the settlement structure in the former Soviet Union is quite different from that in Western countries. There are practically no individual farmhouses, and there is therefore less need for a dense network of minor rural roads that make up an important share of the road network in the West. Finally, there is general road access to settlements and enterprises, although some access roads may be in poor condition, with axle loads typically limited during early spring thaws.

The road network in the Soviet Union was organized into four administrative road classes. *Public roads*, which were the main roads outside urban areas, were administered by the regional public road administrations. The public roads were divided further by level of government into federal/union roads, republican roads, regional roads, and local roads. *Enterprise roads* were roads belonging to organizations such as collective farms and industrial complexes and were the responsibility of the ministries to which these enterprises belong. In Russia the length of enterprise roads is almost equal to the length of public roads. *Private roads* made up a vast network of earth roads and tracks that were not recorded on official registers and for which government budgets were not responsible. Maps and aerial photographs indicate that these roads represent 40 percent of the total road network in Russia. *Urban roads* were administered by urban authorities, similar to Western municipal roads. After the dissolution of the Soviet Union into independent countries, Russia and Kazakhstan reclassified their road networks, but Belarus and Ukraine more or less retained the old classifications, so the post-Soviet classification is not the same in the four countries.

Most of the public roads inherited by the CIS countries were paved. They can be divided into five categories based on traffic volume, as noted in table 5-2. Only a small percentage of the roads were in the highest-use category. There were hardly any roads satisfying the normal definition of a European motorway or interstate highway in the United States (e.g., access control and lane separation). Most of

Table 5-2 Road Categories and Length of Road by Categories
by Republic, 1992

			Km of Public Road			
Category	Traffic Volumes (pcu)	Design	Russia[1]	Kazakhstan[2]	Ukraine[2]	Belarus
I	>14,000	4, 6, or 8 lanes (highway)	2,632	884	1,683	722
II	6,000-14,000	2 lanes 7.5 m	22,691	4,160	12,226	1,417
II	2,000-6,000	2 lanes 7 m	104,308	34,584	25,215	6,572
IV	200-20,000	2 lanes 6 m	317,430	37,762	10,344	31,672
V	>200	1 lane 4.5 m	242,850	3,723	14,631	8,922
Unpaved roads		≈	910,300	5,701	10,605	2,089
Total			≈1,600,000	86,814	167,804	49,305

[1] All roads.
[2] Public roads.

Source: National road authorities.

the network consisted of two-lane roads with a typical lane width of 6 to 7 meters.

The road network also included many physical bottlenecks that reduced traffic speeds. There were, however, few capacity problems outside urban areas. In all four countries the main roads often ran through towns and cities and this lack of circumferential routes contributed substantially to the low travel speeds and high accident rates. There were very few segregated rail crossings, so that rail intersections also limited speed and reduced safety. Many rail crossings were of poor quality, and trains normally passed at extremely low speeds or with severe vibrations of the vehicles.

Many bridges were narrow, especially on local roads; some bridges allowed traffic passage in only one direction at a time. As of the early 1990s, such narrow bridges accounted for 45 percent of the bridges in Russia and 70 percent of the bridges in Kazakhstan. The narrow bridges reduced local traffic speeds considerably and increased accident rates.

Tables 5-3 through 5-6 provide detail on the existing road networks in Russia, Ukraine, Belarus, and Kazakhstan. Western Russia is characterized by a radial network emanating from Moscow, but the east has only a few main corridors. Ukraine's network density is much greater than Russia's, because of higher population density.

Table 5-3 Pavements on Public Roads[1], Russian Federation, 1992

	Total	Cement Concrete	Asphalt Concrete Surface Dressing	Gravel	Earth
Federal	41,014	3,147 (8%)	33,896 (82%)	3,680 (9%)	291 (1%)
National	57,591	1,759 (3%)	43,956 (76%)	10,282 (18%)	1,594 (3%)
Regional	76,970	1,402 (2%)	52,299 (68%)	19,009 (24%)	4,260 (6%)
Local	279,874	3,157 (1%)	114,547 (41%)	112,784 (40%)	49,386 (18%)
Total	455,449	9,465 (2%)	244,698 (54%)	145,755 (32%)	55,531 (12%)

[1] Road classifications as defined before 1992.
Source: Rosavtador, the national road authorities.

Table 5-4 Road Pavements, Ukraine (km), 1992

	Total	Hard Surfaces Including Surface Dressing	Gravel	Earth
Federal	12,486	12,379 (99%)	107 (1%)	0 (0%)
National	18,625	18,132 (98%)	417 (2%)	76 (0%)
Regional	22,585	19,585 (87%)	2,666 (12%)	335 (1%)
Local	114,108	64,759 (57%)	39,155 (34%)	10,194 (9%)
Total	167,802	114,855 (69%)	42,344 (25%)	10,605 (6%)

Source: National road authority.

Table 5-5 Road Pavements, Kazakhstan (km), 1992

	Total	Asphalt	Surface Concrete	Gravel Dressing	Earth
Public roads					
Republican roads	17,284	4,474 (26%)	11,288 (65%)	1,228 (7%)	294 (2%)
Regional roads	69,530	7,244 (10%)	30,878 (44%)	26,092 (38%)	5,407 (8%)
Rural roads	57,000	490 (1%)	2,900 (5%)	7,320 (13%)	46,290 (81%)
Total	143,814	12,208 (9%)	45,066 (31%)	34,640 (24%)	51,991 (36%)

Source: Kazakhstan Ministry of Transport and Construction.

Table 5-6 Road Pavements, Belarus (km), 1992

	Total	Cement	Asphalt	Gravel	Earth
Federal roads	6,383	789 (12%)	5,572 (88%)	22 (0%)	0 (0%)
Republican roads	8,060	75 (1%)	7,333 (91%)	620 (8%)	32 (0%)
Regional roads	7,714	171 (2%)	4,936 (64%)	2,565 (33%)	42 (1%)
Local roads	27,149	576 (2%)	12,324 (46%)	12,236 (45%)	2,013 (7%)
Total	49,306	1,611 (3%)	30,165 (61%)	15,443 (32%)	2,087 (4%)

Source: Belarus Ministry of Highway Construction and Maintenance.

Table 5-7 **Percentage of Hard-Surface Roads by Republic, 1992**

	Russia	Kazakhstan	Ukraine	Belarus
Federal and republican roads	84	91	98	95
Regional and local roads	48	55	62	52

Source: National road authorities.

As indicated in table 5-7, a smaller share of the Russian public road network in Russia had hard-surfacing in 1992, compared with Ukraine, Belarus, and Kazakhstan.[2]

Road Conditions as of the Early 1990s

The primary concern of the road administrations in the four countries during the transition has been dwindling resources for road construction and maintenance. Nevertheless, as of 1992 and 1993, routine maintenance was carried out regularly; potholes and broken edges were not common on the main roads. Established construction and maintenance technologies were not adequate, however, and caused several problems, the most critical being extremely rough surfaces. The construction methods in use had difficulty producing flexible pavements that retain acceptable roughness levels. The quality of the asphalt concrete was generally poor. All-out overlaying is done quite frequently because surfaces deteriorate quickly due to the bitumen-rich mixes and overlay materials that are used. As a consequence, even newly constructed pavements were rougher than would be seen in Western countries, and that roughness increased rapidly over time.

The high roughness levels resulted in high vehicle operating costs. With the expected increase in traffic, particularly of heavy vehicles, and the dwindling funds available for road maintenance, the deterioration of the roads will accelerate, and vehicle operating costs will increase. A main factor in the determination of the structural and functional lifetime of road pavements is the traffic using the road. Particularly important is heavy axle traffic. In a market economy, the road haulers will have a strong interest in increasing vehicle use; this may lead to a substantial increase in axle loads. If these increases occur, public policymakers will have to decide if road strengthening should be accelerated or whether a comprehensive control of axle loads should be introduced instead.

A detailed survey of the Federal road network in Russia was initiated in 1991 by the road ministry. The survey concluded that 35 percent of the roads needed strengthening and 23 percent had inadequate friction. The survey also concluded that 65 percent of the required barriers, 10 percent of the traffic signs, and 86 percent of the road markings were missing. There also was a need for improved maintenance of bridges, particularly in the European region of Russia.

Similar conditions were apparent in the rest of the former Soviet Union, albeit to different degrees. In Ukraine, much effort has been spent on upgrading the main trunk road network to multi-lane standards. According to Ukrainian highway authorities, 85 to 90 percent of the Ukraine public road network could be ranked as "good" in the early 1990s. The road network in Kazakhstan has fewer multi-lane sections than in the other countries and is in better condition than in Russia because of low traffic volumes and lower precipitation. Belarus roads appear better than in the other three republics, especially in the need for overlaying or reconstruction.

Traffic signs, barriers, and guardrails generally were scarce and in poor condition, particularly outside the approaches to urban areas. Galvanizing techniques were seldom used, resulting in guardrails that corrode much faster than in Western countries. There were few road signs, and they were often poor. The production capacity for reflective film is insufficient and of poor quality, which means that films often had to be renewed every year. Road marking was almost nonexistent.

Maintenance

In the early 1990s, a considerable backlog existed in road maintenance. If pavement lives were in the range of 10 to 15 years, as is typical for Western roads, the annual need for resurfacing would have been between 7 and 10 percent. In the Moscow region, 25 to 35 percent of the roads inspected in 1991 required new overlays; this represents a maintenance backlog of approximately 3 years.[3] In Ukraine similarly high percentages of roads required resurfacing. In Belarus and Kazakhstan, the roads appeared to be in markedly better condition.

Table 5-8 Traffic Accidents, 1990-1991

	Fatalities	Injuries	Deaths/ MM Vehicles	Deaths/Billion Vehicle-km[1]
Russia 1990[2]	35,366	214,839	3,150	135
Ukraine 1990[3]	8,975	49,847	N.A.[4]	N.A.
Kazakhstan 1991[2]	2,247	6,607	1,877	64
Belarus 1991[2]	1,304	3,890	1,647	62

Source: [1] Estimated.
       [2] National road authorities.
       [3] MVD Ukrainy (Ministry of Transport and Construction).
       [4] N.A. equals not available.

Road Safety

In all four republics accident rates at the time of transition were very high compared with international standards. Table 5-8 relates the number of fatalities and injuries to the vehicle fleet and total vehicle mileage. The deaths per billion vehicle-kilometers ranged between 62 and 135, which compared with a rate in Britain of approximately 11 fatalities per billion vehicle-kilometers.

In the whole Soviet Union the number of officially reported road deaths was 48,900 in 1980 and dropped to 41,200 in 1985.[4] In the subsequent five years it rose again by 53 percent to 63,400 in 1990. Annual accident data for 1985 to 1990 for the Russian Federation are given in table 5-9. The number of accidents rose by 42 percent in the five-year period, the number of deaths by 56 percent, and the number

Table 5-9 Road Accidents in Russia, 1985-1990

Year	Accidents	Deaths	Injuries
1985	139,000	22,676	148,600
1986	138,600	20,681	150,400
1987	142,700	21,243	155,600
1988	161,300	25,938	176,600
1989	190,000	32,739	207,600
1990	197,400	35,366	214,800

Source: National road authorities.

of injuries by 45 percent, as compared with an estimated traffic growth of 10 percent.

There is considerable potential for implementing policies to improve road safety. Traffic accidents involve a major economic loss to society, both in direct costs (damage to vehicles, roads and property, medical care, administrative services, etc.) and in the indirect costs related to the loss of work and property. For example, based on experience from the United States, the provision of center and edge lines on roads in the former Soviet Union would be economically justified for roads with more than 200 vehicles per day. Experience from other countries shows that a variety of measures such as these may be very cost-effective.

Road Finance and Planning

Much of the historical data published for the Soviet Union on roads expenditure includes both road infrastructure costs and expenditure on vehicles, and therefore is difficult to interpret. Table 5-10 presents estimated road expenditures for the four republics in 1992. Historically, Soviet road expenditures were financed from budgetary allocations to relevant ministries, from special taxes on road users, and from a 2 percent tax on the gross revenue of common-carrier transport enterprises. In 1991, as part of the reorganization of road-sector institutions, road funds were established in each republic to reduce demands on the central government budget and to introduce a higher degree of revenue earmarking. All four republics generally follow the

Table 5-10 Estimated Road Expenditures in the Four Republics, 1992 (MM R)

Item/Country	Belarus	Kazakhstan	Russia[1]	Ukraine
Construction and reconstruction	2,580	249	6,051	5,339
Equipment	—	—	1,405	1,241
Maintenance	6,273	1,516	7,386	10,175
Other	417	369	19,659[2]	—
Total	9,270	2,134	34,500	16,754

[1] Federal road fund only.
[2] Includes R 15.5 billion transferred to regional road funds.

Source: Ministries of roads.

Table 5-11   Truck Fleets and Freight-Carrying Performance of Trucks in the Former Soviet Union, 1970-1990

Item	1970	1980	1985	1988	1989	1990
Freight-carried (billion tonne-km)						
Common-carrier (public use)	64	131	142	143	143	136
Own account	157	301	335	365	378	391
Total	221	432	477	508	521	527
Fleet size (thousands)						
Common-carrier trucks (no.)	627	710	741	727	658	706[1]
Recorded agricultural trucks[2]	N.A.[3]	1,213	1,325	1,453	1,448	1,392
Total	N.A.	1,923	2,066	2,180	2,106	2,098
Common-carrier						
Freight-carrying performance (thousand tonne-km/truck)	102	185	192	197	217	193
Common-carrier average haul distance (km)	17	20	22	21	21	21

[1] The 1990 common-carrier fleet of 706,000 trucks include 12,000 owned by privatized or new private trucking operations.

[2] Recorded agricultural trucks account for approximately one-third of own-account trucks. There were approximately 4.2 million own-account trucks in the former Soviet Union in 1990 by implying a performance of around 100,000 tonne-km per truck compared with 200,000 tonne-km for common carriers. True own-account performance may be greater, as all freight carried by these trucks may not have been entered in the recorded figures.

[3] N.A. = not available.

Source: *National Economy of the USSR 1990,* Goskomstat.

principles of an earmarked road fund, although in Ukraine there is greater intermingling with the general government budget. Significant financing problems persist despite the establishment of the road funds. These problems have increasingly led the governments to consider alternative funding mechanisms for road infrastructure programs, especially limited-recourse private financing.

Trucking Industry

Table 5-11 shows that there were approximately 2.1 million trucks in the Soviet Union in 1990, of which 1.4 million were agricultural own-account trucks. However, these figures reportedly exclude about half of all agricultural trucks owned by state farms and collective farms, and a similar number of own-account trucks used in other sectors. An estimate of the total truck fleet in 1990 would thus be approximately 4.9 million vehicles, not including many military trucks and 1.8 million special vehicles (generally in military use).

Many of the trucks in the former Soviet Union were developed in the late 1960s or early 1970s and compare unfavorably with those designed in other countries. Gasoline engines were used for most trucks right up until the 1980s because of difficulties in obtaining suitable diesel oil and in operating diesel engines under cold winter conditions. However, starting in the 1980s, alternative fuels based on liquefied, or compressed, natural gas began to be used, especially in urban areas. By the early 1990s, these fuels were used in 15 percent of all public-use trucks.

The fleet in the early 1990s contained a wide variety of medium-sized trucks with capacities between 2 and 8 tonnes, but few small or large trucks. Public-use trucks in Russia had an average capacity of 6.4 tonnes. Tippers and tractors with semitrailers had larger average capacities of 9.4 and 12.3 tonnes. Few large semitrailers (over 15 tonne capacity) were used. Most trucks and trailers in the former Soviet Union had open-top bodies, many of which were tippers or dump trucks.[5] Covered trucks and vans had an average capacity of only about 2.5 tonnes and tankers only 4.3 tonnes. Tankers and refrigerated bodies made small but significant contributions to the total fleet. Trucks with other specialized bodies made up less than 10 percent of the fleet.

In Russia, the proportion of public-use trucks that were more than eight years old decreased steadily from 41 percent in 1970 to 15 percent in the early 1990s. In order to achieve this upgrading and to maintain fleet size, approximately 13 percent of the fleet was replaced annually. One effect of this fleet program has been to increase the numbers of large trucks: the proportion of the fleet with more than 8 tonne capacity rose from 5 percent in 1970 to 30 percent in 1992.

Mechanical problems in the truck fleet have been common even when vehicles were new. Truck operators frequently spent two or three months resolving defects following delivery. The lifetime of components was short compared with that in other countries. For example, as of the early 1990s, new engines only ran for approximately 300,000 kilometers before requiring overhaul, compared to up to 500,000 kilometers in Western Europe. The shortage of replacement spares forced operators to make improvised repairs. The condition of the fleet rapidly deteriorated after three years or so, when major repairs or overhauls were required.

Supply of Trucks

There has been a steady decline in truck production since the mid-1980s. In 1986, approximately 920,000 buses and trucks were pro–duced – equivalent to an estimated 825,000 trucks based on past proportions of buses and trucks. According to published production figures, truck production had fallen to 731,000 vehicles in the former Soviet Union in 1989, of which 37,900 were exported. By 1990, production had fallen further to 688,000 units, with 47,000 exported.

The Soviet truck manufacturing industry was organized under the Ministry of Automobile and Agricultural Machine Manufacturing. There were nine principal truck manufacturers in the former Soviet Union.[6] The manufacturers were vertically integrated and their reliance on external suppliers was less than in other countries. For example, 50 percent of components were supplied externally, whereas in western countries the comparable ratio was about 70 percent.

Under the old command economy, transport enterprises were allocated new vehicles according to plan. Each truck manufacturer specialized in its own truck size and held an effective supply monopoly. For example, Ulyanovsk (UAZ) made 2-tonne trucks; Gorkiy (GAZ) made 4.5-tonne trucks; Likhachev (ZIL) made 5- and 6-tonne trucks; Kamskiy (KaMAZ) made 8-tonne trucks; and Minsk (MAZ) specialized in larger trucks and the largest semitrailers. This "monopoly-niche" structure discouraged development of new, improved models, the adoption of more efficient manufacturing methods, and the provision of after-sales service. Transport enterprises often reported difficulties obtaining adequate vehicles, spare parts, and service. Only in the case of KaMAZ was a national support network established to provide spares and maintenance service, but this too was widely deemed to be ineffective. Allegedly, as many as 40 percent of trucks were out of service at any given time, either for maintenance or for other reasons in the early 1990s.

The profile of the manufactured truck fleet reflected the perceptions of road transport needs held by the central planners. No light-

Table 5-12   Exports and Imports of Trucks in the Former Soviet Union
(thousands), 1980–1990

Item	1980	1985	1986	1987	1988	1989	1990
Exports	41.9	39.6	38.9	40.7	36.3	37.9	47.0
Imports	9.7	17.2	17.2	14.7	13.8	13.3	9.0

Source: National Economy of the USSR 1990, Goskomstat.

goods vehicle with a payload capacity of about one tonne was being produced as of the early 1990s, although unsuccessful attempts were made to produce such a model in Yerevan, Armenia. Also, because of the importance attached to using railways for long-distance haulage, few very large trucks with a capacity of about 25 tonnes were produced. Important specialist equipment, such as refrigerator units, also were not produced in sufficient quantities.

Table 5-12 indicates that the Soviet Union imported approximately 14,000 trucks annually until 1990, when financial problems became severe. These trucks made up only about 2 percent of trucks purchased and an even smaller proportion of total capacity. Truck imports consisted mainly of vehicles that filled gaps in domestic manufacture. For example, small vans were imported from Czechoslovakia, Hungary, and Poland. Large tractors and semitrailers were imported, mainly from Western Europe. Other imports from other former Council for Mutual Economic Assistance (COMECON) countries included large TATRA tippers and refrigerated units from the Czech Republic. For international haulage, imported tractors and semitrailers made up almost all the vehicles operated by large enterprises such as Sovtransafto, which for many years had a monopoly of Soviet international road freight activity.

Terminal Facilities

There were 150 main common user terminals with warehouses in Russia in 1992. A similar number were in use in Ukraine, Belarus, and Kazakhstan combined. The main terminals were typically two hectares in size, with most of the area devoted to storing and moving containers. Gantry cranes generally had a maximum capacity of ten tonnes, so that terminals were prevented from using ISO standard containers. Much of this equipment was unreliable and breakdowns

Table 5-13   Volume of Freight Transport by Mode and Sector
              (MM tonnes), 1991

Mode/Sector	Republic			
	Belarus	Kazakhstan[1]	Russia[1]	Ukraine
Rail	110.9	345.0	1,903.0	N.A.[2]
Road (public use)[3]:				
International[4]	0.1	0.0	1.6	N.A.
Intercity[4]	12.7	35.4	121.6	N.A.
Intracity	393.5	579.5	2,568.8	N.A.
Sub total	406.3	614.9	2,692.0	947.5
Road own-account	567.3	1,419.5	12,406.0	N.A.
Total Road	973.6	2,034.4	15,098.0	N.A.
River	18.4	10.6	514.0	N.A.
Pipeline	N.A.	20.6	499.0	N.A.
Air	0.0	0.1	2.5	N.A.
Total	1,103.0	2,410.7	18,016.5	N.A.

Volume of Freight Transport by Mode and Sector
(billion tonne-km), 1991

	Belarus	Kazakhstan	Russia	Ukraine
Rail	65.6	407.0	2,317.0	N.A.
Road (public use):				
International[4]	0.1	0.0	3.0	5.8
Intercity[4]	2.6	5.8	24.8	N.A.
Intracity	4.6	12.7	36.2	N.A.
Sub total	7.3	18.5	64.0	13.5
Road own-account	14.8	23.3	231.7	N.A.
Total Road	22.1	41.9	295.7	N.A.
River	1.7	3.9	195.0	N.A.
Pipeline	N.A.	16.4	1,057.0	N.A.
Air	0.0	0.1	N.A.	N.A.
Total Road	89.5	469.3	3,864.7	N.A.

[1] Kazakhstan figures and Russia own-account figures are for 1990.
[2] N.A. = not available.
[3] All figures are for common-carriers unless otherwise stated.
[4] Intercity traffic is defined as hauls over 50 km and international traffic is to or from
   countries outside the former Soviet Union.

Source: Goskomstat; ministries of transport.

were frequent. Basic warehouse facilities were provided at each terminal but the buildings were often too small for efficient stacking. The provision of refrigerated storage was rare, which was a major reason for commodity losses in food distribution.

As a market economy emerges, increased use likely will be made of ISO containers and other forms of unitized loads using pallets. More efficient loading and unloading techniques also would encourage the use of larger trucks throughout the haul rather than continuing the current practice of transshipment at terminals.

Industry Performance

Data on road freight services in the four republics in 1991 are shown in table 5-13. In terms of tonnes lifted, road transport accounted for the overwhelming proportion of freight carried by all modes, and was itself dominated by the own-account trucking sector. However, lengths of hauls by road are extremely short, typically between 14 and 30 kilometers for common carriers, and between 16 and 26 kilometers for other carriers. In terms of tonne-kilometers, therefore, road transport carried less than 10 percent of all freight with the own-account sector carrying about three-fourths of the road share.

Trucking enterprises were large, averaging more than 200 freight vehicles. These enterprises, moreover, are often units of vast regional organizations owning between 3,000 and 10,000 trucks. By contrast, in Britain only about 10 percent of all trucks are owned by organizations with over 100 vehicles. The average number of trucks per firm is 3.8 in Germany, 6.7 in Holland, and 10 in the United States.

Staffing levels are difficult to interpret because many transport enterprises provide housing and a range of social services. The number of drivers varies between about 1.0 and 1.4 per truck; this demonstrates the common practice of assigning one driver to each truck. This system inevitably reduces annual truck use, which varies between about 30,000 and 50,000 kilometers, much lower than in most Western economies where figures are typically between 60,000 and 80,000 kilometers. With the modest size of trucks used, annual tonnes carried per truck are relatively low, usually about 10,000 tonnes on average.

The road freight industry in the former Soviet Union has failed to meet the needs of many shippers. This situation has led to a growing role for own-account operators, especially agricultural enterprises. The distinction between own-account and common-carrier operators has become blurred, as in many other countries, because the new operators have been able to expand their business by carrying goods for third parties. Enterprises in some agricultural ministries were even beginning to offer limited freight forwarding services by 1992.

The trend toward own-account operations is consistent with experience in heavily regulated environments elsewhere and reflects the need for a "safety valve" to bypass inadequate common-carrier services. However, the proportion of road freight tonne-kilometers carried by own-account operators in market economies is rarely more than 40 percent, and certainly far less than the 70 to 80 percent found in the former Soviet Union. This proportion has been found to increase in market economies when the road transport sector is subject to quantity controls, but to fall in deregulated environments. Entry controls, which restrict competition, tend to lower service quality and encourage customers to opt for own-account transport.

Faced with the difficulties of adapting to a market economy, many enterprises in the former Soviet Union are leasing or even selling their trucks to private individuals. Such developments demonstrate the success of smaller trucking companies in finding markets for road freight services. Although the amount of freight carried by small operators was still low in the early 1990s, it appeared to be growing fast. At the same time, private truck operations were emerging outside of the privatization programs as new operators entered the industry. In theory, there is nothing to stop a person from starting up a trucking business in most of the republics. In practice, there have been very few trucks obtainable apart from privatized or leased trucks, the supply of which is controlled by the transport enterprises. The supply of fuel and spare parts presents other obstacles, and new trucking businesses also need financing both for the fleet and for working capital. The emergence of a new trucking industry has therefore been a slow process.

The main long-term problem may not be the speed but the form of privatization. Timely demonopolization, freedom of entry, and price liberalization would stimulate creation of competitive, efficient enterprises. Existing ministries and public enterprises should be free to compete on a level playing field with new and privatized enterprises but should not be permitted to retain control of the industry or restrain the growth of competition.

Bus Operations

Public-road passenger transport is provided almost wholly by the enterprises formerly owned by the Ministry of Road Transport in each republic. In addition, tourist bus services are provided by other organizations such as Intourist. Ownership of assets devolved to regional or even the district level after 1991.

In a typical regional administration there are between 1,000 and 3,000 buses owned by between 30 and 50 enterprises. These passenger transport enterprises usually have between 50 and 200 buses, but there also are many trucking enterprises that operate bus services as well. Only in certain large cities, however, has administration of bus fleets been separated from that of truck fleets, or have urban and non-urban passenger transport been separated.

The Fleet

There were about 310,000 public buses in the former Soviet Union in 1990. Approximately half of this fleet was used for public transit services. Compared with many other countries, there are few mini-buses in the new republics. There is considerable scope for greater use of smaller buses, as has occurred in market economies after deregulation. These smaller buses offer greater flexibility in matching capacity to demand and in combining some passenger and freight operations such as rural post bus services. These services should increase if subsidies decrease and own-account operators become able to tender for public services.

Supply of Buses

In 1986 approximately 95,000 buses were produced in the Soviet Union. In that year, another 11,200 buses were imported, while 2,900 buses were exported. Imports consisted chiefly of large Ikarus buses from Hungary. By 1991, production had declined to about 76,000, of which less than 20,000 were public-transit vehicles.

As with trucks, production of buses was distributed among seven factories in the former Soviet Union, each one specializing in its own size and type. Similar to the situation in truck production, there was little competition among these factories for each main type of bus. For example, intercity and local transport buses were made by the LAZ plant in Lvov, Ukraine; medium-sized buses by the PAZ factory in Pavlovo, Russia; four wheel drive buses were produced by UAZ in Ulyanovsk, Russia; and large city buses by the LIAZ factory in Likino, Russia.

Industry Performance

Approximately 25 percent of bus travel is rural, 60 percent is urban or suburban commuter travel, and 15 percent is intercity service linking major towns. Intercity buses have tended mainly to serve short trips of about 50 kilometers; longer bus trips apparently are made only where there is no convenient rail service. Although buses play only a minor role in long distance passenger transport in the former Soviet Union, they are the dominant mode in rural transport.

Although the road network offers an alternative means for intercity transport, buses designed for long-distance passengers have never been introduced. As a result, intermodal competition has been minimal. Fares traditionally contained few differentials based on distance or volume, resulting in sharp variations in profitability between routes. There has been a tendency to encourage cross-subsidies, especially from the more dense routes to the less profitable rural or urban routes.

There are usually between 1.5 and 2.0 drivers per intercity bus. About 0.5 mechanics per bus and a similar number of other staff are employed by bus transport enterprises. Staff numbers are increased by ancillary services such as health, recreation, and housing which are provided to employees. All these figures are far higher than those found in Western transport enterprises.

The average proportion of buses out of operation is typically between 20 and 25 percent, usually for maintenance reasons. These levels are rather high compared to Western standards and appear to reflect difficulties getting spares. Vehicle design is also a significant factor, especially the high number of gasoline engines, which require more maintenance than diesels.

Fuel

At the time of transition, the supply of fuel throughout the former Soviet Union was notoriously inefficient. There were few filling stations, they were badly located, and they often ran out of fuel.

Rationing was common, and long queues of vehicles were common-place. In short, as of the early 1990s, motorists were exceedingly badly served; they had to make long detours to find a filling station and then could not rely on obtaining fuel when they got there.

In the early 1990s, the fuel supply and distribution process was virtually unchanged from the central planning era. The monopoly fuel distributor, Goskomneftiprodukt, and its regional operating units continued to enjoy a protected monopoly including ownership of all depots, pipelines, filling stations, and fuel delivery trucks. Refineries were a separate operation under government control but they did not possess discharge facilities suitable for supplying fuel to private distributors, so they were unable to bypass Goskomneftiprodukt. The emphasis in refinery operations continued to be on volume of production based on previous and planned receipts of crude. By international standards, the quality of refined products was low, and the refineries themselves were inefficient. In some cases no attempt was made to repair faulty equipment or leaks, perhaps in part because the administered price of lost oil was so low.

Development of private filling stations was restricted severely by regulations protecting the monopoly position of Goskomneftiprodukt and by the lack of incentives given by price controls. As with the road transport industry itself, an urgent need exists to restructure the fuel distribution industry and provide incentives for private provision of filling stations and distribution services. In addition to ameliorating the current situation – which severely limits new entry and develop-ment of markets for road transport services – private provision of filling stations and other motorist services would remove a significant burden from the public fisc.

Environmental Issues

The global and regional damage to the environment from road traffic is limited compared with the situation prevailing in many western European countries. This limited damage is due mainly to low traffic volumes outside urban areas. However, the modal shifts likely to occur make it essential for the new republics to develop strategies to encourage environmentally sound road transport poli-cies. The main issues to address are vehicle technology, fuel quality and the framework for regulation of environmental impacts of new construction projects. The basic approaches that might be applied are

Table 5-14   Comparison of Specific Emissions from Vehicles in the
Former Soviet Union (FSU) and Western Europe
(WE) (gm/km)

	CO[1]		HC[2]		NO$_x$[3]		Particulates	
	FSU	WE	FSU	WE	FSU	WE	FSU	WE
Gasoline car	16.0	15.0	3.0	2.0	2.4	2.1	—	—
Diesel truck	5.1	4.7	2.7	11.4	11.4	9.5	1.5	1.1
Diesel bus	7.8	2.5	3.4	10.0	10.0	11.0	1.9	0.7

[1] Carbon monoxide.
[2] Hydrocarbons.
[3] Nitrous oxide.

Source: CIS vehicles: NIIAT (State Scientific and Research Institute of
Automobile Transport), Moscow; WE trucks and buses:
Naturvardsverket (Swedish Department of the Environment), report
3285 (Swedish); WE cars: Danish Transport Action Plan, 1990.

adoption of technical standards, use of demand management (especially economic instruments such as pricing), and development of appropriate abatement options for new roads. Many environmental standards and regulations, including those for vehicle emissions, already are in place; in principle, this should ensure a relatively low pollution level from road transport compared with western Europe. However, enforcement measures are weak; pollution levels in practice are much higher than the official regulations would permit.

Vehicle emissions in the former Soviet Union are high compared to Western Europe, as indicated in table 5-14. Table 5-15 presents a comparison of fuel consumption between typical vehicles in the fleets of the former Soviet Union and Scandinavia. Virtually all classes of vehicles, especially gasoline-powered trucks and buses, have a higher level of energy consumption in the former Soviet Union than in Western Europe. Switching to diesel-powered heavy vehicles would save energy and also result in significant reductions in lead, hydrocarbons, and carbon monoxide emissions. Although this would in turn lead to an increase in particulate emissions and possibly also an increase in nitrous oxide emissions, on balance it should prove a net gain for the environment.

Table 5-15   Comparison of Energy Consumption in Typical Vehicles,
Former Soviet Union and Scandinavia
(liters per 100 km), 1992

	Former Soviet Union	Scandinavia
Gasoline car	9.7	8.3
Truck 0.5–25 gasoline	19.0	10.0
Truck 5–8 t diesel[1]	24.0	20.0
Bus 6–7 m gasoline[1]	23.0	15.0
Bus 10–12 m diesel	24.5	20.0–25.0

[1] Truck sizes in tonnes; bus sizes in meters.

Source: Former Soviet Union vehicles: NIIAT, Moscow; Scandinavian trucks and buses: Naturvardsverket, report 3285 (Swedish); Scandinavian cars: Danish Transport Action Plan, 1990.

Policy and Institutional Needs

Structural and institutional changes are needed for both road infrastructure management and the road transport industry. With increased private participation in road maintenance, financing, and construction, the operating functions of the road administrations likely would decrease, and shift from a direct operating to a monitoring and enabling role. If this shift occurs, there will be a growing need for government planning, procurement, forecasting, and financial controls. Better management systems and monitoring methods will be needed to provide current information on traffic, safety, and road conditions.

Because of the network character of transport, a sectoral ministry should administer road infrastructure. However, this structure should not merely supersede the old central road administrations. Other ministries (such as Agriculture) should no longer be responsible for administration of roads. Moreover, most enterprise roads should be transferred to local road administrations. A structure of smaller-scale road administrations, based on economic geography, will help move road investment decisions closer to those who benefit. Such a decentralized structure, while increasing flexibility, also has proved difficult to implement in many Western economies because of a lack of skills at the local level. In the former Soviet Union, local skill-building through training should be encouraged, perhaps with more advanced regions providing training programs for smaller areas.

Road budgets should be focused on maintenance and upgrading of selected corridors. The need for greenfield road development is somewhat limited, and might be accomplished through concessions or other means of project finance. For the most part, the principal immediate concern is that expected increases in traffic will result in worsening road roughness and deterioration with respect to maximum sustainable axle loads. Reviews of pavement management systems and road standards might be undertaken with Western assistance. Some of the current standards appear to be much higher than justified, so that revisions could result in funds being freed for other projects.

In road construction and maintenance, the opportunities for privatization are substantial. To guarantee a sufficient supply of competition among contractors, entry opportunities should be developed and adequate financing mechanisms should be established to structure guarantees and performance bonds. A new system of tendering should be implemented on a consistent basis with some degree of stable funding. Such conditions will help produce a road-building environment conducive to open competitive bidding. International financial institutions might aid in this process by investing alongside road administrations in creating competitive procedures where joint ventures also are encouraged. This structure may be particularly useful in the transfer of technology and managerial capacity.

In road freight transport, the dominant problem is reducing the distortions introduced by spatial monopolies and vertical integration. Care must be taken not to confer privileged status on existing trucking enterprises that have strong incentives to maintain their protected status. To encourage initial efforts at privatization, supporting policies are needed in tariff setting, entry and exit, nondiscriminatory licensing, and the supply of fuel and spare parts. The government should serve in a limited regulatory role. The older organizations, such as the *avtotrans* concerns, should no longer have regulatory responsibility. Most operating restrictions, in domestic and in international haulage, should be proscribed, except for safety regulation.

The trucking enterprises should be divided into smaller units and privatized in that form, although subsequent mergers and acquisitions are likely to occur. Truck auctions could play a key role in getting this policy in place. Another possibility, although not as attractive, would be to have the enterprises convert to leasing companies that provide vehicles for smaller operators. However, such an arrangement runs a grave risk of transforming monopoly operators into monopoly lessors.

Virtually all supporting facilities – freight forwarding, fuel supply and distribution, repair facilities, and smaller terminals – should be privatized immediately. Large terminals continue to be a difficult problem for road and intermodal transport. The key is to emphasize efficiency aspects rather than market power, and to require common-carrier responsibilities for such facilities. Finally, a very effective source of "new" competition in this sector might emerge from increasing the rate of transfer of military transport capacity to the commercial sector.

In passenger transport, public transport must be balanced against the likely long-term growth of car ownership and usage. Privatization or contracting out through leasing of buses might provide substantial benefits. Auctioning off smaller buses and services and contracting out larger operations would increase efficiency and lower both capital and operating costs. Substantial flexibility should be established in setting fare and service levels, subject to certain safety, quality, and access conditions.

Where reduced fare schemes are needed, the government should seek equal competitive conditions, perhaps through operators being compensated on a universal per-passenger basis. If these policy reforms are put in place, a continuing role for public bus service may be preserved, but it will be from a new position in which competition creates new incentives for performance.

The lack of diversity in road vehicles has severely hindered the quality of road transport services. The new republics need to use domestic production, joint ventures, and imports to increase the range of vehicles available, improve fuel efficiency and environmental performance, and raise production to meet growing demand.

In parallel, the development of component facilities and spare parts production and distribution might be best handled not through the vehicle manufacturers themselves, but through third parties, perhaps with licensing authority from the manufacturers. These spare part services can be seen as a key to the development of a decentralized private set of support services, ranging from repair garages to fuel distribution to other roadside services.

Summary

Road transport shares many of the characteristics of the other transport sectors: a supply-oriented system; outdated technologies and a limited range of technological or equipment choices; services and infrastructure controlled by a few large public monopolies; productive choices distorted by low factor prices, particularly for fuel; and neglect of safety and environmental concerns. In at least one important way, however, highway transport appears different from the other modes: any transition to a market economy is likely to produce a larger role for road transport, both for passengers and freight traffic. The sector is well suited for smaller-scale operations and substantial privatization; policy and institutional reforms will be needed to support such restructuring.

Nevertheless, the raw physical capacity of the highway system seems quite sufficient for the immediate future, even if traffic grows at the high end of projections. The existing network is adequate as a basis for future expansion, though there may be a need for selective investment to reduce bottlenecks, alleviate localized congestion, and improve quality. In particular, development of intermodal operations and of road transport support activities are required. More up-to-date technology and related investments are needed to improve both the efficiency and the environmental and safety aspects of road transport.

Notes

1   This chapter is based on COWIconsult and TecnEcon Joint Venture, *Roads and Road Transport Survey: Russia, Ukraine, Belarus, and Kazakhstan* (London: European Bank for Reconstruction and Development, 1993). To the extent possible, the original presentation of the report has been preserved.

2   "Hard-surfacing" is the CIS internal definition, which includes tar and gravel surfaces as well as asphalt.

3   However, such Western standards are based on higher-quality road aggregates, so that effective pavement lives in the new republics may be shorter.

4 An examination of official accident statistics reveals some anomalies. There appears to be an unusually high correlation between the anti-alcohol campaign introduced by Gorbachev and the recorded drop in accidents in the 1980s. Public campaigns against drunk driving reduced alcohol-related accidents and fatalities in both the United States and Western Europe over the same period.

5 For example, in Kazakhstan only 12 percent of ordinary trucks had covered van-type bodies, and for semitrailers this proportion was only 8 percent.

6 See D. Zaslow, "Trucking in the Soviet Economy," *Soviet Geography*, 31 (March 1990).

6

Water Transport [1]

    Water transport has played a less important role in the former Soviet Union than in many other economies, because of climate and geography. Many ports and inland waterways are frozen for long periods, and others are kept open only through extensive ice-breaking operations. Most navigable rivers either run in a different direction than traffic flows, or follow winding routes that often more than double the distances compared with rail transport.

    Water transport in the former Soviet Union encompassed international ocean shipping, inland waterways, river-sea transport, and specialized coastal shipping. Each segment, in turn, was composed of fleets, supporting maritime industries, and infrastructure such as ports, channels, and canals. The principal ports and waterborne transport routes are shown in Figure 6-1. Water transport represented only about 9 percent of total transport volume in the USSR in 1989, and fell to only 2.6 percent of all common-carrier freight tonnage by 1992. However, water transport still plays a vital role for some commodities and for some regions, notably for grain in Ukraine and for oil and coal exports.

    Previous trade patterns were distorted by the Cold War. Excluding oil and gas moving through pipelines, approximately 70 percent of Russia's international cargo transactions used water transport. Although the ports carried a large percentage of non-petroleum trade cargo, the new republics' share of global sea trade was less than 5 percent in 1992. With the opening of the economy to normal international trade, sea trade ultimately will expand.

    In the post-Cold War world, a well-functioning water transport system should help the new republics generate export earnings and bring in vitally needed imports. In the longer term, expanding

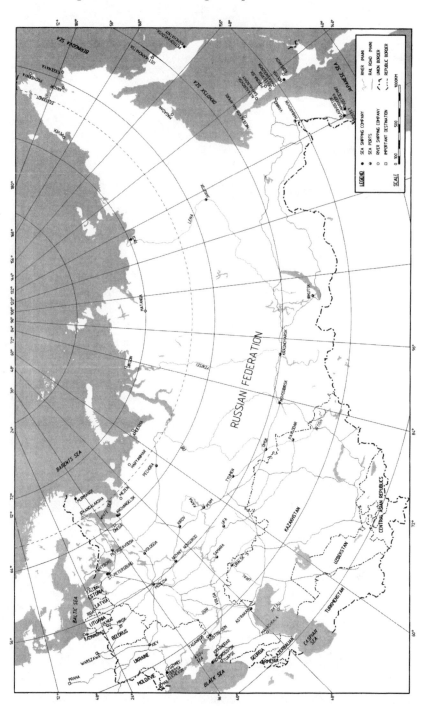

Figure 6-1: Water Transport in the Former Soviet Union   source: Nedeco

international trade, in keeping with less autarkic policies, will place more requirements on water transport, particularly the seaports. There also will be fundamental changes in the composition and direction of traffic flows, to which the entire water transport sector will have to adapt.[2] In light of these expected changes, restructuring the sector and designing an appropriate mix of public and private ownership and activities is essential.

International Maritime

There are 70 seaports in the new republics, of which 26 are classified as major ports. As indicated in table 6-1, nine of the major ports are in Russia, eight are in Ukraine, and one is in Kazakhstan. These eighteen ports handled approximately one-half of the total foreign trade of the former Soviet Union.[3] This concentration of activity was consistent with the centralization of activity that characterized the Soviet planned system. However, a considerable amount of trade moves through now-external ports; the Soviet penchant for specialization meant that many specific use facilities are located in now-independent nations, especially the Baltic countries.[4]

The major ports also were quite specialized. Table 6-1 shows the distribution of traffic volumes of principal commodities across major ports in 1991. The Black Sea ports of Novorossiysk and Tuapse (Russian Federation) and Odessa (Ukraine) were dominated by oil exports. Dry-bulk commodities, principally iron ore and coal, were particularly important in Murmansk and Vostochny in Russia, and in Yuzhniy and Mariupol in the Ukraine. The haulage of grain, dry bulks, timber, and general cargo was spread over several ports. The level of container traffic, both in percentage and absolute terms, was very low.

Traffic Volumes

Oil and petroleum products remain the most important water transport commodity classification. If domestic energy prices move closer to world levels, the proportion of oil available for export is likely to rise. This change would increase volumes through Black Sea ports, Russian facilities at Kaliningrad, and Latvian and Lithuanian ports on the Baltic Sea.

Kazakhstan is a significant oil producer and has transported its output by various means, including pipelines and river-sea vessels

Table 6-1   Major Ports in Russian Federation, Ukraine, and Kazakhstan,
1991

Port	Liquid bulk	Grain	Dry bulk	Timber	Container	General Cargo	Total[1]
				Million Tonnes			
Russian Federation							
Arkhangelsk	—	0.2	0.9	0.2	0.3	1.0	2.6
Murmansk	—	—	6.4	0.1	0.4	0.9	7.8
St. Petersburg	—	5.3	2.3	0.3	0.8	2.2	10.9
Novorossiysk	34.8	6.1	1.5	—	—	2.5	44.9
Tuapse	13.8	0.3	1.7	—	—	0.6	16.4
Nakhodka	4.9	1.3	2.2	2.1	0.1	1.5	12.1
Vostochny	—	—	8.8	0.8	2.0	—	11.8
Korsakov	—	0.1	1.3	0.4	—	0.4	2.2
Kholmsk	—	—	0.5	0.2	—	0.4	6.8
Total	53.5	13.3	25.6	4.1	3.6	9.5	115.5
Ukraine							
Lzmail	—	0.3	4.9	—	0.3	1.8	7.3
Reni	—	0.5	5.4	0.4	—	3.4	9.7
Ilyichevsk	—	1.4	3.7	—	1.2	2.8	15.2[1]
Odessa	18.5	5.4	2.5	—	0.1	1.7	28.2
Yuzhniy	—	—	7.5	—	—	0.7	8.2
Kherson	—	0.3	3.5	—	—	0.4	4.2
Mariupol	0.4	—	8.0	—	0.2	2.8	11.4
Berdyansk	—	0.4	1.0	—	—	0.9	2.3
Total	18.9	8.3	36.5	0.4	1.8	14.5	86.5[1]
Kazakhstan							
Aktau	5.2	—	0.1	—	—	0.1	5.4
Total	77.6	23.0	62.2	4.5	5.4	23.7	207.4

[1] Includes 5.7 million tonnes of ferry traffic through Kholmsk, and 6.1 million tonnes
of rail ferry traffic through Ilyichevsk.

Source: Clell G. Harral, "Economic Reform of Soviet Transport: Issues
and Options," 1991.

from Aktau to Tuapse, across the Caspian Sea to Baku, or to refineries on the Volga. Plans for major development of Kazakh oil and gas fields in Tengiz and Korolev will likely place new demands on export terminals, although where these facilities should be located will only become clear as the industry develops and as key decisions are made on major pipeline projects. Oil movements through Ukrainian ports will depend on the extent to which the republic attempts to become more self-sufficient and whether it chooses to replace Russian supplies with imports from other countries.

Grain has been imported through most of the major ports. Import volumes have depended on the success of the Soviet harvest. Although there is a wide range of opinion as to the prospects for grain transport, it generally is agreed that agricultural reforms will take some time. Within fifteen to twenty years, the republics as a whole may be self-sufficient in grain. Some of the more fertile regions, as in Ukraine and areas of Kazakhstan, may become net exporters of grain.

Although there are some iron ore deposits near Murmansk and near the Black Sea Ukrainian ports, the largest deposits lie around Kursk, midway between St. Petersburg and the Black Sea. Coal exports go mainly to Eastern Europe via the Black Sea ports, and to Japan via the Far East ports, especially Vostochny. The Far East volumes are more likely to be sustained than the European traffic because of greater competition in the latter region.

Most timber exports originate in northern Russia and are exported to Europe via the Baltic and White Sea ports, and to Asia via the Far East ports. Timber also is an important cargo for inland waterways. Shifts toward more timber processing on-site may reduce tonnage volumes (but not values) substantially.

Containerization

Containerization has been very low by international standards. The Soviet fleet, which traditionally carried two-thirds of Soviet trade, had relatively few container ships, and used them in international markets to earn foreign currency. As described in Chapter 4, the rail system lacked facilities for extensive inland container distribution.

Vostochny has been the leading container port, because of its role in the Trans-Siberian landbridge. From 1990 to 2015, container cargo could increase from its Soviet level of 10 percent of general freight traffic to the 1980s' world average of 45 percent. This would result in substantial increases in container traffic at almost all ports.

Port Operations[5]

The ports share several common problems, many of which arise because they have been designed for direct delivery of dry-bulk cargo to and from ships to rail wagons. Almost all cargo is transported to and from ports by rail. In many cases this rail capacity is limited. There is a persistent shortage of rail wagons at port facilities, even though in 1993 there did not appear to be a shortage of rail cars in the economy. The reasons for this situation include poor communication networks (especially electronic data interchange about incoming and outgoing traffic flows); the lack of an effective freight forwarding system; and the lack of incentives for more efficient operations. In addition, the breakup of the railway system across the republics has led to problems of network exchange and the holding back of rolling stock within individual states.

The principal sea access problem is the need to employ ice-breaking equipment, not only for the northern ports and St. Petersburg, but also for the Black Sea (which freezes for up to two months during severe winters). Restrictions on vessel size limit the use of larger ships. As of the early 1990s, only Vostochny and Yuzhniy could handle ships exceeding 40,000 deadweight tonnes. If larger ships are to be serviced, improvements will be needed in provision of deep-water berths, storage facilities, and rail access.

Cargo Handling and Storage

Most ports have sufficient berthing space, but cannot use all berths simultaneously because of a lack of rail access and wagons. This access problem results in very long turnaround times, high berth occupancy rates, and much vessel queueing. An oversupply of berthing space at some ports has become more evident as traffic volumes have declined. However, ship turnaround times have not improved.

The capital equipment used in the ports is capable of achieving acceptable cargo handling rates, but generally fails to do so. One-third to one-half of the mechanical equipment is beyond its depreciable life, according to Western standards. However, because of port overcapacity, low utilization, and acceptable maintenance operations, most of the equipment is in reasonable condition. Cargo-handling operations are slowed more by shortages of rail wagons and by long periods devoted to activities such as hold cleaning, necessitated because of the predominance of general purpose ships. As indicated in table 6-2, utilization rates are very low and equipment failure rates are very high. If higher productivity could be achieved, the surplus of cargo-handling equipment would be more apparent. Cargo-handling rates in bulk trades (such as fertilizers) are low, mainly due to the use of older technologies, such as grab cranes, rather than conveyors, screws, or pneumatic evacuators.

Ports generally have inadequate storage, because of the tradition of loading and discharging directly to rail wagons. Transit shed congestion was made worse by documentation problems and the lack of centrally organized clearinghouses and freight-forwarding operations. Covered storage facilities for grain, with accompanying conveyor operations, are still rare. Port productivity could be increased

Table 6-2 Utilization and Service Levels, 1991

Berth Space

Port	Berths (No.) Available	Used
St. Petersburg	26	18
Novorossiysk	22	22
Vostochny	8	8
Ilyichevsk	24	18
Yuzhniy	7	6
Aktau	12	10

Mechanical Equipment: Time Out of Service, 1991

Type of Equipment	Time for Repairs (%) St. Petersburg	Ilyichevsk	Equipment Utilization (%) St. Petersburg	Ilyichevsk
Gantry cranes	25%	4%	31%	25%
Portal cranes	18%	14%	35%	19%
Straddle carriers	8%	13%	36%	33%
Forklift trucks	5%	9%	25%	17%

Source: CIS Port Authorities.

dramatically by rationalizing the existing storage space and providing new types of storage facilities.

Port Labor

Labor forces for several ports are listed in table 6-3. The staffing levels are high by Western standards. There is no shortage of available workers, and the port workers are well trained for the level of technology and operations. However, considerable retraining is likely to be required to support the introduction of new technology and working practices.

Staffing levels are high in part because the port operators are responsible for a range of social provisions such as housing, education, and health care. These tasks add about 40 percent to port labor costs. Direct labor accounts for approximately 35 to 40 percent of total operating costs, while social costs account for another 15 percent. The large labor forces result in low productivity levels, but are not the primary cause of operating delays.

Environmental Issues

The major environmental issues relate to the handling of dangerous goods; discharges and spills; dredge spoil; and air pollution and dust. The former Soviet Union was a signatory to several international conventions on the handling of dangerous cargoes, but the republics still operate on the basis of their own classification and handling rules. Most of the ports have booms and oil-spill removal equipment. Systems exist for the collection and treatment of waste, but most are only capable of treating oily residues and are unsuitable for chemical

Table 6-3 **Port Employment, 1990-1991**

Port	Numbers Employed
St. Petersburg	6,500
Novorossiysk	3,800
Vostochny	3,100
Murmansk	2,700
Nakhodka	4,500
Vladivostok	4,200

Source: Maritime Transport Research Institute, Moscow.

residues. The overboard dumping of dry-bulk residues and residues from hold cleaning can cause serious sediment and contaminant pollution. The open air storage of dry bulks and grain results in dust and air pollution problems.

Organization and Management

Before the dissolution of the Soviet Union, maritime ports were the responsibility of the Ministry of Merchant Marine (Minmorflot). Like the vertical relationships in other sectors, the ports were managed by individual shipping companies.

Initial steps in port restructuring reflect quite different approaches in the different republics. Most ports in the Russian Federation have been established as independent business units, reporting directly to the Ministry of Transport. Some of the ports, particularly those in the Far East, have already involved the private sector, mainly through asset leasing. There also are private stevedoring operations.

Ukraine has established a Ministry of Transport, but executive control of port operations initially remained with the Black Sea Shipping Company. Under policies advanced in the early 1990s, the strong link between port and shipping activities would be continued with proposals to establish a holding company (Ukmorflot) reporting directly to the Council of Ministers of Ukraine, bypassing the Ministry of Transport.

Kazakhstan has established an entirely new port management organization. The Aktau International Sea Transport Company was created in May 1992 as an international joint-stock venture with public, private, and foreign capital. The Ministry of Transport and Construction holds the largest share (27 percent). There are 20 other stockholders, each with 8 percent or less.

Finances

In the Soviet system, identical tariffs were set for "similar" ports, based on average costs plus a profit margin of approximately 60 percent. Costs included historical cost depreciation, but no interest payments or return on capital investment. The transition from this system of rigid state controls to a semi-autonomous structure has been rapid. Maritime ports now have almost complete financial independence. They are allowed to retain profits, must pay taxes, and are expected to finance their own investments. The main restrictions are related to tariff setting and retention of foreign exchange, but even these restrictions were relaxed in late 1992.

Three significant changes in port tariffs in Russia and Ukraine began to become evident early in 1993. First, average rates increased between 15 and 20 times through June 1992; these increases reflected inflation and the declining value of the rouble. Second, the proportion of the tariff that was required to be paid in foreign exchange has been increased. Each port appears to have its own policy on this matter. Third, some ports introduced tariff surcharges earmarked for funding new investments.

Some ports experienced serious cash flow problems in 1992 and began to have difficulty meeting wage payments. None of the ports had sufficient reserves to invest in projects designed to expand capacity, improve quality, or lower costs. Tariffs were too low to generate sufficient funds for equipment replacement. To overcome this problem, both Russia and Ukraine established maritime banks to act as clearinghouses for payments as well as to provide investment funding.

The future financial position of the ports will depend on several institutional factors. Most ports are local monopolies with high entry barriers. Privatization and relaxation of barriers to entry could increase competition and reduce the cash flows expected from tariff deregulation. As a result, several large investment projects may have difficulty obtaining financing, either internally or from public sector institutions such as State banks. Foreign investment is thus likely to be sought, but much remains to be done to provide a sound investment environment. For example, although the ports are entitled to use former State assets, it is not clear which organizations own these assets, nor is there any consensus procedure for valuation.

Inland Waterways

Inland waterways account for only about 3 percent of total domestic freight tonne-kilometers. Although the physical infrastructure is substantial, the network is little used because of the assignment of major markets to rail. There have been few incentives to use the most cost-effective types of vessels and operating practices, or to ensure that the associated cost savings are reflected in tariffs. The large margins of spare capacity and the large labor force have made restructuring difficult. The inland ports remain strongly linked organizationally and economically to the large shipping companies, even though they are technically independent. The waterway organizations have strong regional identities, are large employers, and have been extremely vulnerable to political intervention. As a result, any reform program must address a range of structural, operational, institutional, and investment problems.

Within Russia, there are four main types of waterways, with different operating aspects. The first and most important waterways are those created in the 1930s by the damming of large rivers for electricity generation. The second major type is a network of canals built to link the major river systems to each other and to the seaports. However, this network often follows circuitous routings and thus has difficulty competing with rail transport. The third type of waterway consists of the Siberian rivers that are primary supply lines for northern regions, but are frozen for long periods and have very high dredging costs. Finally, there is a fairly extensive network of secondary waterways with light traffic volumes and high maintenance costs.

In Ukraine, the inland waterway network is much smaller and is centered around the Dnepr River and its electricity-related reservoir system. Many secondary waterways in Ukraine have been closed since 1980 as a result of the Chernobyl nuclear accident.

Traffic Volumes

Table 6-4 shows the volume and composition of inland waterway traffic between 1980 and 1990 to 1991. Both Russia and Ukraine estimate that inland waterway traffic declined 30 to 50 percent from the late 1980s to 1992, mainly because of reduced activity in the construction industry. Construction materials and aggregates accounted for approximately 80 percent of Russian waterborne traffic in tonnes, and 45 percent in terms of tonne-kilometers. Such materials represented 85 percent of Ukraine traffic and 65 percent of Kazakhstan traffic. Much of the aggregate being hauled was material dredged from the same inland waterways.

Construction materials moved short distances, with an average haul length of 200 kilometers, compared with 880 kilometers for other bulk cargoes. In Ukraine, construction materials moved only an average of 25 kilometers, compared with 550 kilometers for other bulks.

Table 6-4 Inland Waterway Traffic, 1990–1991

| | Inland Waterway Traffic Volumes | | |
	1980	1985	1990–1991
Million tonnes			
Russia	568	633	669
Ukraine	51	57	60
Kazakhstan	N.A.[1]	N.A.	11
Billion tonne-kms			
Russia	245	262	233
Ukraine	11	12	10
Kazakhstan	N.A.	N.A.	N.A.

Commodity Mix (Excluding Construction Materials)

| | Traffic (MM tonnes) in 1990–1991 | | |
	Russia	Ukraine	Kazakhstan
Timber	51	—	1
Oil	34	1	1
Coal	17	1	—
Grain	7	1	—
Iron ore	6	2	—
Fertilizers	5	—	—
Iron and steel	3	1	—
Minerals	2	—	—
Cement	1	—	—
Total	126	6	2

[1] N.A. equals not available.

Source: River Transport Research Institutes, Moscow and Kiev.

The Fleet

As of the early 1990s, the inland waterway fleet consisted of almost 9,000 vessels in Russia, 800 vessels in Ukraine, and 400 vessels in Kazakhstan. Approximately 35 percent of the fleet was self-propelled. These self-propelled ships hauled 60 percent of the total tonne-kilometers but were more expensive to operate than barge tows of similar capacity, as shown in table 6-5. The fleet is also quite old, as shown in table 6-6. Only Ukraine made a considerable investment in its barge fleet in the 1980s. However, a large surplus of capacity in the early 1990s suggests that replacement needs are likely to be small.

The productivity of the inland waterway fleet is very poor. Utilization is low, and port congestion and low handling rates mean that turnaround times are long. The productivity of barge tows is further reduced by the standard practice of keeping tugs and barges permanently coupled. As a result, tugs spend 55 percent of their time in port, compared with 10 to 20 percent in western Europe. Moreover, only about half the time in port is spent handling cargo; around 30 percent of the time is spent waiting for port services such as rail wagons or storage.

Inland Ports

There are approximately 3,000 river ports in Russia, most quite small. The eleven largest ports handle less than 5 percent of the total traffic. By contrast, Ukraine has many fewer ports, and the ten largest ports account for 80 percent of all traffic.

The principal problem in the inland ports is the lack of storage space. The space that does exist remains full for extended periods. This lack of space increases the need for direct loading and discharge to rail wagons. Other factors that reduce productivity include the shortage of modern discharging equipment for rail wagons for bulk cargoes; the predominance of low-capacity cranes; and shortages of small equipment.

Table 6-5 Comparative Costs of Self-Propelled Vessels and Barge Tows (1990)

	Self-propelled Vessels[1]	Barge Tows[1]
Capital cost (MM Rb)	3.5	1.7
Operating costs (Rb per day)		
In port	950.0	730.0
Sailing	1,600.0	950.0

[1] For capacity of 6,000 dwt.

Source: Estimate based on material supplied by the River Transport Research Institute, Moscow.

Table 6-6 **Average Age of Fleet, Russia and Ukraine, 1990-1991**

	Average age (years)				
	Self-propelled Vessels			Barges	
Russia	Dry bulk	Liquid bulk		Dry bulk	Liquid bulk
	19	17		14	17
Ukraine	Long-distance	Local		Long-distance	Local
	22	28		8	12

Source: River Transport Research Institutes, Moscow and Kiev.

Organization and Management

In Russia, the inland waterways are managed by Glavodput, a consortium of fourteen inland waterway associations reporting directly to the Ministry of Transport. Inland shipping operations are carried out by 21 large inland shipping companies. These companies previously owned the ports, and were themselves controlled by a separate Ministry of River Transport. Although the various enterprises involved in river transport in theory are now independent, this is not yet true in practice. The Ministry of Transport continues to appoint senior managers of the shipping companies. The shipping companies still coordinate the business operations of all enterprises, including ports and ship repair yards. The firms also continue to finance the social obligations of all the enterprises.

In Ukraine, there is a single body responsible for inland waterways (Ukrechflot). This organization originally reported directly to the Council of Ministers of Ukraine, but now reports to the newly established Ministry of Transport. Ukrechflot coordinates traffic flows and assets, recommends tariffs, sets technical standards, determines business policies, and is responsible for social obligations. There also are two river shipping companies, the Dnepr River Shipping Company and the Danube River Shipping Company. The privatization of the Dnepr Company has been moderately successful, in part because the company managed substantial international trade activity under the Soviet regime. This privatization, though, retains strong organizational linkages to the government; for example, the head of Ukrechflot also was head of the Dnepr River Shipping Company.

In Kazakhstan, the river shipping companies are responsible for all port-related operations and report directly to the Ministry of Transport and Construction. Their activities are quite small relative to those in Russia and Ukraine.

Finances

Tariffs vary by shipping line, by type of cargo, and by geographical area, apparently taking into account some cost differences between ports. Since May 1992, ports and shipping companies in Russia have been free to set their own rates, with the provision that these rates be no more than 35 percent above costs. As of 1994, this pricing flexibility was not yet fully implemented.

Tariffs do not appear to cover replacement costs of assets, although this is not an immediate problem because of surplus capacity. The most important financial problems relate to maintenance. The cost of dredging and other works is high, and traditionally has been financed by a mixture of central government grants and revenue from selling the construction aggregates that have been dredged. The grants have been largely withdrawn and income from such aggregates has fallen sharply with the decline in the economy.

River-Sea Transport

Approximately half of the inland shipping companies in Russia and the Dnepr and Danube Shipping Companies in Ukraine operate river-sea services. These services are a specialized form of inland waterway transport using the same inland ports as waterway-only operations. These vessels must be able to navigate river networks as well as traverse seas or large lakes. This requirement calls for different hulls and sea transport capabilities, compared with barges or coastal ships.

There has been a growing demand for this type of transport since transition. It has also been more profitable than other types of inland waterway traffic, accounting for only 16 percent of tonne-kilometers and 4 percent of tonnage, but 35 percent of net revenues. Furthermore, unlike other inland waterway traffic, it has more potential to earn foreign exchange. Greater fleet utilization is also achieved, because vessels can be redeployed when many rivers are frozen. Finally, the use of river-sea vessels could rise substantially as seaport transport links are no longer limited to rail. Few of the major ports currently have any links to the inland waterway system, and thus river-sea vessels may have a growing role to play in transshipment operations as these connections are developed.

In 1990 and 1991, Russian river-sea vessels handled approximately 17 million tonnes of international cargo, and 5 to 6 million tonnes of domestic cargo. In Ukraine, such operations handled about 2 million tonnes of international freight and 4 million domestic tonnes. The international routes go mainly to Scandinavia, Poland, and Germany from the north, and to Bulgaria, the former Yugoslavia, Turkey, and Greece from the Black Sea. The most important domestic routes are in the Caspian Sea, around the Gulf of Finland, and from northern Siberia to the Far East.

The Russian river-sea fleet in the early 1990s had approximately 500 vessels with a total capacity of 1.3 million deadweight tonnes (dwt). The Ukrainian fleet totaled 71 vessels with a capacity of 184,000 dwt. The average vessel had a capacity of about 2,600 dwt. The average age of Russian vessels was estimated at 19.5 years, whereas the Ukrainian fleet was much younger at 8 years. The majority of the hulls had been imported from eastern Europe or were locally built.

Coastal Shipping

Coastal shipping services have been important in the Arctic and Far East regions, often providing the only links to remote areas. In the Black Sea, coastal ports are used to redistribute grain imports from Novorossiysk to smaller ports. The total volume of cargo in 1990 and 1991 was 29 million tonnes, broken down by commodity in table 6-7.

Coastal shipping in the Arctic and Far East requires costly ice-breaking operations and the use of strengthened hulls.[6] Alternative supply routes are difficult and expensive, so that it is likely that such services will be maintained. The services are undertaken by Russia's maritime shipping companies with cost-plus tariffs as administered by the Ministry of Transport.

Nonetheless, fundamental changes may occur if Russia's northern waters are opened up to international shipping. For example, direct foreign supply routes from Japan may replace domestic services to locations such as Kamchatka. Also, the use of a northeast passage between Europe and the Far East could become more economical if and as ice-breaking costs are spread over larger volumes.

Table 6-7   Coastal Shipping Traffic Volumes

Traffic by Shipping Company, 1990 (MM tonnes)

Commodity	Murmansk	Northern	Arctic	Far East	Sakhalin	Kamchatka	Primorsk	Novorossiysk	Total
Petroleum	0.03	0.05	0.02	0.34	0.04	0.12	4.73	0.02	5.35
Coal	0.50	0.02	0.10	1.69	1.72	0.62	—	—	4.65
Ore	1.23	—	—	0.12	—	—	—	—	1.35
Grain	—	—	—	0.04	0.02	—	—	0.65	0.71
Other bulk	0.07	0.18	0.02	1.37	0.93	0.31	0.08	0.11	3.07
Timber	0.04	0.03	0.17	0.07	0.54	0.17	—	—	1.02
General cargo	0.98	0.37	0.14	2.85	6.82	1.67	—	—	12.83
Total	2.85	0.65	0.45	6.48	10.07	2.89	4.81	0.78	28.98

Source: Institute of Complex Transport Studies, Moscow.

Institutional Issues

The basic needs in water transport are increased competition, privatization, investment in new technology, more focus on commercial success, and coordination with other transport modes. Policy recommendations sometimes differ for seaports and inland waterways.

Because seaports involve much integrated planning, port authority structures might be established to own port assets and lease them to private operators. The authority also could license and coordinate activities on a nondiscriminatory basis; enforce technical and safety standards; and perform common services such as channel maintenance and security and fire service, perhaps through outside contracting. In parallel, port reform should seek privatization of stevedoring, cargo-handling, and warehousing services. Similarly, shipping lines and shippers should be privatized as soon as possible. Noncommercial services might best be handled through private provision, perhaps through competitive bidding.

Competition should be encouraged within ports by separating operating activities; between neighboring ports; and, for long-haul traffic, by developing more competition between groups of ports in different regions. Increased competition is likely to emerge almost inevitably, because it was constrained in the past not by commercial considerations but by centralized planning of cargo movements.

Many of the old planning roles increasingly will become the province of the individual ports themselves.

Relatively few regulatory controls on pricing, services, or market areas are likely to be needed, so long as interport competition is encouraged by breaking up the old spatial monopolies. The principal places where competitive conditions are unlikely to be achieved are at some inland ports, which may be too small to be independently viable or which have spatial monopolies with little alternative land transport competition. The potential of intermodal competition must also be considered. Future regulation appears best limited to vessel navigation and safety standards, environmental protection, and technical operating standards and practices.

Summary

Some seaports will have an increasingly important role to play as the economy becomes more open to international trade. The exact role at particular ports will depend on changes in the volume, direction, and commodity mix of traffic. Major changes will be needed in the way cargo is handled, especially in containerization and in limiting the practice of direct delivery to and from railcars. Privatization efforts may help improve efficiency and increase access to investment capital.

The future role of inland waterways is less clear, given substantial excess capacity, declining major markets, and an already small market share. Inland waterways are likely, though, to play a major role in some areas and in some niche markets. Commercialization and more rational pricing should improve the competitive position of inland waterways relative to rail transport. River-sea transport is a special niche market that apparently evolved in the Soviet Union to avoid port congestion and double handling; these are transshipment aspects that may become more important in any market-oriented system. Coastal shipping serves areas of strategic importance in the North, and could be affected by greater commercial activity between Europe and the Far East. Across all sectors, the performance and success of waterborne transport will be affected by the extent to which foreign shipping operations are permitted to compete for both international and domestic cargoes.

A striking aspect of waterborne transport in the CIS is the extent to which efficiency could be improved by making relatively simple organizational changes or a few focused small investments. Expanded port storage space, and more provision for trucking and rail access would be particularly helpful – especially if combined with a major expansion of containerization. Much could be achieved by simply reallocating space by usage and better scheduling. Like the other modes, basic physical capacity and available human resources appear to be more than adequate. Because of the existing overhang of excess capacity relative to current demand, there will inevitably be severe financial problems and widespread bankruptcies. Restructuring water transport will result in major reductions in labor forces and forced retirement of capital assets, especially aging parts of the shipping fleet. Again, restructuring along with tighter and more commercially-oriented management appear to be the keys.

Notes

1 This chapter is based on Nedeco Consultants, *Waterborne Transport Survey: Russian Federation, Ukraine, Kazakhstan* (London: European Bank for Reconstruction and Development, 1993). To the extent possible, the original presentation of the report has been preserved.

2 Most production in the Soviet Union was traded internally, with international trade limited primarily to Eastern Europe, Cuba, and other Asian and African allies.

3 According to the Institute of Complex Transport Problems in Moscow, Russia, Ukraine, and Kazakhstan generated 55 percent of total Soviet foreign trade of 400 million tonnes in 1989.

4 For example, Riga was one of only two ports with modern container facilities, and Ventspils, Latvia, was the major oil export terminal. Tallinn and Odessa served as the Soviet Union's major grain storage facilities. Some of these facilities had begun to charge hard currency for port traffic by 1992.

5 This section is based on studies of the ports of St. Petersburg, Novorossiysk, Vostochny (Russia); Ilyichevsk and Yuzhniy (Ukraine); and Aktau (Kazakhstan). The studies were conducted by Nedeco as part of the sector survey.

6 The cost of ice-breaking operations in 1990 amounted to 130 million roubles, or about 4 to 5 roubles per tonne at 1990 exchange rates.

7

Air Transport[1]

Although air transport shares many of the problems confronting other sectors, several factors are unique to the industry and will influence any transition to a market economy. First, to a greater extent than in the other modes, pricing distortions have resulted in a much larger industry than could be afforded in a market economy. Second, the long distances and isolation of many communities make air transportation particularly important in several of the republics, particularly Russia and Kazakhstan. Third, Soviet aviation was characterized by tight vertical integration of activities that are usually separated elsewhere. Airline operations, airports, air navigation, and regulatory functions all were largely under the control of Aeroflot.

The transition in air transport is complicated further by the close linkages between civil aviation and the defense sector. Much of the airspace is controlled by the military, but the influence of defense activity goes far beyond air navigation. Aerospace was viewed as a showpiece of Marxist technology. The Soviet Union manufactured and flew its own aircraft. There was virtually no role for foreign subcontractors or for the variety of production technologies and other innovations described in chapter 3. Soviet commercial aircraft are unique in design, construction, and operation, and share few commonalities with Western manufacturers. This inheritance introduces a multitude of certification issues for aircraft, as well as difficulties in integrating air navigation technologies with neighbors in Europe and Asia.[2] Finally, as a Soviet foreign policy instrument, Aeroflot "showed the flag" in many cities around the world, operating many uneconomic routes. Although this situation is true for many national "flag carrier" airlines, few had a greater burden than Aeroflot.[3]

Industry Overview and the Soviet Legacy

Air travel represented 37 percent of all intercity passenger traffic in the former Soviet Union in 1990, a share more than twice that of the United States, and three times that of Western Europe. This extremely high proportion was the result of vast distances, exceedingly low fares, and the underdevelopment of road transport alternatives.

Air transportation was chronically underpriced. Fares were set low and were related to an average worker's weekly pay, so that air travel was affordable for large segments of the population. In 1989, before the worst of Russian inflation had occurred,[4] seats on domestic flights from Moscow cost approximately 40 percent less than the lowest fare for American cities a similar distance from Chicago.[5] Fares in comparable European markets were roughly 2.5 times greater than those charged by Aeroflot in 1989.[6] Given this fare structure, it was not surprising that demand chronically exceeded supply.[7]

In the 1980s, Aeroflot perennially was the world's largest airline. Table 7-1 presents traffic and operating data for selected major airlines. In 1991 all divisions of Aeroflot carried slightly more than 128 million passengers. With many restrictions on travel and routes,[8] a relatively limited role for international travel was characteristic of

Table 7-1   Operating Statistics for Selected Airlines, 1991
(scheduled traffic only)

Airline	Flights (thousands)	Passengers (MM)	Revenue Passenger-kilometers (billions)	Passenger Load Factor (%)
Aeroflot	758	128	209	85
Air Canada	143	9	22	68
Air France	179	13	33	67
American	853	76	131	62
British Airways	247	23	63	69
Japan Airlines	99	23	52	71
Lufthansa	374	24	42	61
Singapore	35	8	33	73
United	690	62	132	66

Source: International Civil Aviation Organization, Traffic 1987–1991.

Aeroflot: in 1991, only about 3 percent of passengers and 7 percent of revenue-passenger kilometers (RPKs) were on international services. By contrast, in the United States international travel comprised 11 percent of passengers and 33 percent of RPKs in 1991.[9]

Aeroflot also was responsible for all air freight services. Cargo traffic volumes for Aeroflot and selected Western carriers are shown in table 7-2. The bulk orientation, along with low fuel prices, resulted in air freight playing a much different and more extensive role than in Western economies. In the former Soviet Union, air freight involved heavy volumes carried short distances. The figures are striking: Aeroflot carried approximately five times the tonnage of Air France in 1991, but only two-thirds the freight tonne-kilometers. The large role for air freight was aided by Soviet aircraft designed for large bulk transport, such as the Antonov-124 and Antonov-225.[10]

Air Passenger Travel by Republic

Table 7-3 presents passenger data for Russia, Ukraine, Kazakhstan, and Belarus during 1990, 1991 and 1992 for domestic and international flight operations. Data were not available to distinguish domestic and international traffic for the four states, but it is likely that the percentage of international traffic was similar to the 3 to 5 percent share of the former Soviet Union. Of course, new inter-republic "international" travel has increased.

Table 7-2 **Freight Traffic, 1991 (scheduled services)**

	Tonnes Carried (thousands)	Tonne-kilometers Performed (MM)
Aeroflot	2,470	2,351
Air France	485	3,230
American	413	1,290
British Airways	384	2,120
Japan Airlines	717	3,360
Lufthansa	718	4,106
Singapore	314	1,740
United	463	1,773

Source: ICAO.

Table 7-3   Changes (%) to Passenger Trafficon Selected City-Pairs, 1990–1992[1]

City Pair	1991–1990	1992–1991
Alma Ata – Moscow	5.6	-27.0
Alma Ata – Ust Kamenogorsk	23.2	-5.7
Moscow – Karaganda	3.4	-15.6
Alma Ata – Karaganda	-3.2	-13.2
Minsk – Simferopol	-1.6	-47.0
Minsk – Moscow	8.7	2.4
Moscow – Tselinograd	-3.5	-5.3
Moscow – Ust Kamenogorsk	-0.6	-18.4
Minsk – Sochi	1.1	-32.8
Moscow – Odessa	-8.5	-57.3[2]
Moscow – Kiev	-17.0	-32.0[2]
Alma Ata – Odessa	7.7	-85.3
All Russia	-1.0	-24.4
All Belarus	-1.0	-31.0
All Ukraine	-5.9	-10.0
All Kazakhstan	-7.5	-23.5

[1] 1992 versus 1991 based upon first quarter except as noted.
[2] May and June 1992 versus May and June 1991.

Source: Aerodevco.

The Aeroflot Organization

As a Production and Commercial Association reporting to the Ministry of Civil Aviation, Aeroflot operated as a holding company with separate subsidiaries for international operations, domestic aviation, and other enterprises. The separation of international from domestic operations centralized control over foreign exchange and international travel, and ensured compliance with International Civil Aviation Organization (ICAO) standards and recommended practices on international flights.

The domestic operations of Aeroflot were controlled from Moscow but operated as 31 decentralized regional directorates. Many of these regional units were extremely large and operated autonomously. The regional directorates also operated all airports, air traffic control

(ATC) systems, and associated worker social support activities, resulting in a set of vertically integrated spatial monopolies. Accounting and managerial systems also commingled operations of airlines, airports, and air navigation. As a result, little heed was paid to variations in airline operating costs or revenues in each region. For example, unlike ICAO standards in which air navigation charges are based on costs, Aeroflot established a uniform set of fees. The resulting cross-subsidies are hard to determine, though, because market-oriented revenue and cost accounting data are limited.

Aeroflot owned more than 8,000 aircraft in 1990, including about 1,500 commercial jets, with the rest of the fleet ranging from regional turboprops to crop dusters. The Aeroflot jet fleet was approximately 2.5 times larger than that of American Airlines and about 4 times the size of British Airways. However, in 1992 only about 60 percent of this fleet was active at any given time, compared to 85 to 90 percent reliability achieved by most major Western carriers. Compared with other large airlines with similar service networks, the Soviet fleet had a preponderance of older, narrow-body aircraft of quite limited range. With little diversity in types and size of aircraft, little attempt was made to match capacity to market size. The fleet characteristics also reflect the Soviet legacy of underpriced fuel and a producer orientation.

Effects of the Soviet Breakup

The breakup of the Soviet Union led to a dismemberment of the Aeroflot enterprise along the lines of the regional directorates. In essence, the directorates initially assumed control of aircraft, airline operations, airports, and air navigation in their respective regions. Each region in effect became its own civil aviation conglomerate. Officially, Aeroflot's fleet was divided among the republics according to traffic demands and schedules, but in practice, the republics assumed operating control of whatever assets were available and wherever the planes happened to be at the time. This dissolution went even further in the larger republics, which saw independent aviation operations established at the subregional level: for example, the 21 regional directorates of Aeroflot in Russia devolved into more than 100 enterprises.

Aeroflot attempted to coordinate the operations of these new airlines, but this did not prove easy.[11] ATC and airport coordination apparently were maintained, albeit with some difficulty. Unfortunately, the transition was accompanied by a breakdown in network aspects such as clearinghouses, interline connections, and integration of air traffic control systems.[12] To make matters worse, Aeroflot's centralization of production facilities made it extremely difficult for many of the new regional aviation conglomerates to obtain access to spare parts, training and maintenance facilities, and other equipment and personnel needs. Moreover, many of the new enterprises either were unable or chose not to adopt the prior Aeroflot policies with respect to licensing, certification, inspection, safety regulation, and other regulatory structures and practices. In short, aviation fragmented into a collection of "baby-flots," which controlled much aviation activity in their respective regions, competed only on a limited basis, and made few efforts to re-establish network aspects necessary for a well-functioning air system. Indeed, there were few incentives to do so.

The disintegration of the Aeroflot system in the early 1990s led to increased independence for the former regional divisions and to the entry of many newly formed charter services and quasi-scheduled operations. In addition, independent, private airlines were established in some regions. Many of these carriers offered services only for hard currency, and some were able to use this funding as security for leases of Western aircraft. Many of the airlines in the regional departments formed joint stock companies and applied to the Ministry of Transport for operating authority.[13] At the end of 1993, there were 89 registered scheduled commercial air carriers in the Russian Federation alone, with an estimated 103 airlines providing some sort of regular commercial service.

Traffic and Finances

Load factors, passenger volumes, and RPKs fell slightly from 1990 to 1991, and then dropped precipitously in 1992. The sharpest declines were in domestic services and in inter-republic travel. Considerable traffic also shifted from air to rail in 1992, mainly on short-distance routes. Historically small price differentials between the modes widened considerably, particularly on short hauls. For example, in 1990, the Minsk to Moscow air tariff was 18 roubles compared to 14 roubles by rail (hard class). By summer 1992, the air fare on the route had risen to 445, while the railroad fare increased only to 120 roubles. Consumer prices overall increased by a factor of

25 between 1990 and mid-1992, so that in this market the air fare moved in line with overall prices, while inflation-adjusted rail fares dropped sharply. Overall, though, air fares lagged behind general inflation. In Russia and Belarus, ticket prices between 1990 and mid-1992 rose by a factor of 18; Ukraine's fares increased by a factor of 20; only Kazakhstan's fares kept pace with inflation. Nevertheless, the demand-decreasing effects of falling personal incomes overwhelmed the effects of the decline in the real price of air travel, resulting in substantial traffic declines in virtually all domestic air markets, as shown in table 7-3.

The volume declines and lagging real fare adjustments created increasing financial difficulty. Operational costs grew by factors of 30 to 36 between 1990 and 1993, placing severe financial pressure on the carriers. Much of the large increase in airline costs was prompted by the rapid increases in fuel prices after 1990, although they still had not reached world levels. In 1990, Aeroflot had purchased fuel for 64 roubles per tonne, approximately 2 percent of the world price.[14] By mid-1992, at 35,000 roubles per tonne, it was still paying only 20 percent of the world price at then-prevailing exchange rates. Flights were canceled frequently for lack of fuel; some cities lost services completely. Effective January 1, 1993, the Russian Federation decided to halt air subsidies, although a program to cover 50 percent of Russian Aeroflot's fuel expense remained in place.

Traffic Forecasts

Table 7-4 shows passenger traffic forecasts for the four states based on alternative economic scenarios.[15] Actual levels of traffic for 1990 are shown along with a forecast of what traffic might have been in 1990 if the former Soviet airlines had been operating under "normal" international conditions in a market economy with negotiated bilateral agreements. The 1990 actual level of 194.4 billion RPKs was approximately 78 percent higher than what might have been expected (109.3 billion RPKS) in a market economy based on the Soviet Union's GDP. There was some variation across republics, with Ukraine's air transport sector roughly 48 percent larger than might be expected, Russia's 80 percent higher, Kazakhstan's 83 percent above norm, and Belarus's 126 percent higher.[16]

The traffic declines of the early 1990s are unlikely to be recouped for about 20 to 25 years. In the long run, Aerodevco Consultants

Table 7-4 Passenger Traffic Forecasts, 1990–2015 (billions of revenue passenger-kilometers)

Year	Russia Base	High	Low	Ukraine Base	High	Low	Kazakhstan Base	High	Low	Belarus Base	High	Low	Total Base	High	Low
Actual															
1990	159.5	—	—	16.0	—	—	13.2	—	—	5.5	—	—	194.4	—	—
Hypothetical Market Economy															
1990	88.7	—	—	10.8	—	—	7.2	—	—	2.4	—	—	109.1	—	—
Forecast															
1993	62.7	63.1	58.4	7.4	7.4	6.9	5.0	5.1	4.7	1.7	1.7	1.6	76.8	77.3	71.7
1995	61.9	56.2	52.1	7.2	7.7	6.2	4.9	5.4	4.3	1.7	1.8	1.4	75.7	81.1	64.0
2000	77.6	85.0	55.4	8.8	9.4	6.4	6.0	7.3	4.3	2.0	2.2	1.6	94.4	104.0	68.0
2005	93.7	106.4	61.4	10.4	11.5	6.9	7.1	9.4	5.4	2.4	2.7	1.8	113.5	130.1	75.5
2010	110.3	131.2	71.0	12.0	14.0	7.8	8.2	12.2	6.3	2.8	3.3	2.0	133.5	160.7	87.2
2015	128.0	161.7	81.9	13.8	17.1	8.9	9.4	15.7	7.4	3.3	4.1	2.3	154.5	198.5	100.6

Source: Aerodevco. Hypothetical market economy figures based on average GDP/RPK relationship for ICAO-reporting countries. High, low, and base cases derived from different assumptions about the speed and strength of economic recovery.

estimate that overall traffic volumes under a market economy will be 20 to 30 percent lower than those which might have been achieved had the command economy with its subsidized inputs, fares, and relative prices of modes continued, as shown in table 7-4. Similar cargo forecasts, presented in table 7-5, suggest that the rationalization of air freight will be about the same as for passenger travel, with demand by 2015 reaching only about 80 to 85 percent of 1990 levels.[17]

These forecasts also suggest that commercial aviation in the former Soviet Union is likely to experience substantial reallocations of traffic flows, even under the most optimistic of circumstances. The largest decreases should be experienced on short-haul markets, which can be expected to lose substantial mode share to road transport. Accordingly, many investments in airport capacity expansion or major refurbishment projects would seem difficult to justify.

Other Aspects of Commercial Aviation in the former Soviet Union

The Quality of Services

The quality of service provided by airlines in the former Soviet Union was notoriously poor. In the Soviet system, passengers and freight merely represented a demand on system resources. Few in the system benefited directly from serving passengers or freight customers. The problems were legion. Flights were continually oversold and had lengthy waiting lists, because of severe underpricing and no financial incentives to increase frequencies. Little effort was made to coordinate schedules or improve connecting flights. The system relied heavily on nonstop and through flights, often on less than a daily basis. After the breakup, these old problems persisted while new ones were added, including passengers forced to purchase separate one-way tickets (especially for inter-republic travel) because airlines refused to honor tickets issued by other carriers.

Safety

Fatal accident rates for air carriers in the former Soviet Union rose in 1991 and 1992 from the levels achieved in the late 1980s, when the USSR's accident rate was about twice that of the U.S. rate.[18] In 1991 and 1992, however, the accident rate in the former Soviet Union rose to 3.2 times higher than that of U.S. carriers. Unofficial reports for 1993

Table 7-5 Air Cargo Traffic Forecasts, 1990–2015 (billions of revenue tonne-km)

Year	Russia			Ukraine			Kazakhstan			Belarus			Total		
	Base	High	Low	Base	High	Low	Base	High	Low	Base	High	Low	Base	High	Low
Actual															
1990	2,438	—	—	164	—	—	125	—	—	64	—	—	2,791	—	—
Hypothetical Market Economy															
1990	1,155	—	—	292	—	—	69	—	—	59	—	—	1,575	—	—
Forecast															
1993	769	775	705	191	193	181	42	43	38	35	35	32	1,038	1,045	956
1995	757	818	614	188	202	162	40	48	34	34	38	28	1,019	1,106	838
2000	980	1,087	652	246	262	174	56	78	42	48	53	34	1,330	1,480	902
2005	1,215	1,403	731	308	337	197	74	111	55	63	72	43	1,660	1,923	1,026
2010	1,467	1,779	863	374	428	233	92	157	69	79	96	53	2,012	2,460	1,218
2015	1,738	2,255	1,018	446	543	275	111	220	87	97	127	66	2,392	3,145	1,446

Source: Aerodevco.

and early 1994 suggest a worsening trend throughout the CIS republics.

Data on total accidents per 100,000 flight hours from 1986 to 1992, presented in table 7-6, indicate that accident rates increased after the Soviet Union dissolved. The average rate[19] for the period before the Soviet Union was dissolved was 0.072 fatal accidents per 100,000 flight hours, whereas for the two years after the dissolution it was 0.112 fatal accidents per 100,000 flight hours, or 55 percent higher. Despite the magnitude of this increase, it is based on only two years' exposure and could have resulted from random fluctuations in the number of accidents from year to year. In sum, there is rising concern that safety performance in the former Soviet Union, which improved over the 1980s, deteriorated markedly in the first half of the 1990s.

Flight Safety Inspections

The effectiveness of flight safety inspections is perhaps the most serious air safety concern in the wake of the Soviet Union's dissolution. Government safety inspections are responsible for maintaining the integrity of flight standards and ensuring that other factors do not affect system safety. *Air Safety Week* reported in December, 1992 that the Department of Air Transport of the Russian Federation had only 17 inspectors, compared with 2,500 in the United States.

Several other negative influences on safety apparently have emerged, including regional conflicts, lack of enforcement of codes and regulations, the appearance of new commercial operators, an

Table 7-6   Accident Rates for USSR/Former USSR Scheduled Passenger Services, 1986–1992

Year	Fatal Accidents Per 100,000 Flight Hours
1986	0.139
1987	0.056
1988	0.084
1989	0.000
1990	0.079
1991	0.106
1992	0.118 (estimated)

Source: Civil Inter-State Aviation Committee (MAK).

exodus of newer aircraft and more experienced flight crews to international flights (leaving older planes and less-experienced pilots flying domestic services), and cuts in expenditures on air safety and reliability programs.[20]

Aviation Infrastructure

The quality and performance of aircraft, ATC equipment, and airport infrastructure in the former Soviet Union is often below Western standards. Nevertheless, this infrastructure is in many cases adequate to meet the demands of a downsized civil aviation sector for the medium term, especially if some refurbishment and upgrading is undertaken.

Aircraft

Commercial aviation in the former Soviet Union operated almost exclusively with Soviet-built equipment. The basic types of aircraft and their performance characteristics are shown in Table 7-7. In comparison with Western equipment, the Soviet fleet generally was heavier, about 20 to 30 percent less fuel efficient, and had less range. These significant economic and environmental shortcomings of Soviet-designed aircraft are likely to make them increasingly obsolete as fuel prices rise to world market levels. Noise problems prohibited operation into some foreign destinations even in the early 1990s, and these conditions have since become even more restrictive. Spare parts are a problem because many aircraft systems were designed for complete replacement rather than modular repair. To make matters worse, spare parts production declined dramatically in the early 1990s.

The fleet also has a preponderance of aging narrow body aircraft such as the Tupolev 154 (TU-154) and Tupolev 134 (TU-134). The TU-134, TU-154 (and its derivative the TU-154M) generated over 70% of total station departures and 68% of total seat-kilometers of capacity in 1991. There was only one wide-body aircraft in the fleet, the Ilyushin 86 (IL-86). Wide-body aircraft are usually most effective on very long routes, where their crew and fuel productivity more than offset longer station stops. In contrast to the rest of the world's use of wide-body planes, the IL-86 was operated mainly on short stage lengths, partly because of range limitations.

Table 7-7 Performance Comparisons of Soviet and Western Aircraft

Aircraft Type	Passengers	Gross Weight (lbs)	Range (n mi)
Tupolev 134	64/72	99,200	1,907
Fokker 28	55/85	73,000	1,704
Boeing 737	103	110,000	2,500
Tupolev 154	128/167	198,416	1,565
Boeing 737-400	146/170	138,500	2,487
Airbus 320	164/179	162,040	2,305
Ilyushin 86	234/350	458,560	2,235
Boeing 747-400	496/592	800,000	8,406
McDonnell-Douglas MD-11	250/400	602,500	7,988
Airbus 310	218/280	330,695	5,113
Boeing 767	216/290	300,000	3,639

Source: Official Airline Guide, Thomas Cook, Inc., July 1993.

In the Soviet fleet there was a notable gap in the 100 to 150 and 180 to 250 seat ranges. Somewhat suggestively, these ranges (along with 50 to 75 seat aircraft) also were those aircraft sizes that were undersupplied during the regulated era for commercial aviation in the United States and other countries. With liberalization in many air markets worldwide, airlines can match their capacity to fluctuations in demand and provide markets with a better trade-off between aircraft size and flight frequency.

Unfortunately, most of the "baby-flots" cannot afford newly produced Soviet aircraft, even of older designs. Escalating operating costs, especially for fuel, leave few resources for fleet renewal. To meet this problem, the Civil Aviation Research Institute (Gosniiga) in Moscow has examined the feasibility of replacing the engines of Soviet-built aircraft with western designs. It found that the total cost of the installations is prohibitive for 20-year-old airframes. This finding suggests that a fundamental need for aerospace and aircraft manufacturing in the new republics is to catch up with Western technologies that are much more sensitive to energy efficiency and operating requirements for commercial operation.

Another organizational issue is the need for "enterprise integration" among aircraft suppliers. Soviet aircraft enterprises commonly had largely separate and independent design bureaus and production organizations. Better links are needed between design, production, and commercial activities such as sales and service. This goal might be met, at least in part, by introducing technology- and production-sharing joint ventures such as those described in chapter 3. Indeed, the principal Russian and Ukrainian aerospace enterprises have sought affiliations with Western aircraft, engine, and avionics firms.[21] Entry of third-party parts and equipment suppliers also should be encouraged to relieve spare parts shortages and to establish a competitive after-sale environment so that airlines do not remain captive customers of manufacturers.

Equipment and Support Facilities

Airports and ground-handling operations in the former Soviet Union generally are characterized by inefficient design, high maintenance downtime, excessive manpower, and a heavy burden of unserviceable equipment at most airports. Western aerospace firms make greater use of modular designs, techniques to monitor operations, redundant design provisions, and statistical quality control.

Air Navigation

Soviet airspace dwarfed all other national airspaces in the world, but suffered from many deficiencies. Civilian air routes are often circuitous because of large areas reserved for military use. These nondirect routes greatly increase operating costs. Air routes usually consist of a series of many short legs. Since flight crews must contact controllers at each flight segment, this system significantly increases the workload both in the air and on the ground. These problems are especially troublesome for international overflights, because most controllers have only a limited command of English (the worldwide official language of air navigation).

Although the former Soviet republics are largely in compliance with ICAO Standards and Recommended Practices for Air Navigation, some problems remain. Many specific navigation aids do not meet ICAO standards, and only can be used by aircraft equipped with special Soviet receivers, which most Western aircraft lack. There also is a prevalence of non-directional beacons and other antiquated ground-based navigation aids.

Overflights

Overflight aircraft normally do not require ground-based navigation aids because they are able to operate with self-contained equipment. They do require that ATC be equipped with communications and secondary surveillance radar to maintain aircraft separation and operations. Without this equipment, flight corridors can become saturated at peak periods and can be hazardous. Given the long and busy air routes between Europe and Asia, overflight services from the republics, especially Russia, could prove an important source of savings for international airlines as well as a source of added revenue for air navigation.

Revenue generated from international overflights is collected in hard currency centrally by Moscow. En-route fees are not calculated using ICAO cost-based formulas, but rather are negotiated separately with individual international airlines. The level of fees is influenced by the number of technical stops, the type of onboard equipment, and the number of overflights. There also are departure and air navigation fees. These charges are often only a paper entry among the new aviation enterprises, so in effect many airlines paid no user charges in the early 1990s.

The potential revenue from overflight charges is difficult to estimate, given uncertainty about demand and the effects of route resectoring and design. Table 7-8 shows Aerodevco revenue forecasts based on the traffic scenarios described earlier in this chapter. Russian overflight revenues are forecast to be U.S. $337 million by 2002. The amounts for Ukraine, Belarus, and Kazakhstan are considerably lower, because of combinations of smaller airspace and thinner traffic routes. Overall, these revenues could be particularly attractive for limited-recourse or non-recourse project finance.

Airports

The Soviet Union had several thousand airports of all sizes. Approximately 200 received scheduled services by jet and turboprop aircraft that required the full complement of airport support activities. Of these airports, 150 are in Russia, 21 are in Ukraine, 21 are in Kazakhstan, and 7 are in Belarus. Smaller airports support agricultural, forest fire, pipeline, small charter, search and rescue, and emergency medical services. Many do not have paved runways, operate only in clear (visual flight rules) weather conditions, and are

Table 7-8   Estimated Potential Overflight Revenue for Russia, Ukraine, Belarus, and Kazakhstan, 1993–2002 (MM nominal U.S. $)

	Russia		Ukraine		Belarus		Kazakhstan	
Year	CIS Airlines	Other Airlines	CIS Airlines	Other Airlines	CIS Airlines	Other Airlines	CIS Airlines	Other Airlines
1993	47.7	117.4	4.6	14.1	12.1	6.6	5.4	21.2
1997	61.6	157.2	5.8	20.2	15.2	9.3	7.7	30.6
2002	90.2	247.0	9.1	32.0	20.4	23.9	12.2	48.7

Source: Aerodevco forecasts.

closed during the long winter season. As in other countries, some of these small airports are considered a public service and often provide the sole transport access to many communities.

All the major airports were part of the Aeroflot Production and Commercial Association and thus followed Aeroflot practices. This made it difficult to operate them as profit centers, and to develop commercial opportunities which would lead (eventually) to financial sufficiency. For example, an airport usually did not charge its "home" airline for fuel, air traffic control, passenger servicing, and ramp handling. These costs generally were passed on to other airlines. In 1992, fees for international carriers were approximately twice that for domestic carriers.

Most airports in the new republics have terminal buildings which are ill-prepared to welcome and process passengers in comfort. Terminal buildings were designed to funnel passengers on and off aircraft in the fastest and cheapest manner possible, with little regard for comfort, commercial activity, or connecting convenience. Most airports also lack dedicated departure and arrival gates or loading bridges. Airport property has not been developed to attract third-party investment in hangars, catering services, freight forwarders, and other aviation services.

Institutional and Policy Reforms

Two distinct types of restructuring are required in the aviation sector. First is the separation of regulatory and operating functions, with the transport ministries retaining their oversight and enabling roles. Some progress had been made by 1993, although in many cases this was more "on paper" than in practice. The drafting and effective implementation of air codes for each republic is extremely important to institute procedures for licensing, certification, safety, security, and bilateral service agreements. A single, uniform set of policies is not necessary; in fact, such a structure may restrict entry and reduce competition. However, the codes and operating requirements should allow for mutual recognition and harmonization, similar to the ongoing efforts throughout Europe.

The other key institutional need is to deal with the legacy of the Aeroflot structure. The aviation sector presents an extraordinarily difficult problem, because there is a need for consolidation in some areas, but a need for separation and demonopolization in others. To begin with, it is essential to separate air navigation, airports, and airline activities. The breakup of Aeroflot along the lines of the old regional directorates has produced a set of spatial monopolies that reduce effective competition and create incentives and opportunities to exploit other domestic and international carriers that use the controlled airports and other aviation services.

A basic trend in civil aviation worldwide has been to decentralize and to allow multiple participants where possible. In air navigation, this trend has led to corporatized state enterprise structures responsible for ATC operation, investment, and financing. Although air navigation in the former Soviet Union has sufficient overall capacity, there are many bottlenecks and a concomitant need to upgrade and refurbish equipment. Much of this can be accomplished through project finance structures that marshal funds secured by air navigation charges. Such charges, though, should move toward the ICAO cost basis used in much of the rest of the world.[22] Some regulatory oversight also will be needed to ensure that airlines and airports have equal access on terms that reflect the costs imposed on the system. Suppliers of air navigation equipment also might benefit from joint ventures similar to those described above for aircraft.

Airports present a different problem from air navigation. Within each region, airports have network aspects, but the extent to which airports need to be centrally controlled can be overstated. In particular, there is little to justify a single ownership structure for airports and air navigation; these are largely separable activities. Moreover, if each airport operates its own airline, it is likely to take advantage of its monopoly power when providing landing rights and services to other airlines. Although larger airport systems should be self-sufficient financially, the danger is that this geographical scale may reinforce the establishment and use of spatial monopoly power. In many countries, this issue is dealt with through economic regulation of the airport enterprise, whether it is structured as a corporatized, governmental, or private organization. Some initiatives to reduce the need for regulation have been attempted either through bidding for concessions for specific airport activities, or by introducing competition among airports within a given metropolitan area. For example, Baltimore-Washington International Airport in the United States competes with Washington's National and Dulles Airports.

Moscow faces a similar choice in the organization of airports in its region. Counter to this competitive orientation, the reorganized Aeroflot Russian International Airlines in Moscow has established several joint ventures ranging from hotels to catering to air terminals. These joint ventures represent a major extension of Aeroflot's monopoly powers and do not bode well for the transition to a more competitive and commercially oriented aviation sector.[23]

A single corporatized structure sometimes may be more "bankable" from the standpoint of financing, not because of the underlying economic justification, but rather through the conferral of monopoly power. Even if a single corporatized structure is chosen, opportunities remain for introducing inter-airport competition through competitive contracting for airport concessions, either for the operation as a whole or for individual functions such as parking, services, and ground handling. For smaller airports that are not viable commercially, subsidy requirements might be minimized by contracting out such services on a bid basis, in which the bidding is for the amount of subsidy needed. This approach has been used increasingly in many countries, resulting in savings compared with the prior policies of cross-subsidizing small airports with the revenues generated by large ones.

The airline situation in the former Soviet Union is quite different from that of air navigation and airports. Instead of demonopolization, the need is for consolidation; the traffic and travel needs of the new republics do not require the 200 or more airlines that now provide some sort of service. As fuel costs and air fares rise to market levels, many of these airlines likely will fail or be absorbed by their remaining brethren. However, this consolidation should come about through the economics of the airline industry, rather than having survival be the result of having an enterprise control airports or other activities that may cross-subsidize the airline itself. There is a concomitant need for bankruptcy and other reorganization procedures to reduce the economic costs of consolidation and rationalization.

Financial and clearinghouse relationships should be re-established between aviation enterprises. A service organization is needed to handle reservations for passengers and freight, for operating information, and for inter-airline account clearing. To facilitate transition to a market, this service organization must be available to all enterprises, in order to provide information for consumers and incentives for airlines and airports to participate. Also, it should encourage the development of supporting activities such as travel agencies and freight forwarders, which are essential to creating ongoing incentives and pressures for commercialization.

Summary

In many ways, Aeroflot represents a stellar example of the complex set of problems and needs facing transition economies. Civil aviation in the new republics inherited many problems from the Soviet era. The chaotic economic picture, together with the sociopolitical developments of the early 1990s, severely tested governmental commitment and capabilities. Since the breakup of the Soviet Union, air traffic levels have fallen on most routes by between 20 and 50 percent. The governments often have simply made up airline shortfalls, without objective subsidy criteria. The existence of monopolies on many routes and the lack of pro-competitive policies have further complicated the situation.

The major problems faced by civil aviation in the four republics include: a limited knowledge of how to manage in a commercial environment; fragmentation of the industry into untenably small operators; ineffective coordinating institutions; outmoded technologies; past underinvestment in some aspects of the system; critically weak financial performance; a massive decline in demand; and shortages of key materials such as fuel. Major strengths include dedicated and experienced professionals, considerable technical capability, and well-established airframe and powerplant industries. The key policy problem is how to preserve and build upon these strengths while substantially restructuring the industry to attenuate its many weaknesses.

This restructuring should be predicated on separation of airport, air navigation, and airline activities, both to enhance competition and to better assess investment needs and capacities. Outright privatization then could be sought for airlines, subject to safety and soundness regulation. A competitive airline industry without captive airports also is likely to produce better investments in upgrading and replacement of aircraft, because of incentives to tailor the fleet to the nature of the markets being served. Air navigation and airports are more difficult to privatize. In these cases the objective should be to introduce commercial considerations wherever possible, through concessions, subcontracting, and efforts to enhance competition between airports. There also are opportunities for investments in improving quality of service and in reducing bottlenecks in air navigation. Many of these investments might be financed using private capital in limited- or non-recourse structures.

Notes

1   This chapter is based on Aerodevco Consultants Ltd., *Civil Aviation Sector Survey* (London: European Bank for Reconstruction and Development, 1993), supplemented by the authors with considerable assistance from B. Berman, a member of the Aerodevco project team. Berman's contributions are of particular importance in the sections on aviation safety.

2   For a discussion of these issues, see J. Moxon, "Testing Times," *Flight International* (December 15–21, 1993): 25–29.

3   In 1991, the international network of Aeroflot Soviet Airlines was responsible for 113 bilateral agreements covering 134 stations in 102 countries.

4   The World Bank noted that an average domestic ticket price in Russia in February 1992 was 250 roubles, about U.S. $2.50 at then current exchange rates.

5   Based on purchasing power parity estimates for 1989 from the IMF.

6   Amounts based on the average of black-market buying and selling rates for the rouble in Moscow, from "The Economy of the Former USSR in 1991," (Washington: IMF, 1992): 85.

7   Gosniiga traditionally forecast two demands when examining future capacity requirements: passengers actually traveling and "unsatisfied demands." Unsatisfied traffic consistently amounted to about one-fourth of the traffic actually carried.

8 In the Soviet era, virtually all international flights arrived in and departed from Moscow, consistent with visa and travel constraints.

9 Direct European comparisons are not meaningful given the smaller size of the countries. Taking Western Europe as a whole, about 16 percent of passengers and 42 percent of RPKs were outside of the region.

10 The Antonov AN-225 has a cargo capacity of 500,000 pounds and 42 million cubic feet. By comparison, a Boeing 747-400 freighter has a weight capacity of 220,000 pounds and 23 million cubic feet of cargo volume.

11 Economies of scale are limited for airlines, although some network and density economies exist.

12 To help deal with these problems, in 1992 the republics of the CIS formed an Interstate Civil Aviation Committee (MAK) to develop policies for airspace control, certification, and safety regulation. Unfortunately, MAK failed to become an effective organization and largely was marginalized by 1993.

13 An example is Air Ukraine, structured as a joint venture between the Ukrainian Civil Aviation Agglomerate and private parties, which operates leased Western-built aircraft and charges fares only in hard currency.

14 Based on an exchange rate of 20 roubles per U.S. dollar (average of black-market buying and selling rates for the rouble in Moscow in 1990). From "The Economy of the Former U.S.S.R. in 1991," (Washington: IMF, 1992): 85.

15 Regression models were developed by Aerodevco Consultants to forecast international and domestic revenue passenger-kilometer demand for air travel in Russia, Ukraine, Kazakhstan, and Belarus. This was done by comparing each republic's situation to other nations internationally. The models basically estimated traffic according to the GDP and to the geographical area of each nation. No other explanatory variables were found to be of influence. Base case GDP forecasts assumed a stabilizing of the economy by 1995 at about two-thirds of 1990 GDP, with subsequent growth of 4 percent annually. In addition to the base case, high and low forecasts were developed, with changes in the timing of stabilization and in subsequent growth. The low case assumed contraction until 1996 and that GDP will not regain 1990 levels until after 2010. The high case is based on a 1994 economic trough and GDP achieving 1990 levels by the end of the century.

16 These Aerodevco estimates are based on relationships between commercial aviation demand and GDP, estimated for ICAO reporting countries. The model does not include other factors, thus implicitly assuming that average worldwide relationships would hold in the former Soviet Union.

17 The passenger and cargo models have different estimates for the relation to economic activity. Business passenger travel is estimated to have a GDP elasticity of 0.88, personal travel 1.0, and cargo 1.14. These estimates are broadly consistent with other studies of air transport elasticities.

18 This is true for rates based on departures, flight hours, or passengers. Most accidents occur during takeoff or landing periods, so departure-based accident rates are preferred for comparative purposes.

19 Simple averages for the entire period, not the average of annual rates.

20 A. Velovich, "A Safe Place to Fly?" *Flight International* (January 12–18, 1994): 13.

21 For example, Yakovlev has worked with Allied-Signal; Rolls-Royce with Tupolev; Pratt and Whitney with Ilyushin; and Rockwell-Collins with both Tupolev and Ilyushin.

22 Air navigation charges generally are not established on the basis of willingness-to-pay, although there are increasing opportunities for price competition among alternative air routes over different countries.

23 An example of the potential for decreasing competition was the Russian Federation government decision to allow Aeroflot International to retain Sheremetyevo Airport in Moscow so that Aeroflot's hard currency earnings could be used to pay for improvements there.

Part III

Policy Issues

8

Corporatization and Privatization

The modal analyses in part II suggest that the major transport need in the new republics is institutional reform. In particular, the vertically integrated monopoly conglomerates inherited from the Soviet system should be restructured to enhance competition, managerial incentives, and service quality. Similar problems in other parts of the world, though markedly less acute, have led to much experimentation with and movement toward corporatization and privatization. For example, the worldwide spread of privatization since the late 1970s attests to an ongoing re-evaluation of whether many public sector economic activities might be more effectively supplied privately. Regulatory developments and initiatives, particularly in contestability theory and the role of potential competition, franchising, and price-cap regulation, have begun to at least raise the possibility that public provision may no longer be necessary to achieve social goals in activities imbued with a substantial public interest.

This chapter describes organizational and institutional choices in restructuring the transport sector in the former Soviet Union. Unlike either mature market economies or developing countries, the transition economies begin with a structure that combines aspects of both ministerial provision and public enterprise. These structures generally exist in an environment without a commercial orientation (either from substitutes, from customers, or from suppliers). Thus, the starting point is quite different in the former Soviet Union than it is for public enterprise reform in other parts of the world. Transport frequently involves long-lived investments and issues of networks, scale, and scope, so that the choices made about ministerial, corporatized, or privatized provision will play a central role in determining performance and efficiency.

Corporatization

Corporatization represents something of a hybrid or compromise between privatization with regulation, on the one hand, and continued government operation on the other. With corporatization an activity typically is spun off from a government ministry and established as a separate corporate entity, often to be operated (at least ostensibly) on a commercial basis, with less interference from political interests. The corporatized enterprise is expected to have better defined and focused managerial responsibilities than a typical government ministry, and to have access to private capital markets on commercial terms.

In the West, corporatized structures also have been created following government takeovers or nationalizations of previously private activities. Corporatizations can vary in the extent or degree of government ownership, because some shares of corporatized firms may be held privately. Rarely, though, does the government control less than 51 percent of the voting stock of a corporatized enterprise.

One view, common in former command economies, is that corporatization is a "way station" between ministerial control and privatization i.e., a mechanism for restructuring before transfer to private ownership. The alternative view is that corporatization is a strategy to gain the benefits of privatization, especially in restructuring pre-existing contracts in factor and product markets, without ownership transfer. This second view also holds that retention of government ownership and control leads to benefits of concentrated ownership, such as reduced pressure for short-term performance, and a superior ability to provide and sustain activities imbued with a substantial degree of public interest.

These contrasting views suggest several questions. Is the hybrid character of a corporatized public enterprise better able to meet multiple objectives, or is it merely subject to increased commingling of commercial and social goals? Can changing the organizational structure of an activity (the agent) be effective if the same principal (the government) remains in place? Or is corporatization likely to fail because the governance structure of "ministers as shareholders" probably will be comprised of members representing the same range of limited, parochial interests that made departmental or ministerial provision ineffective?

Corporatization efforts, especially when viewed as preludes to eventual privatization, generally have proceeded sequentially. An initial, and usually rather necessary, effort is made to separate regulatory and operational activities. Second, non-commercial functions are separated to the extent possible. Operational scope commonly is limited. In most cases, the corporatized enterprises' charters define commercial activities by mode, by vertical function (e.g., infrastructure provision or operation), by market, by product, or in other ways. In practice, most newly-formed corporatized state enterprises have reduced the range of their operations, spinning off peripheral activities, closing marginal facilities, and concentrating more on core operations. Third, if accompanied by separation of activities within a given transport sector, most corporatized structures also help introduce a more commercial orientation and reduce entry barriers by weakening both spatial monopolies and vertical integration.

Once this sequence is complete, managers of the corporate enterprise usually are expected to run the remaining activities on a commercial basis. In addition, corporate enterprises often are required to finance themselves without recourse to state support, either by internally generated cash flows or from commercial private-sector capital sources, and to pay taxes and dividends to the government.[1]

In many cases, attempts are made to institute more "arm's length" structures for performance monitoring and accountability. Managers are held responsible for decisions about activities, production, pricing, marketing, and investment within performance goals set by ministers (or by appointed boards of directors, modeled after private-sector corporate governance). The longest experience with this approach has been in France, most recently with contract plans for the state railways. Although these agreements have led to greater clarity about objectives, they can be broken by acts of government policy.[2] Also, contract plans commonly are not legally enforceable and thus cannot substitute as a control mechanism between government and the corporate enterprise.[3] As pointed out by Foster,[4] contract plans are easier to specify and are more effective if the time period is short, if required capital investment is either not long-lived or not industry-specific, and if the quality of the good or service can readily be described and priced. Above all, contract plans require that the government not change its mind about what it wants from the enterprise.[5]

Corporatizations, like privatizations, seemingly have a better chance of success if they operate in a commercially competitive environment, with privately provided substitutes or alternatives. This phenomenon raises an obvious question; why were these activities not successful as department structures while in the same operating environment? One answer might be that corporate status allows more managerial flexibility with respect to factor and product markets; corporatization then makes it evident that the real problem lies with broader government policies and practices. A dynamic commercial environment, however, may not have existed previously, in which case the government should seek sectoral reforms such as deregulation to place additional competitive pressure on the state enterprise. Above all, merely replacing a dominant government department with a dominant state enterprise should be avoided.

Operational Problems and Definition of Goals

Most state corporatizations face mixed objectives. Beyond commercial goals, these often include social service provision, safety, and regional development. Even when statutory corporations have a clear commercial purpose, additional non-commercial objectives often are added (such as "long term returns to the community" as in the case of the New Zealand Forestry Corporation). Although the goal typically is to replace mixed, inconsistent, discretionary and frequently non-monitorable objectives with clear, commercial, measurable ones, this often does not occur.

The enterprise, when under department or ministerial status, has a regular and close daily involvement with ministers on policy matters and operational issues. Under the corporatized structure, ministries typically become shareholders. This system theoretically places them in a position to monitor returns and seek performance outcomes but not be actively involved in business strategy.

State enterprise boards can reasonably argue that their role is to act as shareholder representatives – mainly to assign management responsibility, to see how well the enterprise does its job, and to react by intervening for further restructuring if necessary. From the government's perspective, however, assets held by public enterprises remain part of the public's (or taxpayers') assets and, arguably, should be no less exempt from legislative accountability than any other government asset. This view almost inevitably results in government consultation and required approval for major decisions. As noted by Foster:

> If the State is to be regulator, shareholder, and client, among other roles ... that implies either incoherence in performance or [requires] distinct parts of government performing the various roles; and in both cases there is bound to be a greater possibility that the separation of interests will be blurred.[6]

Government involvement is likely to be greatest during the transition from a ministerial to a corporatized structure. In fact, this involvement has sometimes been so extensive that it is common for the "transition period" to become the permanent state of affairs. Ministerial actions have ranged from changing objectives, to modifying financial and dividend policies, to restraining investment or disinvestment plans. Moreover, even though the state enterprise accounts may no longer be subject to legislative appropriations, in practice they usually remain subject to review by elected parliaments.

Ministers and other government officials are first and foremost political decision makers. Ministers may be less interested in monitoring and improving commercial performance and economic efficiency than in having a public enterprise – especially a profitable one – embark on non-commercial activities that benefit particular political constituencies. If these constituent benefits then become vested, ministers may be even less willing to serve as activist monitors in responding to dynamic changes in the economic environment.

Boards of corporatized enterprises often embody a range of interest groups, including labor, suppliers, and customers. In this environment, the objective of commercial success is likely to be attenuated. There have been a few cases, though, of charters specifically prohibiting or delimiting political appointments. Corporatized state enterprises, even with an "independent" board, usually still experience considerable political and ministerial involvement. A sequential principal-agent problem occurs, from the public to the legislature to the ministers to the enterprise board to the state enterprise itself. In short, a new, and often much more tortuous chain of principal-agent problems is created as efforts are made to define how to "monitor the monitors."

To help mitigate this problem, some forms of capital market monitoring can be introduced, such as partial equity shareholdings, non-recourse debt financing, or operating and performance contracts that specify both financial penalties and rewards. However, experiments with nonvoting equity shares, or "equity bonds" with payments linked to profits, have not been promising. The problem may arise from deficiencies in the design of the securities (e.g., the structure of the claims is too muted to induce active monitoring), or from not being issued in sufficiently large quantities to be effective.[7] Another possibility is that multiple holders of large blocks of equity may be less effective as monitors, either by canceling each other out or by increasing the "free rider" incentive relative to a single large shareholder.[8] The result is to reduce the likelihood of achieving needed restructuring through corporatization.

Privatization

Arguments for privatization,[9] commonly made in the West, may not apply all that easily or effectively to transport in the former Soviet Union. Certain preconditions usually must be met to make privatizations economically and politically successful.[10] Unfortunately these preconditions are often lacking in the former Soviet Union.

Willig has identified a set of basic characteristics about the relationship between the structure of an economy and the success of privatization.[11] First, effective reform requires a suitable set of institutions, legal structures, and a strategy tailored to the particular circumstances of the sector and the country. Second, a commercially oriented institutional framework is required. Third, there should be a microeconomic structure oriented toward competition. Fourth, there must be an effective regulatory structure in the case of enterprises with substantial market power. Within these broad features, the effectiveness of privatization is conditioned by the characteristics of the sector.

For example, competition in the markets in which privatized firms buy and sell is highly desirable, indeed almost indispensable, if privatization is to succeed. Competition appears vitally important in encouraging the cost savings or efficiencies that often motivate privatization. Furthermore, competition reduces the ability of private firms to exploit monopoly or market power to raise prices or restrict supply. To benefit from privatization, it helps to have competitive markets for important inputs as well as in downstream markets, so that any newly privatized entity is not held captive to sole-source suppliers or customers.[12]

Evidence that a competitive environment facilitates privatization has been found in a wide variety of case studies. For example, bus transit privatization is easier and generally more successful wherever bus ridership per capita is relatively high, because the market then can support multiple companies. In the new republics, where bus ridership per capita is high, bus privatizations thus should be workable. At a minimum, operating activities that are potentially amenable to competition and private provision (airlines, intercity buses, trucking, shipping, and intermodal activities) should be separated from infrastructure provision, which commonly is characterized by some degree of spatial monopoly and network characteristics (airports, air navigation, roads, and some port operations).

The key is to create as many incentives for efficient provision as possible. For example, even if a spatial monopoly exists, infrastructure costs and efficiency may be improved by contracting out operations under a performance-related incentive contract. Moreover, a competitive and efficient transport operating sector will itself produce ongoing pressures to lower the costs and to improve the performance of infrastructure providers.[13]

A special aspect of transport reform in the former Soviet Union, unlike in the Western market economies, is the opportunity to "go private" right from the start with activities undersupplied in the prior command economy. These activities include services for consumer goods and intermodalism, which often have low intrinsic entry barriers so that companies can be started and operated effectively on a small scale (e.g., in trucking, freight forwarding, and warehousing). In turn, a more dynamic trucking sector likely will pressure highway authorities to meet its needs. The threat of intermodal competition also is likely to produce incentives for improving rail operations and infrastructure. Privatization not only can spur improved performance in its own specific industry, but among suppliers, customers, and other transport modes as well.

Privatization also is much easier to implement when the efficiency gains from privatization are large; there is simply "more in it" for all concerned. Such gains should occur if the private sector is inherently more efficient than the public sector. Experience suggests, however, that too many economic rents available for expropriation can hinder privatization by creating strongly opposed vested interests, as in the case of U.S. airports.[14] Likewise, in the CIS republics, some transport privatizations appear likely to be both highly profitable and highly controversial.

Efficiency gains from privatization are not limited to cost reduction. Enhanced and innovative services are often as important. For example, where bus transport has been privatized and deregulated (as in Britain and many developing countries), innovations such as minibuses and microbuses and express services have prospered and proliferated. Similarly, enhanced telephone services are widely recognized as major benefits of telecommunication privatizations and deregulations.

Privatization also is easier to implement when little or no government subsidy has been required. Subsidies invariably complicate privatization efforts by extending the nature and scope of the political discussion.[15] Subsidy debates tend to be especially intense in transport situations in which few alternative modes are present, high initial and ongoing investments are involved, and future demands are uncertain. For example, new urban rail passenger lines are built by the public sector in most countries, because the heavy subsidies typically required make private provision highly risky and controversial. New private highways often face similar handicaps, especially development roads extending into thinly populated areas. It is far simpler and easier if a privatization can be financed (including investment needs) solely from available tolls, fares, or other direct-revenue sources.

A subsidy, however, need not be a bar to privatization. For example, in the United States and Britain unprofitable bus routes have been contracted out to private operators, through bidding procedures which seek the lowest possible subsidy.[16] Similar contracting practices have been used in many countries for remote air services.

Privatization also is easier when few redistributions or transfers of benefits among groups occur. For example, concerns about wage declines and job losses have complicated privatization efforts in bus transit, highway concessions, and rail transport, and are undoubtedly some of the greatest difficulties to be faced in the CIS. Under public enterprise, monitoring of effort was difficult, performance generally was not rewarded, the possibility of being fired was small, and unions often were able to impose labor-intensive work rules that resulted in higher costs, lower productivity, but easier jobs.[17] Similarly, any loss of subsidized service associated with privatization and deregulation clearly will be perceived (especially by those who formerly used the subsidized services) as at least a partial offset to any gains created by privatization and deregulation. In short, fewer political frictions will arise to impede privatization if not too many transfers or redistributions result. In the former Soviet Union, where so many benefits are tied to the place of employment, redistributions may greatly complicate privatization efforts.

Privatization works best when there are relatively few externalities involved. In the West, by far the most common and contentious externality concern is environmental damage. Like redistributions, externalities generate political interest and a need for political adjudication. The complexities of these issues have been particularly evident in attempts to privatize airport and highway development in the United States and Europe but also have proved important in bus system privatizations.

Finally, the success or failure of privatization or corporatization also can be conditioned by the general economic milieu in which such programs are undertaken. These larger considerations fall into cyclical and secular aspects. There will also be differences, sometimes quite sharp, among programs for privatizing existing state enterprises and those for private construction of infrastructure.

The private sector, motivated by profit, arguably should be more responsive to consumers and more efficient than transport ministries or public enterprise managers. For example, the private sector should seek out more cost-effective designs or operating strategies. Similarly, the private sector may have more flexibility and incentive to adopt innovative schemes for pricing its services, thereby reflecting the variations in costs that different users impose and the benefits that different users receive. Private firms generally have a better record of responding to customer needs and developing suitable new products or services in a timely fashion when needs or technological capabilities change.

Private transport also may be able to tap into additional sources of financing and managerial capacity. If private operations can finance their projects in the private capital market and repay their investors without recourse to scarce tax resources or public funds, required investments might be made in the transport sector without raising additional taxes or increasing public-sector debt. This need not displace other investments, moreover, if financed with foreign sources or other capital not otherwise normally available for domestic investment.

Although the usual experience has been that privatizations do improve economic performance, it still is unclear whether private ownership *per se* is essential to the design of effective incentive structures. In theory, many of the conditions leading to successful privatization also ought to create the same opportunity for efficient public enterprise reform. Issues of monitoring, management information, multiple objectives, viability, and freedom to determine factor mix, diversification strategies, and capital needs and sources may be present (to varying degrees) in both private and public enterprise.

In practice, however, ownership does appear to matter. Foster[18] identifies five aspects that support the superiority of private ownership. First, the process of privatization engenders more evaluation, review, and investigation than corporatization, because equity stakes are not present in the latter case. Second, it is harder for a private entity to shift risks to taxpayers. Third, more financial market disciplines are present and active. Fourth, the threat of takeover or bankruptcy is more credible. Fifth, privatization is a more irreversible process than corporatization because of legislative requirements and because a new set of ownership interests, sometimes international as well as domestic, likely have been created. Although the evaluation and risk-shifting aspects are open to some debate, the more powerful arguments are the exposure of the private enterprise to the full range of financial, legal, and market disciplines and the greater incentive to restructure given the enhanced irreversibility of privatization.

Macroeconomic Considerations

Both corporatization and privatization may affect macroeconomic performance by influencing inflation rates. As noted in chapter 2, the inflation problem in the former Soviet Union is primarily due to the lack of effective central bank control over the money supply. State enterprises have exploited this control vacuum by extensive inter-enterprise lending. As long as either state banks or the cooperative or private banks validate these credits by accepting them as collateral, enterprise losses are likely to continue or even expand. Privatizations or corporatizations have some attraction as a means of reducing these demands for inter-enterprise credits and public subsidies, both through efficiency gains and by possibly altering the incentives and political expectations of management. Privatization might be particularly helpful by hardening the soft budget constraints that typify so many state enterprises.

Arguments about macroeconomic effects need not rest there, though. If associated with the introduction of competition, improved managerial incentives, and opportunities to retain profits, privatizations and corporatizations may stimulate technological improvements.[19] One of the principal dynamic features of a market economy is the duplication of activities by different firms in an industry. When a given technology or industry is at an early stage of development, firms are likely to perceive different opportunities and pursue different strategies to compete. This competition among approaches helps spur innovation; once a "dominant" technology or marketing system emerges, the range of approaches is reduced as the industry matures.[20] In socialist economies, this competition among alternative approaches has been much less prevalent. With incentives to reduce duplication, Gosplan was more prone to select technologies based on limited information and experience and to force their adoption. Privatization or corporatization, by creating smaller, more autonomous organizations, could induce more competition among technologies, with resulting benefits for economic growth.

Other, more secular macroeconomic considerations that will influence the success or failure of privatizations mainly pertain to the stage of economic development. For example, highway privatization is likely to be most successful, both politically and economically, at the "takeoff" stage when an economy is just becoming a modern consumer society.[21] Some of the new republics might reach this stage by the turn of the century. Automobile ownership and usage are likely to grow rapidly, and highway limitations and congestion will emerge. Until then, though, self-financing projects may be difficult to find, because vehicle ownership rates are too low.[22]

Pitfalls Facing Transport Privatizations in the Former Soviet Union

When matched up against these conditions for successful privatization, the transport sector in the former Soviet Union offers a very mixed outlook. As the sector existed at the time of the Soviet breakup, competition in factor and product markets was virtually nonexistent. However, this situation may change rapidly. Except for some aspects of railroading, transport operations are for the most part inherently competitive, especially in water and road transport. Even though most modes require interconnection and clearinghouse activities for efficiency, these networks often can be provided separately from the associated transport activity, such as air navigation or highway systems. Indeed, experience suggests that it takes a heavy hand of government to suppress competition in road, water, and to a lesser extent, in air transport.

That heavy hand clearly existed in the former Soviet Union. So which should come first: market reforms or privatization? On the one hand, given the importance of competition in realizing efficiency gains from privatization, it would appear best to restructure first. On the other hand, in circumstances with relatively few market institutions, privatization might be deemed a prerequisite, or at least a great help, in establishing competitive markets. Without prior market reforms, however, some privatizations might freeze in place existing structures that impede entry. This hazard is quite real in the former Soviet Union. Nevertheless, properly designed and executed privatizations can be useful in undoing the vertical integration that inhibits entry and sustains monopoly in transport in the former Soviet Union. Furthermore, the Soviet legacy of spatial transport monopolies reinforced the tendency toward regional autarky among industrial and commercial enterprises. How fast these regional markets merge into national and global markets could depend on the nature and speed of transport reforms, in particular how fast road and rail transport can be restructured.

In transport, as with much of privatization in the new republics, there was at least an initial presumption that the existing legal enterprises were the appropriate economic units for privatization. However, no particular reasons exist for believing that these organizations, or various combinations of them, have the attributes of viable firms in a market economy. At the same time, too much cynicism about the consequences of privatizing such enterprises may be unwarranted; a wave of post-privatization merger and restructuring proposals might be expected, as the new organizations redesign themselves to meet changing opportunities. The key may be the degree to which the spatially oriented transport enterprises can enter each other's markets, in a fashion similar to the regional telephone companies in the United States or what is likely to occur with enhanced route freedoms for airlines of the European Union.

An important issue is the prospective use of holding companies as an organizational structure for privatization. Unlike single-enterprise privatizations, holding company structures help preserve the integrated structures of the old associations or ministries. In short, the holding companies may help retain the familiar (and often unwanted) features of the old regime. Also, by reducing opportunities for external shareholders, such structures effectively give managers and employees more control than would result if activities were separated and ownership was more dispersed.

Proposals have been made to create "financial-industrial groups" along Japanese or European lines. These proposals fail to recognize that the starting points are quite different. Multi-industry enterprises only have worked well when they have been carefully built over time and out of viable economic arrangements rather than political constructs. In the market economies of Japan or Europe, these groups arose from smaller enterprises becoming affiliated into a network. Affiliations and competitive behavior were conditioned by the presence of other such groups or from unaffiliated firms. In the new republics of the former Soviet Union, these competing groups largely do not exist; as a consequence, such organizational structures would be positioned much more effectively to preclude entry. Moreover, such groups likely would soon be deemed "too big to fail," and thus would continue to operate as if they faced soft budget constraints. Ultimately, large transport enterprises should restructure themselves so that they are economically and financially viable. This restructuring is much less likely to occur if financing is captive. External financing is needed to play both modernization and monitoring roles. In that vein, creating new credit sources to facilitate small enterprise start-ups in the former Soviet Union could be very useful and possibly a means of reducing the power of monopolies in road and water transport.

As far as having relatively large efficiency gains available for harvest, transport in the former Soviet Union should do well. Adopting "best practices" used elsewhere could provide a period of substantial productivity gains for most modes. Reduced traffic volumes, however, may offset some of these gains through loss of scale economies or underutilized capital investment. Some of the losses associated with reductions in transport volume may be recaptured through improved logistics in the rest of the economy.

Doing without government subsidies also may be difficult, especially for the airlines. Regulation of fares, even of a lingering kind, can create a substantial need for subsidies in a highly inflationary environment such as that experienced in many of the republics in the early 1990s. That need would be even more pronounced if government mandates continued socially attractive, but highly unprofitable, services. Attempts should be made to identify these social functions, to make their costs more transparent, and to create opportunities for their private provision.

Redistributions are likely to be extremely troublesome when privatizing transport in the former Soviet Union. With the disintegration of central administrative authority, control of many enterprises apparently has moved to managers and workers. These transport enterprises face the usual service abandonment, tariff changes, and potential unemployment problems encountered in the Western economies when adopting privatizations, as well as intense fears about lost retirement and other fringe benefits. This tie-in undoubtedly has much to do with the slow pace and stiff opposition to many privatization proposals in the former Soviet Union. A possible use of some of the efficiency gains from privatization might be to "buy out" some of these benefits.[23] Indeed, some financial schemes proposed for privatization recognize these possibilities by reserving some equity shares for zero- or low-cost acquisition by retirees and employees. If carried too far, though, buyouts of welfare benefits and other fringes might reduce the efficiency gains from privatization.

Environmental issues and other externalities are likely to play a lesser role in privatizations in the former Soviet Union than in the West. First, and most importantly, any transport privatization is likely to be associated with a move toward more cost-based factor prices, particularly for energy. Such price rationalizations virtually will force improvements in efficiency and should have an immediate beneficial effect on the environment. Adoption of newer technologies also is likely to reduce pollution, both from vehicles and from the production of transport equipment. Second, the needs in the transport sector often do not involve large capacity expansions, which typically involve major environmental disputes. Third, the rationalization of the transport sector and overall industrial change are likely to reduce dramatically the volumes and distances of freight haulage, thereby greatly reducing associated environmental effects. Of course, environmental concerns could re-emerge, especially after energy prices have achieved world levels and automobile ownership has become more widespread. At that point, the pattern of environmental disputes may begin to assume many of the characteristics of those in Western societies.

Summary

Neither privatization nor corporatization is a solution to all transport problems in the former Soviet Union, but, carefully and selectively used, they can help. Above all, properly done, they could assist in solving the most difficult of all transport problems in the former Soviet Union – dismantling and restructuring the vertically integrated monopolistic conglomerates inherited from the prior regime. Unfortunately, done poorly and too hurriedly, they also could freeze in place these same enterprises, with all that would mean in terms of obstructing further reforms.

Restructuring and privatizing transport in the former Soviet Union will be difficult. The upheavals for labor, management, and users, will be profound. Some possible policies for alleviating these dislocations can be identified but no pervasive "escape" is apparent. Unemployment created by privatization of state-owned transport enterprises will only be partly offset by jobs in new firms and activities. Regulatory regimes (as described in the next chapter) might be implemented that would protect legitimate consumer interests while still preserving investment incentives for both domestic and foreign investors. Furthermore, the efficiency gains potentially available from privatizing transport loom so large that redistributions or transfers that leave many people much better off may be at least conceivable. However, all groups face wrenching adjustments, and many workers will lose jobs and incomes. The redistributions created by transport reform and restructuring will be large, in part because the new republics have little of the institutional infrastructure of a market economy so useful in creating the competitive conditions that help extract and distribute efficiency gains from privatizations.

Some advisers argue for a more modest approach: widespread or near universal corporatization in lieu of privatization. Advocates of corporatization contend that retention of state ownership, albeit in a new form, can convert the government into an effective monitor, avoid valuation problems, improve commercial performance, and preserve public benefits. While corporatization may be an improvement on ministerial status, gains are likely to be greatest when corporatization is viewed as a "way station" to eventual privatization. An open question, emerging from contestability theory, is whether the threat of privatization (or departmentalization) is sufficient to induce improved performance from a state enterprise.[24] In fact, though, corporatization often ends up as the permanent structure, with all the problems of state ownership appearing over time.

In transport, corporatization often can and should be bypassed in favor of privatization. Bypass appears warranted for most trucking, water transport, and airline activities, as well as many warehousing and intermodal operations. In situations involving some infrastructure investments, externalities, or network issues (e.g., air traffic control, airports, or railways), the establishment of public corporations may improve incentives for upgrading and for operational improvements, especially if common-access features reduce the incentives for private organizations to make such investments. When creating such corporatized structures, however, commercial institutions and competitive relationships should be introduced where possible. Examples include opportunities for multiple public airport authorities in Moscow, or competing port authorities on the Black Sea or in the Russian Far East.

Finally, lack of competition, substantial subsidy requirements, and opposition to redistributions are all likely to be at least as troublesome barriers to ownership reforms in the new republics as in the West. However, the potential efficiency gains are probably greater and environmental conflicts less difficult. All in all, considerable privatization and corporatization could and should occur in the transport sectors of the former Soviet Union, even though the benefits may sometimes be difficult to harvest and the political obstacles may be formidable.

The outlook is more mixed for private long-term investments in transport infrastructure other than highways. Raw capacity appears sufficient, in some cases for a long time. There are, though, important needs for upgrading the quality of equipment and infrastructure in some applications, particularly in air and rail. These involve very specialized niches such as containers and container trains, landbridge services, air reservation systems, and payment clearance systems. These niche investments are likely to occur privately only if these activities are separated from control by the transport enterprises inherited from the old Soviet system. For these activities restructuring is the key reform; the choice of organizational design should be based on whether privatization or corporatization is most likely to accelerate that process.

Notes

1 These sources of finance have had a major effect on the success of new public enterprises. Debt and capitalization have been major issues in the restructuring process. Explicit government guarantees on debt usually have been withdrawn, although an implicit guarantee may still persist. Some newly corporatized enterprises have experienced long periods of losses under their old structures and thus entered the transition burdened by debt payments or lack of investment capital. In some cases, the government has written off debts early in the transition or assumed debt later on. In other cases, reductions in debt have been achieved by minority share issues in private capital markets. Corporatized enterprises with unrestructured debt often argue that such burdens place a constraint on their investment and restructuring capabilities. .

2 See C. D. Foster, *Privatization, Public Ownership, and the Regulation of Natural Monopoly* (Oxford: Blackwell, 1992), 362–365.

3 See J. Nellis, "Contract Plans and Public Enterprise Performance," World Bank Working Paper PPR WPS-118 (October, 1988).

4 C. D. Foster, *Privatization, Public Ownership, and the Regulation of Natural Monopoly*, 364.

5 The consistency of objectives also will depend on the stability of the government and the associated ministers. Longer tenure may increase the likelihood of policy and contractual consistency, although then a need may arise to ensure that the objectives are in the public interest.

6 C. D. Foster, *Privatization, Public Ownership, and the Regulation of Natural Monopoly*, 340.

7 These aspects are discussed by A. Boot and A. Thakor, "Security Design," *Journal of Finance* 48, 4 (September 1993): 1349–1378.

8 See R. Zeckhauser and J. Pound, "Are large shareholders effective monitors?" in R. G. Hubbard, ed., *Asymmetric Information, Corporate Finance, and Investment* (Chicago: University of Chicago Press, 1990): 149–180.

9 See C.D. Foster, *Privatization, Public Ownership, and the Regulation of Natural Monopoly*; J. Kornai, "The Principles of Privatization in Eastern Europe," *De Economist* 140, 2 (1992): 153–176; D. Lipton and J. Sachs, "Creating a Market Economy in Eastern Europe: The Case of Poland," *Brookings Papers on Economic Activity* 1 (1990): 75–133; S. Fischer, "Priva-

tization in East European Transformation," in C. Clague and G. Rausser, eds., *The Emergence of Market Economies in Eastern Europe* (Cambridge: Basil Blackwell, 1992); R. Frydman and A. Rapaczynski, "Markets and Institutions in Large-Scale Privatization: An Approach to Economic and Social Transformation in Eastern Europe," in V. Corbo, F. Coricelli and J. Bossak, eds., *Reforming Central and Eastern European Economies* (Washington, D.C.: The World Bank, 1991); R. Frydman, A. Rapaczynski, and J. S. Earle, *The Privatization Process in Central Europe* (two vols.) (Budapest: Central European University Press, 1993).

10 See R. E. Kranton, "Pricing, Cost Recovery, and Production Efficiency in Transport: A Critique," World Bank Working Paper WPS 445 (June, 1990); J. S. Vickers and G. K. Yarrow, *Privatization: An Economic Analysis* (Cambridge, MA: MIT Press, 1988); D. Gayle and J. Goodrich, eds., *Privatization and Deregulation in Global Perspective* (New York: Quorum Books, 1990); R. Vernon, The Promise of Privatization; John Donahue, *Public Ends, Private Means*; J. A. Goméz-Ibañéz and J. R. Meyer, *Going Private: The International Experience with Transport Privatization* (Washington, DC: The Brookings Institution, 1993); S. Kikeri, J. Nellis, and M. Shirley, *Privatization: The Lessons of Experience* (Washington, DC: World Bank, 1993).

11 R. D. Willig, "Public versus Regulated Private Enterprise," *Proceedings of the World Bank Annual Conference on Development Economics* 1993, 155–170.

12 Even in markets where optimal scale is large relative to the size of market, or where domestic competition does not exist due to other entry barriers, reducing tariffs and other international trade barriers may enhance competition and thereby reduce opportunities for predation.

13 See R. Kranton, "Pricing, Cost Recovery, and Production Efficiency in Transport: A Critique," 29–30.

14 J. A. Gomez-Ibañez and J. R. Meyer, *Going Private: The International Experience with Transport Privatization*, chapter 13.

15 In the new republics the continuation of subsidies to state enterprises has been at the very heart of political debate.

16 In these cases, contracting out has the objective of minimizing subsidy costs for a specified level of performance.

17 R. Kranton, "Pricing, Cost Recovery, and Production Efficiency in Transport: A Critique," 32–33.

18 C.D. Foster, *Privatization, Public Ownership, and the Regulation of Natural Monopoly*, 350–365.

19 The potential of this "technology gap" was first pointed out by A. Gerschenkron. For a discussion of the problems of innovation in the Soviet economy, see J. Berliner, *The Innovation Decision in Soviet Industry* (Cambridge, MA: MIT Press, 1976); M. Weitzman, "Soviet Postwar Eco-

nomic Growth and Capital-Labor Substitution," *American Economic Review* 60 (December 1970): 676–692.

20 J. Berliner, *The Innovation Decision in Soviet Industry.* See R. R. Nelson, "Capitalism as an Engine of Progress," unpublished mimeo, 1990; also R. R. Nelson and S. G. Winter, *An Evolutionary Theory of Economic Change* (Cambridge, MA: Harvard University Press, 1982).

21 See J. A. Gomez-Ibañez and J. R. Meyer, *Going Private: The International Experience with Transport Privatization,* chaps. 6 and 7.

22 Furthermore, in the early stages of a consumer economy, automobile ownership will not have reached a level sufficient to generate major environmental concerns. Any redistributions due to highway development also are likely to be of only minor concern.

23 See O. Blanchard, S. Commander, and F. Corecelli, "Labor Markets in Eastern Europe" (Washington, DC: World Bank, 1993).

24 Potential competition is a less effective disciplining device in product markets than actual competition. The effects of potential organizational restructuring on existing performance are unclear, although the market for corporate control has induced restructuring independent of actual merger or acquisition bids. See W. J. Baumol, J. C. Panzar, and R. D. Willig, *Contestable Markets and the Theory of Industry Structure* (San Diego: Harcourt Brace Jovanovich, 1982); W. G. Shepherd, "'Contestability' versus Competition,"*American Economic Review*, 74, 3 (June 1984): 572–587.

9

Regulation[1]

Since the mid-1970s, there has been growing recognition that transport services can be provided under a wide range of ownership and operational structures, including direct ministerial provision, public enterprise, contracting out of operations, and privatization. Given the scale, spatial and network aspects of many transport activities, however, shifts from public to quasi-public or private provision also confer the risk of merely transforming public monopolies into private ones. This problem generally has been managed in market economies by instituting regulatory oversight of privatized transport.

Two broad types of regulation can be identified: economic and non-economic. Economic regulation is concerned with the governance and control of market power, and thus is concerned with prices, services, profits, and anticompetitive behavior. Non-economic regulation generally is focused on such matters as safety and minimum performance standards. Just as separation of transport operations from infrastructure provision is often a good idea, so is the separation of economic from noneconomic regulation.[2] When the commingling of both types of regulation occurs in market economies, it often involves conflicts of interest and attempts to use economic constraints to subsidize non-economic goals, such as universal service, uniform pricing, or protection of specific consumer groups. For example, safety regulation conducted by a transport ministry, although quite common, also creates potential conflicts of interest; ministries often perceive themselves to have responsibility for promotion and development of the industry, whereas a regulatory role may require disciplinary actions.[3]

Nevertheless, the establishment of governmental institutions to enforce basic laws and safety standards is usually essential. As reliance on private producers and markets in the former Soviet Union has increased, organizations must be established to ensure public safety, with appropriate investigative and enforcement powers. Moreover, because an efficient transport network requires integration across what are now national boundaries, these organizations may require multi-state charters or coordination. This approach helps foster integration of "common use" resources (such as air navigation) and facilitates integration of operating practices and regulations with those of international transport, particularly with the rest of Europe.

In both economic and non-economic regulation, the underlying philosophy should not be direct control; rather, broad principles and constraints should be established within which transport activity can be conducted. Regulation should seek an enabling role – providing a basic set of rules and guarantees and then allowing transport activities to take place within this framework. In practice, making the governmental transition from provider or active controller to "enabler" has been difficult everywhere. Accordingly, this is where much of the rethinking of regulation has occurred.

Economic Regulation of Newly Privatized Firms in the 1980s

Historically, enterprise nationalizations in market economies fell into two main categories: failing firms and firms with substantial market power (monopolies or near-monopolies). When many of those nationalized firms subsequently were returned to the private sector in the wave of privatizations that occurred in the 1980s, many organizations with dominating market positions were among those privatized. For newly privatized firms with dominant market positions, governments often believed it necessary to introduce economic regulation along with privatization. Some of these regulatory frameworks have been far reaching, in many cases resulting in a substitution of private (albeit regulated) monopoly for public monopoly.

That problems have arisen with this newly instituted regulation should not be too surprising. As Baumol has observed:

> Problems … have arisen primarily from inexperience with economic regulation, its pitfalls, and the practices that will keep

its social costs within reasonable bounds. For the nations that have the nationalized firms to be privatized are obviously those which in the past have chosen nationalization over regulation as the instrument for control of monopoly power. Thus, it is hardly accidental that the privatizing economies are the ones least prepared to carry out a regulatory regime … in a number of cases, they have simply repeated many of the mistakes of U.S. regulation that it has taken decades to begin to ameliorate.[4]

The new republics will encounter many of these same problems as they move from tight command and control relationships toward a market economy. As part of the regulatory framework developed in such transitions, a tendency often springs up to proscribe managerial discretion, sometimes even beyond the constraints imposed on the managers of the same enterprises when in the public sector. An ambivalence also may arise about whether regulatory bodies should introduce or encourage competition, and if so, to what degree. In practice, few industries or activities are subject to such scale or network economies that viable entry at some scale or stage of the activity is impossible. Potential entry, however, does not guarantee effective competition, especially if regulatory restrictions impede actual entry.

Another problem is a tendency for regulators to continue cross-subsidies by requiring universal access or service availability. This universality often is achieved via a "trade-off" for monopoly power, because monopoly profits are used to fund the subsidies. These cross-subsidies can have marked effects on the prices of goods or services quite beyond those that universal access seeks to promote. For example, subsidized transport to remote territories may induce greater levels of investment and industrial activity that then provides political support for continuation or extension of the subsidy.

A continuation of monopoly through regulation, even if not mandated by technology or scale economies, also may be chosen by governments to ease the financing of newly privatized enterprises. A monopoly often tends to be more "bankable" than a highly competitive firm. This phenomenon is particularly common in telecommunications privatizations,[5] but also is likely to characterize ports and airports. Moreover, the perceived financial security of monopoly enterprises gives both lenders and suppliers incentives to push for the creation or extension of spatial monopolies, especially when financing infrastructure.

Fortunately, for the new CIS republics physical capacity is abundant, so few major transport infrastructure projects are contemplated. The physical capacity currently available in the former Soviet Union might be regarded as a sunk cost, financed by public funds, so no capital cost recovery seems warranted. The main immediate need seems to be financing maintenance of existing infrastructure. Fuel taxes are among the lowest cost sources of tax revenue for governments, and are commonly used to fund highway maintenance. Furthermore, because of negative environmental externalities, a fuel tax may improve rather than distort resource allocations, especially where fuel is subsidized or cheap, as in most of the former Soviet Union. Accordingly, a flat tax on fuel in the new republics might be a good way of financing transport improvements as well as maintenance.

Regulatory Motives and Goals

Governments traditionally worry that private enterprises may have monopoly power in some markets, thereby hurting consumers and inducing economic inefficiency. Furthermore, if market power arises from scale or network economies, the private firm may be able to forestall entry by threatening to cut prices below those of potential competitors. To the extent that this threat is credible, actual prices may remain above costs, but no additional entry will occur.[6]

In industries characterized by large joint, fixed, or overhead costs (as is common in transport), the allocation of costs to particular activities can be inherently arbitrary. Regulators often are attracted to setting prices equal to fully allocated costs in the belief that these will ensure the firm's solvency. Unfortunately, the fully-allocated costs and the prices that emerge from them may bear almost no relation to the different demand conditions facing each product. Furthermore, because these prices are "cost-plus" in character, they can reduce incentives for cost reduction and improvements in efficiency. Indeed, many of the problems resulting from using fully allocated costs to guide pricing in Western economies have striking parallels with the administrative allocations of revenues, operating expenses, and investment costs that marked the Soviet economy.[7]

The problem of allocating joint costs sometimes has been handled by assigning price markups in inverse proportion to demand elasticities.[8] Such inverse-elasticity allocations theoretically can minimize the distortions of moving away from marginal cost pricing while still recouping all costs. The history of transport regulation in market economies has been characterized by many rates set well above costs, commonly justified by highly inelastic demands and a perceived need to charge relatively low- and below-cost rates elsewhere (to achieve social or political goals such as network standardization or rates closer to marginal costs where these were well below average costs).

Eventually, the original cost and demand conditions sustaining any such cross-subsidy almost inevitably are undermined by technological innovations, changes in market demographics and tastes, or the emergence of competitive alternatives. Indeed, the existence of very high markups in some activities creates incentives to find substitutes. Unfortunately, regulatory proceedings in Western countries tend to be legalistic, bureaucratic and political, and thus are slow to adapt to these changes. Regulatory inertia is such that in some cases regulatory powers have been used to impede technological innovation, or to restrict competition that might introduce lower costs or new technologies. Specifically, even though change might be beneficial to consumers, regulatory opposition often arises because change undermines the arrangements that sustain cross-subsidies or other politically sanctioned redistributions.

A common outcome of transport regulation in market economies is a systematic attrition of profitable activities and an almost equally systematic expansion, or at least a continuation, of unprofitable ones. Such trends cannot be sustained indefinitely by private enterprises. Indeed, this has been the causative mechanism leading to public ownership of many private railroads and transit operations in the West. Absent deregulation, the principal alternative to such nationalization is systematic withdrawal of private capital from the regulated industry via bankruptcy, service abandonments, diversifications into other industries, and the like. In a market economy, the consequences of inflexible, lagging regulation that ignores technological and dynamic changes are clear: neither taxpayer nor long-run consumer interests are well served. Hence, the search for better regulatory regimes often has led to straightforward deregulation.

Regulatory Alternatives

If regulation is too lax, consumers will be charged more than is necessary and an activity will be underutilized. If regulation is too stringent, private investment will not be forthcoming. The hallmark of successful regulation is to strike a balance between protecting the public from excessive charges and allowing investors the opportunity to earn a reasonable rate of return on their investment (recognizing and adjusting for the risks they are assuming).

Regulatory procedures also should be clear from the outset. If the regulatory environment is perceived to be inconsistent and prone to opportunism, investments in long-term capital projects that character-ize much of transport may not be made. Even minor uncertainties about future regulation will add risks; investors will insist on a higher rate of return as compensation. Foreign investors are likely to be particularly sensitive to such regulatory uncertainties, because they are usually less familiar and comfortable with the internal political situation.

The best form for regulation depends in part on whether a single investment or continuing investment is required. Many infrastructure concessions, for example, are commonly thought of as a single investment, particularly terminals, airports, tunnels, bridges, or en-tirely new expressways. The initial investment is the only major investment contemplated during the life of the concession (other than routine maintenance), especially if additional facilities are not needed until after the end of the initial concession period. Additional rounds of investment then might be awarded as new concessions.

Many activities do require continuous investment. Almost no transport technology is static. For example, air navigation or comput-erized reservation systems require continuing upgrades. Similarly, almost all privatized state enterprises are likely to have a continuing need for investment. Indeed, these initial needs may be substantial, as a "catching up" period is not uncommon.[9]

One of the most common regulatory schemes is to target the allowable rate of return on investment. Under such regulation, widely practiced in the United States, private enterprises petition a special regulatory body, usually a state public utility commission, when they seek an increase in tariffs. The request triggers a rate-of-return investigation in which the regulatory commission calculates the return being earned or proposed by the utility and compares it to returns earned by private companies in competitive industries facing similar risks. If the utility's actual or proposed return is higher than that in comparable industries, the tariff increase is denied or reduced. The underlying assumption is that the returns earned in other comparable but competitive industries are determined by market forces; they are just high enough to attract the capital needed but not so high as to generate excess profits. In the former Soviet Union few benchmarks exist for doing such comparisons, so the application of such a regulatory system would be difficult.

The American system, oriented as it is to ensuring a continuing incentive to invest, appears potentially well suited for industries in which continuing improvements and investments are required, such as telephone or electricity systems or some transport operations. One of the major drawbacks of the American system, though, is the need for frequent rate-of-return proceedings and revisions. Selecting the appropriate rate of return is a difficult and often controversial task. In particular, good estimates of the capital employed, and of the capital needed, must be made. In the former Soviet republics, as elsewhere, these data needs might not be met easily. If the regulators overestimate or underestimate the needed rate of return, the regulated company will have incentives to over- or under-invest.[10] The informational burden on the regulated company and the government is therefore substantial, especially in inflationary periods when tariffs require frequent adjustment. Privileged and asymmetrical access to information and the requisite expertise to understand it often favor the regulated enterprise over the regulator.

Two additional drawbacks are the tendency of the American system to reduce incentives to control costs and of regulatory authorities to be "captured" by the incumbent firms in the industry.[11] When this happens, the system may degenerate to "cost-plus" regulation and may inhibit new entry or technological change.

Great Britain recognized many of these difficulties when designing regulatory structures for its privatization initiatives in the 1980s. Under the British approach, a company's average tariffs are allowed to increase each year at the rate of the retail price index (RPI) less an estimate of the expected rate of productivity improvement (X).[12] This estimate X is revised periodically (every 3 to 5 years) based on a new investigation by the government agency responsible for the industry.[13] The British have used this approach with various public utilities privatized during the 1980s, including electricity, telecommunications, water supply, and airports.

If the rate of return is greater than the returns earned in private companies in competitive industries facing similar risks, X is increased for the next period. If it has been less than that earned by other comparable industries, X is reduced. British companies under *RPI-X* regulation also have a strong incentive to control costs because the rate of return is not capped during the period between investigations.[14] If the company can reduce its operating costs during that period, it keeps the profits from so doing. The RPI-X approach also attenuates tendencies to overinvest or underinvest, or toward other forms of inefficiency often produced by American rate-of-return regulation.[15]

One potential difficulty with adopting the British scheme in the former Soviet Union is the reliance on market prices as the starting point for regulation. Embedded in a market economy, nationalized British firms paid market prices for most of their inputs and did not face soft budget constraints to the same extent as enterprises in the former Soviet Union. Under the Soviet command economy, prices often bore little resemblance to any market reality. Some of the prices charged by nationalized British industries may have had similar characteristics, but not to the same degree. Nevertheless, in the absence of any firm knowledge of what the prices would be in a new market equilibrium in the former Soviet Union,[16] historical prices probably provide the only sensible point of departure. Furthermore, the British scheme provides a flexible adaptation to general inflation which, if need be, always can be made more sensitive by simply increasing the periodicity of RPI adjustments. The inflation index also might be designed to give greater weight to inputs of major importance, such as fuel.[17]

The British approach does not, however, entirely eliminate the need for periodic rate-of-return investigations. To meet this problem, the State of California devised a variation of rate of return regulation for four private toll-road concessions that the state awarded in the early 1990s. California's highway franchise agreements established a maximum rate of return; different returns were set for each concession in recognition of the different risks faced. The concessionaire is largely free to set toll rates as long as the maximum rate of return is not exceeded.[18] The franchise is for 35 years. Once the concessionaire has earned the targeted maximum return, any excess largely goes to the state (or the concessionaire can transfer the road to the government ahead of schedule). The state's regulatory role is thus auditing the accounts to ensure that the returns are within the maximum or, more precisely, to determine when and if the target rate of return is achieved.

An improvement on the California scheme might be to mandate profit sharing above certain rates of return rather than capping the return. Under this approach, for example, if the target return was 18 percent, the government might receive 50 percent of any excess return between 18 and 25 percent, and 80 percent of the excess return over the 25 percent.[19] A Puerto Rican toll bridge was successfully financed under regulatory terms similar to these. By not capping the rate of return completely, incentives are provided for the concessionaire to continue to operate efficiently even if the project is very profitable. If the return simply was capped, the concessionaire would have no incentive to control operating costs once returns exceeded the cap.

A primary advantage of the California/Puerto Rico approach is that it controls the rate of return relatively directly rather than indirectly. Moreover, the formula for regulation can be stated fairly simply in the concession or privatization contract. Other than auditing revenues and confirming the rate of return, there is no need for continuing controversial regulatory investigations (although it would be subject to some of the deficiencies and perverse incentives of traditional rate-of-return regulation).

The California/Puerto Rico approach also has at least two potential drawbacks. The less serious is that this approach is applied more easily to single investments than to investment concessions requiring several, almost continuous, infusions. Although the rate of return initially negotiated might be satisfactory for the initial investment, there is a danger that it might prove inadequate (or excessive) for future investments. This problem might be attenuated if rates of return are specified in real (i.e., net of inflation) rather than nominal terms, or, if inflation remains high and persistent, by specifying returns in hard currency.

Another potentially serious problem might arise from all excess profits going to the government and thereby to general taxpayers rather than directly to consumers or users. In theory, reductions in tolls or regulated rates might be made as an alternative to payments to the government, but this would complicate the concession contract.[20]

The California/Puerto Rican approach might be adapted to privatizations of enterprises as well as to infrastructure and other such concessions in the former Soviet Union. Target rates of return also might be used as elements in deciding competitions for concessions (including privatizations of state enterprises). Bidders might be selected on the maximum rates of return they required and the profit sharing they proposed above the threshold rate of return (as well as other possible criteria). If rate reductions instead of government sharing in excess profits was preferred, then the British *RPI-X* system of regulation would be preferable. The British approach also might make more sense for regulating former state enterprise monopolies, because they are likely to require continuous infusions or renewal of capital. Furthermore, *RPI-X* requires a bit less information to be implemented. It also has the flexibility to better adapt to inflation and provides more continuity and stability in transition economies.

Competition and Antitrust Policy[21]

Antimonopoly laws in the former Soviet Union generally are modeled after European Community policy. They are primarily concerned with dominant market positions rather than cartelization and exclusionary practices.[22] The 1991 Russian Antimonopoly Law, for example, gives the government jurisdiction over the creation of new private entities by privatization and by merger. The substantive standards are to prevent dominant positions and transactions that may lead to "a material limitation of competition."[23] The Russian law also prohibits anticompetitive actions by government agencies, although these provisions apparently have been ineffective in dealing with Production and Commercial Associations and politically power-ful state enterprises.

Another aspect of Russian competition policy is price and product regulation. Following the price decontrols in early 1992, Goskomtsen was authorized in August 1992 to regulate prices of those firms with more than a 35 percent market share. In Russia, rail- and sea-freight tariffs were limited to overall inflation rates, while air freight, river, and truck transport prices were limited to result in no more than a 35 percent profit margin.[24] Rail passenger fares remained subject to fixed government tariffs, and passenger air fares were subject to a 20 percent profit constraint.[25]

Moving regulatory structures in the new republics away from detailed price controls will be difficult.[26] Citizens and many enterprises appear comfortable with price controls, partly because in the old regime they did not serve an important allocative and value function. As observed by Joskow, Schmalensee, and Tsukanova, " ... pervasive regulation could be more of a threat to economic efficiency than pervasive monopoly."[27] The need is for movement away from price regulation, in part through recognition that many of the dominant market structures in the former Soviet Union are the result of history rather than innovation, natural monopoly, or other economic sources.

Regulatory policy should promote competition rather than just define, regulate, and restrain monopolies. Overall, policies are needed that promote competition in the transport activity itself and in the sectors that are heavily dependent on that transport. This principle is at the heart of demonopolization programs in rail, road, and water; these initiatives would be strengthened further if competitive supplier and customer markets also were encouraged.

Transport generally has been included on lists of "national interest" industries, which then may become prime candidates for extensive regulatory oversight. In this setting, it is critical to limit the ultimate scope of regulation by separating natural monopoly segments (e.g., some infrastructure) from inherently competitive activities (e.g., most operations in road, water, and air transport). Accordingly, these issues must be addressed in an integrated fashion. Encouragement of new entrants in the inherently competitive modes is particularly important. The ministerial and holding company or association structures aimed at preserving network activities must be addressed lest they become permanent institutional arrangements for perpetuating artificial monopolies. In these industries, issues of federal versus local control also need to be assessed. In particular, where transport networks now cross international borders that were once internal to the Soviet Union, regulatory structures should take into account their historical linkages while moving toward greater harmonization with international standards.

Summary

Transport regulation is not something easily done well, and is especially difficult when capacity is scarce. Fortunately, transport in the former Soviet Union will not face many of these problems, at least for a while, because of the inheritance of a surfeit of capacity.

Regulation is, though, a bit like privatization. It works best when there is plenty of competition in most of the surrounding economy, thereby providing a rich set of yardsticks and relevant information for determining how a competitive market might work in the regulated sector. Clearly, the new republics face major deficiencies in this regard. Competition also has a tendency to seep outward. A regulated industry surrounded by competition may over time reduce its need for, or even possibility of, effective regulation. The best regulatory strategy in the new republics therefore is to move away from price regulation and to promote competition wherever possible.

Notes

1   This chapter draws heavily from the ideas in J. A. Goméz-Ibañéz, "The Political Economy of Highway Pricing and Congestion," *Transportation Quarterly* 46, 31 (July, 1992): 343–360; and from J. A. Goméz-Ibañéz and J. R. Meyer, *Going Private: The International Experience with Transport Privatization* (Washington, DC: Brookings Institution, 1993). We are indebted to both *Transportation Quarterly* and The Brookings Institution for allowing us to draw extensively from these sources. Professor Goméz-Ibañéz' help was of particular importance in the pricing and regulatory alternatives sections of this chapter. Although any virtues in these sections owe much to him, any remaining errors or mistakes are strictly the responsibility of the authors.

2   For a discussion of the pitfalls in mixing social and economic regulation, see C. D. Foster, *Privatization, Public Ownership, and the Regulation of Natural Monopoly* (Oxford: Blackwell, 1992): 291–323.

3   C. D. Foster, *Privatization, Public Ownership, and the Regulation of Natural Monopoly*, 316–323.

4   W. Baumol, "On the Perils of Privatization," C.V. Starr Center for Applied Economics Economic Research Report 93–22, New York University (May 1993): 10.

5   In infrastructure privatizations that require major capital investments that are irretrievable once sunk, a competitive tendering of license rights that restrict competition for some period of time may present the best prospects for attracting foreign investors and thereby obtaining necessary funding, technology, and management expertise.

6 This market would be characterized as imperfectly contestable, in that potential competition does not exert the same competitive effects as does actual entry. See W. B. Tye, *The Transition to Deregulation* (New York: Quorum Books, 1991).

7 Prices based on short-run cost and demand conditions also can create regulatory problems, especially if self-sufficiency of the regulated enterprise is deemed desirable.

8 F. Ramsey, "A Contribution to the Theory of Taxation," *Economic Journal* 37 (1927): 47–61; H. Hotelling, "The General Welfare in Relation to Problems of Taxation and of Railway and Utility Rates," *Econometrica* 6 (December 1937): 242–269. Similar pricing rules for individual enterprises were derived by W. Baumol and D. Bradford, "Optimal Departures from Marginal Cost Pricing," *American Economic Review* 60 (1970): 265–283.

9 Such a situation characterized some of the privatized water companies in Britain in the mid-1990s.

10 This is the so-called Averch-Johnson effect named after the seminal contribution of H. Averch and L. L. Johnson, "Behavior of the Firm under Regulatory Constraint," *American Economic Review* 52, 4 (December 1962): 1052–1069; Also W. J. Baumol and A. K. Klevorick, "Input Choices and Rate-of-Return Regulation: An Overview of the Discussion," *Bell Journal of Economics* 1 (1970): 162–190; A. L. Kolbe, W. B. Tye, and S. C. Myers, *Regulatory Risk: Economic Principles and Applications to Natural Gas Pipelines and Other Industries* (Boston, MA: Kluwer, 1993).

11 See G. Stigler, "The Theory of Economic Regulation," *Bell Journal of Economics* 2, 2 (Spring 1971): 3-211; J. Q. Wilson, *The Politics of Regulation* (New York: Basic Books, 1980).

12 The regulatory regime created in Hungary for its telecommunications sector is based on X equal to zero, to increase the attractiveness of modernizing investment. In situations of excess capacity, such a structure would attenuate incentives for cost reduction and productivity improvement.

13 Usually that government agency is assisted in its investigation by the Monopoly and Mergers Commission, Britain's antitrust enforcement agency.

14 Incentives might be created to let costs "creep up" just before the review so as to create a justification for a smaller X in the next period.

15 See J. Kay, C. Mayer, and D. Thompson, eds., *Privatisation and Regulation: The U.K. Experience* (London: Clarendon Press, 1986); C. Graham and T. Prosser, *Privatising Public Enterprises* (London: Clarendon Press, 1991).

16 H. Hunter, ed., *The Future of the Soviet Economy, 1978–1985* (Boulder, CO: Westview Press, 1978); H. Hunter and J. Szyrmer, *Faulty Foundations: Soviet Economic Policy 1928–1940* (Princeton, NJ: Princeton University Press, 1992).

17 There is also a tendency to leave certain costs outside the formula for "cost pass-through." See C. D. Foster, *Privatization, Public Ownership, and the Regulation of Natural Monopoly*, 209.

18 California does not cap the return entirely. Concessionaires can earn higher rates of return if they meet certain performance criteria, such as increasing carpooling on their road. These "incentive returns" are themselves capped (at 6 percentage points above the basic return), and are "earned out" by the concessionaire and the California government sharing equally in free cash flow after the target rate of return has been achieved.

19 Thus, if an actual project return of 30 percent was achieved, the concessionaire would receive 22.5 percent and the government the remaining 7.5 percent.

20 The main problem is that the rate of return would have to be calculated for the hypothetical case of higher rates to determine whether any reduction requested by the government was no greater in value than its share of the excess profits would have been. This calculation would require assumptions about the elasticity of demand with respect to rates, a figure which is likely to be uncertain and therefore potentially controversial.

21 This section is based on P. Joskow, R. Schmalensee, and N. Tsukanova, "Competition Policy in Russia during and after Privatization," *Brookings Papers on Economic Activity: Microeconomics 1994* (1994): 301–381.

22 For a detailed discussion, see R. Pittman, "Some Critical Provisions in the Antimonopoly Laws of Central and Eastern Europe," *The International Lawyer* 26 (Summer 1992): 485–503.

23 As defined in Articles 17 and 18. See R. Pittman, "Some Critical Provisions in the Antimonopoly Laws of Central and Eastern Europe," 485–503.

24 Margins are defined as a percentage of production costs, not as a percentage of sales as in western accounting practice.

25 P. Joskow, R. Schmalensee, and N. Tsukanova, "Competition Policy in Russia during and after Privatization," 31–32.

26 Many of the statutory controls are evaded or are nonbinding. If the system survives, however, there likely will be increasing pressure to make it effective.

27 P. Joskow, R. Schmalensee, and N. Tsukanova, "Competition Policy in Russia during and after Privatization," 51.

10

Toward a Market-Oriented Transport System

Transport in the early 1990s in the former Soviet Union was far from being determined by market forces. Indeed, so great were the distortions bequeathed by the command economy of the Soviet Union, it is even difficult to project what a market equilibrium might have been. About the best that can be done is to compare transport in the new republics with what happened elsewhere, controlling as much as possible for economic, demographic, and other differences that always complicate international comparisons. Moreover, this process is further complicated because transport activities commonly are sheltered from market forces everywhere, not just in the former Soviet Union.

Even with these imperfections, transport markets elsewhere are almost certainly the only guide to projecting the strengths, weaknesses, and future of transport in the new republics. What then are the lessons conveyed by these international comparisons? Are there any discernible patterns in the modal experiences in the former Soviet Union that are distinctively different from experiences elsewhere? What might these patterns portend about likely future development and about strategies for a successful transition to a market-oriented transport sector?

Answering these questions is best started by reviewing the modal surveys (in chapters 4–7) to identify common elements or patterns. Four major generalizations emerge: sufficient raw physical capacity is already in place; quality needs to be improved; price structures must be revised to reflect economic costs and market demands; and considerable organizational restructuring is required. These common elements have roots in the Soviet system, a legacy of a closed economy, subsidized energy, and an orientation to producer needs – all factors that are changing in the transition to a market-oriented system.

Physical Capacity

A most striking, and somewhat unexpected, finding in all the modal surveys is that the raw physical capacity of the transport system is substantial and probably sufficient to meet most needs in the immediate future. The scale and basic capacity of transport infrastructure is largely in place; there is little need for large greenfield investments. Even the relatively underdeveloped road transport sector has no immediate need for a capital program similar to the European or American motorway systems developed in the post-World War II period.

In large measure this surfeit of capacity is a legacy of the Soviet system. The Soviet economy was conspicuous for generating far more freight transport per rouble (or dollar) of national income than Western countries, though far less passenger travel. This imbalance should change if economic transition takes hold, prices move toward world levels, and competition begins to shape the economy. Under the old regime, rail and aviation services were particularly under-priced and were organized as almost completely vertically integrated monopolies. In transition, both modes should experience a permanent loss of market share to road transport, in both passenger and cargo markets. Indeed, the air, rail, and water sectors are overdeveloped relative to market-justified demand, even under macroeconomic scenarios of rapid recovery and growth. Only the highway mode is likely to grow in volume. Aviation, being well suited to the geography of Russia and Kazakhstan, also should regain growth and eventually (probably some time after the turn of the century) achieve activity levels as great as those of the Soviet period.

There are some immediate bottlenecks in all modes. These constraints are for the most part limited and might be remedied without extreme difficulty. Most are related more to vehicular needs (aircraft, trucks, buses, and rail rolling stock) than to right-of-way or infrastructure. There is, however, an extensive need to catch up on deferred maintenance. Many roads need overlays; rail tracks and ties should be replaced; many runways and airport aprons need to be repaved; and on the roads, center and shoulder lines should be repainted, guard rails erected, and so forth. Many of these repairs, as a byproduct, will increase the effective capacity of the transport system, further reducing any need for special projects to expand physical capacity. Network and interchange operations which may have been in place but have been weakened should be restored. Such activities as clearinghouses, reservations systems, and network information systems are candidates for investment and financing through user charge systems.

Only road infrastructure is likely to require additional physical capacity in the short term. Road congestion has been limited to the major cities and near environs. However, road surfaces are rough and pavements are vulnerable to any growth in traffic volumes and to increased truck axle loads, so that pavement strengthening warrants priority over new construction. In addition, institutional and organizational reforms are critical to ensure that construction and maintenance are achieved at lower cost through competitive tendering for projects.

Road safety is a cause for concern: highway death and accident rates are very high. Improvements will require a comprehensive approach that encompasses striping, signals and cross barriers, safer vehicle design, educating and testing drivers, and strengthening traffic enforcement. Many of these investments promise to yield substantial benefits in the near term at low or moderate cost. Indeed, much of the transport system is at a stage at which many small incremental improvements and investments are likely to yield large capacity and efficiency gains. By contrast, most large projects might be deferred. For example, an international motorway network linking Moscow, St. Petersburg, Minsk and Kiev with each other and with Western Europe will no doubt be justified once any transition is largely completed, but there are higher priorities before then.

Transport in the former Soviet Union uses much more energy per unit of output than transport in the West, with attendant additional pollution. The most direct immediate remedy to this problem is to move energy prices nearer to world levels. In the longer run, however, a more active environmental policy will likely be needed. For example, a rapid rise of private car ownership might be expected, given the severe suppression of demand in the past. The potential market in the former Soviet Union is placed at approximately 2 to 3 million new cars per year; this estimate may even prove low. To avoid accompanying environmental and congestion problems, governments must clarify policies concerning taxation and fuels. For example, exhaust emissions can be reduced by introducing unleaded gasoline and catalytic mufflers, although the cost will be high and replacement of the present fleet will take many years.

Both European and North American experiences strongly suggest that the service advantages of the highway modes make them highly attractive to consumers and shippers; this attraction is not easily overcome by providing expensive (and often redundant and subsidized) alternatives. Accelerated development of the highway mode also will pose some difficult environmental trade-offs and questions that will not be resolved easily. The other modes, however, are often not, on close inspection, as environmentally benign as first supposed. For example, operational fuel savings often are offset by greater energy consumption in construction. The most effective environmental strategy for transport in the former Soviet Union in the immediate future almost surely will be to get prices right, in particular those for energy and, to a lesser extent, for congestion costs in urban areas.

Service Quality

A second major finding in all four modal surveys is that the quality of transport, in stark contrast with quantity, is markedly inadequate. Too often, as one (anonymous) observer has put it, transport was run on a "holding pen concept of demand management"; that is, transport services often were delayed until sufficient demand accumulated to fill available capacity. These delays tended to maximize use of transport capacity but created very wasteful logistics. Basic inventory requirements were inflated and "just-in-time" logistic systems remained well beyond reach.

The underlying cause, of course, traces back to two pervasive problems of command-control economies: the lack of good price signals for guiding managerial decisions, and the absence of concern for customers' willingness to pay for quality aspects of products and services. In their absence, Soviet transport managers developed a steadfast orientation to production goals (such as utilization rates and volume of throughput), irrespective of costs or quality. That orientation persists but might be expected to slowly erode as competitive pressures emerge.

One particularly helpful step toward achieving better quality transport in the new republics would be an increase in intermodalism –

the use of different modes for particular trips or shipments, each specialized in its best or most efficient applications. Given the long distances involved for many major market segments, the economic prospects for intermodalism are greater than in most regions of the world. This intermodalism should go well beyond simple container- ization, as desirable as that would be. For example, with a properly enhanced intermodalism, the role and character of terminal facilities would be rethought. A common observation about seaports and river ports in the republics is that their efficiency is greatly hampered by overreliance on rail as the connecting land mode. In the same vein, many airports and railroad stations may not have been well located in relation to local urban transport.

Quality also could be improved greatly by adoption of more functional specialization. For example, greater use of unit trains for moving basic commodities such as coal, fertilizers, grains, ores, and chemicals would reduce the cost of moving these commodities and would "clear the tracks" to provide better service for passengers and higher-value commodities. Similarly, the implementation of more "liner trains," dedicated to carrying containers, would directly im- prove service for the higher-value goods and would reduce the demands placed on classification yards. In turn, general cargo services carried in more conventional box and flat cars would be improved. In the same vein, more dedicated container ports, ware- housing, and staging areas would help improve water and highway transport. In many cases these changes will be as much a matter of reorganizing spatial uses as adding spatial capacity. Specialization can often create quality improvements without using additional resources, because it is a matter of improving design and layout in lieu of additional investment.

Better communications and management information systems also would help improve quality. Recommendations for such improve- ments are found in all the modal reports. For the rail mode in particular, better communications are almost indispensable to im- proving service by permitting trains of varying speeds to be dis- patched safely over high-density trackage. Better traffic control improves both the quality of rail operations and the available capacity through better utilization of existing networks. For water transport, better information management would contribute to improvements in scheduling and turnover at berths and piers, and reduce the frequency of long delays caused by mismatches of waterside and landside capacities. Outmoded cargo-handling systems and the lack of information technology reduce effective capacity, raise costs, and present a substantial obstacle to increased international trade. For aviation and passenger rail, the institution of modern reservation systems would reduce the need for rationing by queue, would moderate peak-period capacity constraints, and would enable better matching of demand with available capacity.

Price Reforms and Implications for Investment

A third major generalization about transport in the former Soviet Union is that price reform is vital for all modes but especially for rail and for urban transit (in which tariffs were held constant for decades despite rising costs). Although it is hard to predict where prices and costs might be established in long-run equilibrium, the relative prices for transport likely will rise, particularly for rail and air. Tariffs more closely tied to costs should reduce intermodal distortions and provide better signals for new and replacement investment. Given the substantial public investments in the transport sector, cost recovery must be relatively consistent across all sectors.

A move toward market-determined energy prices is particularly needed. This change will create needs for technological modernization. Rail rolling stock, motor vehicles, aircraft, and ships are outmoded, with energy consumption, operating costs, and performance characteristics that are much worse than in the West. The vehicular deficiencies, to the extent that they occur, are related mostly to shortages of specialized vehicles that render better or more efficient services: very large intercity tractor-trailers; small urban delivery vans; rail flat cars for containers; large hopper rail cars for unit-train bulk movements; replacement of two-cycle diesel engine technology; tank cars and trucks; environmentally acceptable aircraft suitable for international services; river-sea dual-use ships; and container handling equipment at ports. Above all, though, there is a large potential market for truck manufacturers, particularly for light commercial vehicles (vans and pickups), large tractor-semitrailer units, and trucks with specialized bodies, as well as for spare parts.

Transport equipment manufacture suffers from the same problems endemic to other Soviet industries: collapse of integrated production;

dramatically reduced ability to pay for new equipment by operators; poor design and efficiency; and inadequate quality control. Existing transport equipment still needs to be maintained and rehabilitated, with corresponding needs for spare parts and the like. Fortunately, in most modes, the decline in demand has provided a grace period for restructuring and upgrading the equipment. An opportunity also exists for organizational restructuring in that much of the current need might be supplied by new, smaller, more focused and efficient enterprises, especially in providing maintenance and aftermarket spare parts and components manufacture. In the longer term, such facilities may develop licensing relationships with foreign suppliers and in so doing may begin to develop export markets. These joint ventures should facilitate technology transfer, including much-needed locomotive and engine replacement programs.

To illustrate, truck production in the Soviet Union was concentrated in five large factories, while most buses were produced in Hungary and Ukraine. As discussed in chapter 5, light and heavy trucks and diesel engines need to be produced. Given shortages of hard-currency funds available in the short term, importing such vehicles is unlikely. However, this may provide an opportunity for the domestic industry to improve its technology and product through a variety of cooperative agreements. Indeed, toward that end, the truck and auto manufacturing industries have begun to organize into joint stock companies, a first step in enabling foreign affiliations.

In commercial aviation, the principal design bureaus and production facilities are located in Russia. The aircraft fleet is aging and fuel-inefficient. The major problems lie in engine technology, but airframes and avionics also suffer from performance or compatibility issues. Aircraft and engine manufacturers are well suited for joint ventures, and maintenance and rehabilitation needs for planes may be met through new intermediate enterprises that provide components and overhaul services. Although there is some evidence that maintenance facilities are lacking, this may not be true once demand reflects market-oriented pricing. In addition, defense conversion may offer additional hangar and overhaul facilities, although some financial aid may be required. Airports and air navigation require ongoing upgrade programs; these should be well suited for project finance or some limited-concession arrangements, because these projects are likely to generate foreign currency revenues.

The shipping fleet also is aging and requires improvements in communication, propulsion, and cargo-handling facilities. Shipbuilding and repair facilities are outmoded; a growing share of Russian overhaul and maintenance is being sent to foreign yards. In time, foreign shipowners and yards may link their more modern technologies with skilled, but low-cost, Russian labor. Such joint ventures could help generate export earnings and have spillover benefits for other industries such as steel.

Existing cargo-handling systems and the lack of information technology reduce capacity, raise costs, and present a substantial obstacle to increased international trade. Cargo-handling and intermodal equipment is outdated or in short supply. Given the specialization of production under Soviet planning, many of these products were made outside the Soviet Union in Eastern Bloc countries, and there is thus a need to develop new suppliers, most likely through conversion of facilities or diversification of other manufacturers. Again, foreign affiliations through licensing, co-production, or joint ventures would be appropriate for modernizing this sector without placing undue financial or investment strains on the economy.

In the short term, the need to maintain and repair existing equipment will require re-establishing many of the previous production relations on a commercial basis. However, this task should no longer be the sole province of the ministries and vertically integrated state enterprises. Spare parts and components manufacturing and associated repair facilities could be done in privatized factories and in facilities converted from defense uses.

Organizational Restructuring

A fourth major generalization about transport in the new republics is that all the modes need considerable organizational restructuring. Even assuming that macroeconomic and financial stability might be achieved, the former Soviet Union still faces a formidable task in developing enterprises with the incentives and competence to create a modern and efficient market economy. Transportation, like most sectors of the old Soviet economy, suffered from an industry structure dominated by vertically integrated monopolistic conglomerates. One enterprise typically would have responsibility for all activities associated with a particular mode in a particular geographical region –

vehicles, right-of-way, terminals, supplies, maintenance, and so on. Such a structure created very large and difficult-to-manage enterprises that would have been hard to challenge or influence, even if entry of smaller and more efficient firms had been legally permitted – which it generally was not.

The problems created by this structure were further complicated by superimposing on these enterprises responsibility for many, if not most, social services. Hospital and medical care, retirement, recreation, vacations, housing, child care and education often were provided, at least in part, by the enterprise for its employees. Sometimes even more specialized benefits were provided. For example, as in much of the rest of the world, free or low-cost travel was often available for transport employees and their families. More unusually, employees, and many retirees, of Soviet railways and their families enjoyed free or very low-cost telephone service. This tie-in of the social safety net and other fringe benefits to the enterprise was hardly unique to the Soviet system,[1] but was almost certainly more extensive than almost anywhere else.

The evolution of the planned economy limited the failure of enterprises that would otherwise be nonviable, for product, scale, managerial, or other reasons.[2] Given the orientation toward output and production, the planning ministry sought to structure industries in a way that simplified the chain of commands for the execution of economic activities. As an extension, the socialist enterprise was not faced with the risk of losing demand for its products, because its "customers" were little more than the predetermined next step in the production process. In contrast to market economies, in which vertical integration may reduce flexibility and induce the loss of alternative suppliers, integration in the planned economy was limited only by administrative convenience. Since transport played such a key role in this economic system, this inheritance is a particularly difficult one to remedy.

Thus, the problem of socialist organization transcends the commonly expressed concern about the monopolies created by the planned economy. Not only were units of the economy developed without heed for flexibility, but because each unit was extraordinarily dependent on its "supplier" and its "customer," they had incentives to develop close ties with the suppliers of their inputs and the recipients of their outputs. In terms of institutional integration,[3] each unit invested heavily in "asset specific" niche investments that made enterprises almost totally dependent on each other for survival.[4]

Many entrenched interests, for both labor and management, were best served by continuity. This continuity perhaps was achieved or accepted more easily in transport than many other sectors because, unlike some sectors, the demand or need for many transport services persisted after the breakup. In addition, transport appeared relatively profitable under the old regime. Most intercity rail and highway activities, shipping, and Aeroflot generated apparent surpluses (revenues greater than operating costs) under the old Soviet rules, tariffs, and input prices. As long as essential inputs were available at subsidized levels, such surpluses enabled enterprises to continue to operate under long-established practices.

Of course, the magnitude of this "profitability" depended on the accounting conventions employed. Two central distorting factors stood out in the Soviet transportation system. First, fuel prices were exceedingly low by world standards (one percent or less of world prices in some instances) and capital investment was underpriced in many applications. Since transport of all types, especially when right-of-way is included, tends to be both fuel and capital intensive relative to most economic activities, these distortions were important.

Second, Soviet transport, like transport in many other parts of the world, was often thought to have special responsibilities to further certain political and social goals, even if this required incurring losses. One such responsibility was the provision of "universal service" or "universal access" to the transport network.[5] This objective was largely implemented, as in other countries, by a system of implicit cross-subsidies from larger or more dense markets to smaller or thinner ones. The locales of these losses were much the same in the former Soviet Union as elsewhere: services to "show the flag" internationally and to tie remote areas into the national system, urban and suburban transit, short-haul rail passenger services, and perhaps some special services to outlying defense posts or perimeters. The existence of such cross-subsidies should not be interpreted as evidence that such societal goals are unworthy. Such activities, however, do not survive easily in a competitive marketplace; privatized organizations are unlikely to provide universal access without either explicit subsidy or regulatory mandate.[6]

Indeed, whatever the type of privatization or its motive, privatization almost always involves a shift in government orientation, at least relatively, away from operating responsibilities and toward monitoring. Privatization also usually requires that some sort of contract between the government and the private sector be established. Such contracts require, in turn, that property and other legal rights be defined. Arrangements cannot be as casual as when dealing with another governmental agency; no longer is the budgetary incidence simply a matter of transferring from one government pocket to another. With privatization, government also needs to specify procedures (preferably competitive bidding) for determining who will receive franchises, concessions, or contracts.

For some privatizations of state enterprises the only plausible purchasers – for political, economic or managerial reasons – may be existing management or employees. In such cases, employee buyouts or management buyouts are often undertaken. Even in advanced market economies with fully functioning and competitive financial markets, such buyouts can be subjects of abuse or unfair advantage so that governments are compelled to assume oversight responsibilities (e.g., to avoid insiders taking advantage of their ostensibly greater knowledge of the enterprise's status and operations).[7] Transition economies usually have less than fully developed financial institutions so the possibilities for abuse can be substantial; thus, considerable government involvement is required. Sometimes, too, government may have to help with the financing, particularly when extensive employee ownership is desired or if debt assumption is required.

Not surprisingly, as noted in chapter 9, regulatory concerns often first come to an economy as a byproduct of privatization. When an industry is nationalized or government-owned, government usually has direct control of prices, production goals, and other major economic decisions. Industries imbued with a public service or utility aspect, and also believed to have a tendency toward natural monopoly, thus have been particular targets of nationalization, even in Western economies that are otherwise market-oriented. When privatizations place previously government-owned monopolies or utility operations under private control, governments often feel that some kind of regulatory oversight is needed to protect consumer interests. In essence, regulation is substituted for direct government control, with one form of government activity substituted for another.

But as pointed out in the last chapter, regulating transport can be as difficult as operating it. The traditional corporate governance problem, the principal-agent relationship between owners and managers, assumes additional complications under regulation.[8] With regulation and privatization, two principals are involved instead of one: both the government regulators and the private stockholders are principals trying to condition the behavior of management agents. In such circumstances, establishing the proper managerial incentives can be quite difficult.

In the new CIS republics, fortunately, only the rail mode should have market power sufficient to warrant economic regulation. Properly privatized to provide for ease of entry of new competition, the water, air, and road modes all might be developed with reasonably competitive structures, reducing or eliminating any need for major regulatory oversight. Furthermore, in the long run, with the development of intermodal competition, even economic regulation of rail might be greatly reduced or largely eliminated.

To avoid the need for regulation and its attendant complications, corporatization sometimes is advocated. Unfortunately (for reasons discussed in chapter 8), corporatization sometimes combines much of the worst of both government ownership and regulation. Specifically, corporatization may achieve only a few of the reforms or efficiency improvements achievable through privatization, while nevertheless exposing the government to a disguised regulatory role. With corporatization, the government more or less retains operating and financial responsibilities while acquiring some new oversight duties that often introduce potential conflicts of interest. Furthermore, corporatization may create a sequential principal-agent problem that is more complex and troublesome than the well-known governance problems of private corporations.

Organizational Reforms by Mode

A large role almost certainly lies ahead for private initiative and investment in the transport system of the former Soviet Union. This is especially true in road transport, and to a lesser degree in water and air transport. There may, however, be merit in the State retaining ownership of some of the basic transport infrastructure, especially the rail and road network, and (with some nuances) ports and airports. It is also necessary to identify and separate specific functions that are more appropriately provided by a single body, such as air navigation. These functions could be provided by government or some quasi-public entity, or by cooperative joint ventures among the users. The requisite reforms are different for the different modes, although for at least two modes (road and water) the prescriptions are quite similar.

Road and Water

These two modes require easier and enhanced entry and resulting greater competition in supply. As one step toward these ends, the highway and water modes would benefit from substantial decentralization. Highway and water transport are naturally competitive modes, with little in the way of scale or scope economies except for some components of infrastructure. They lend themselves well to small-scale entrepreneurship, providing the flexible services demanded by the small and medium-sized companies that can be expected to emerge in a market economy. Unfortunately, the Soviet legacy created interlocking obstacles to this pattern of development, including restrictions on ownership, the supply of vehicles, fuel and spare parts, and credit – all of which impede transition. For highway and water activities, organizational restructuring should precede privatization in most instances, since immediate privatization runs a great risk of perpetuating the inefficient Soviet structures. Fuel distribution also will have to be demonopolized, either by extensive entry from new suppliers or from fragmentation and divestiture of existing enterprises. Controls on retail fuel margins also need to be removed, if private transport firms are to have adequate access to fuel.

Vehicular manufacture, maintenance, fuel supply, terminal, and other support activities must be separated from the basic carrier functions, as well as from each other. Breaking up these vertical structures will facilitate entry into these operations, and increase efficiency in the activities themselves. The requisite entry might be achieved without such divestitures but will almost certainly be more difficult in their absence. One particularly promising possibility would be to roll back the large trucking and water conglomerates to their basic carrier functions and then convert them into leasing companies. These leasing enterprises then should be required to make their vehicles available to all and let the market sort out the questions of scale.

The resultant industry structure would probably be many individual owner-operators of trucks and barges and only a few large-scale operators. These multi-unit operations would concentrate in a few market niches that require specialized vehicles and terminals, ranging from parcel delivery to bulk tankers. Even these markets should be moderately competitive. Government, therefore, should be able to keep regulation of water transport and trucking to a minimum.

Similar organizational and restructuring principles apply to buses. Intercity bus services should be privatized. This segment of the industry generally has operated without subsidy, and privatization should not be difficult. Urban public transport, however, is incurring massive financial deficits in the former Soviet Union as in the rest of the world, because city governments try to hold down fares while input costs escalate. About the only exceptions to these deficits occur when government takes a step back, reduces its involvement both in ownership and in fare regulation, and allows the private sector to provide these services with little interference (as in Britain outside of London, Chile, Sri Lanka, and Morocco).[9] In most instances a high priority is to change the process of determining and managing subsidies. There is a need to set objectives and procedures, including contracting out essential services to whichever private or public enterprise bids to provide such services for the lowest subsidy.

Separation of construction and maintenance enterprises from state ownership should be implemented. This separation will give these enterprises stronger incentives to perform efficiently and will give ministries more incentive to quality and performance criteria. This change will require the appropriate ministry to promulgate procurement regulations and the newly privatized contractors to learn the art of bidding and contracting. With proper incentives, the search for less costly construction techniques should be stimulated. Reorganization of the road construction industry into competing enterprises facing competitive tendering should spur both lower costs and higher quality. Nonetheless, road building in much of the former Soviet Union is likely to remain somewhat more costly than in most other countries because of geography and climate.

In contrast to the road sector, water transport after the transition should be of less importance. Rivers and canals, because of geography and climate, play a lesser role than in many countries. This role is likely to be further diminished in a market economy. Nevertheless, inland water transport – by rivers, canals and coastal shipping – should continue to have an important role for low-value commodities, particularly for construction aggregates and timber. This sector also will provide an important competitive check on rail, which, for reasons outlined below, will have more of a tendency toward monopoly than any of the other modes.

The Russian Federation also is likely to be concerned, as its predecessors have historically been, about access to international waters. Russian international trade historically has relied on Baltic and Black Sea ports, some of which are now foreign territory and the use of which required at least partial payment in hard currency as of the early 1990s. The extent to which it is warranted to pursue large port investments within Russian territory to replace this capacity, rather than working to improve commercial relations with neighboring countries, is a sensitive topic. On purely economic considerations, coordination with the neighbors clearly would be the preferred policy. It might be good foreign policy as well.

Better coordination with land transport also is needed at Russian and Ukrainian ports. Some modest investment in storage facilities would aid this coordination, particularly for containerized intermodal operations. Achievement of such operational improvements also would be helped by decentralization and by the entry of private investors to operate terminals within the ports.

Rail

Before the transition began, the Soviet rail system performed by some measures one-half of the world's rail freight transport and one-fourth of the world's rail passenger transport. The Soviet railway ministry was by these measures the largest industrial organization in the world. The Soviet system was also one of the few publicly owned rail systems in the world that required no subsidy. It was highly efficient in carrying coal, iron ore, and other bulk raw materials among a few giant monopoly manufacturers of low-value products, especially at long distances.

However, a market economy places greater emphasis on meeting consumer demands and those of associated light industries. This emphasis will increase the importance of serving many geographically dispersed small and medium-sized factories competing with one another to produce high-value goods. These enterprises will demand transport services of the kind road transport traditionally has been good at and rail has not. Rail traffic in the former Soviet Union in 1992 was down by 20 to 30 percent from 1990 levels, and continued to fall through 1993. Much of the lost traffic is unlikely to return. Unless services are cut back and made more responsive to users' needs, the large financial losses that first appeared in the early 1990s will continue.

Rail, because of its extensive network requirements, is much less naturally competitive than the water or highway modes. For railroads around the world, intramodal competition between railroads is limited. However, intermodal competition, between rail and other modes, can be extensive, as it is in North America, Europe, and much of the Pacific Rim. Generally speaking, most societies believe, perhaps not always wisely, that at least some regulation is required of railroad activities until or unless this intermodal competition becomes effective. There is no obvious reason why the former Soviet Union should be an exception.

Meanwhile, there is a strong continuing tendency everywhere for railroads to be spatial monopolies. Attempts can be made, as in the United States and Canada, to discipline these monopolies by providing for as much interchange as possible between neighboring railroads and other modes. These interchanges should be encouraged for competitive reasons and to provide better service, in particular for intermodal activities and traffic originating on one railroad with destinations on another. At a minimum, information systems are needed to establish payment settlements and to keep current records on location and use of equipment (rail cars) that must be interchanged or otherwise shared.

A program of institutional reform is needed to restructure the railways so that they may play a down-sized and more specialized role. This program also will require substantial efforts to retrain managers and redeploy redundant labor. If the republics commit themselves to such reforms, investments would be warranted in technological modernization and in selected remedial maintenance (though not to expansion of the network). Although there is little or no need for railroads to be in many of the manufacturing and other support activities in which they are sometimes involved, the core activity of rail transport may nevertheless necessitate a fairly extensive organization to be efficient. Accordingly, for the rail system in the CIS, in sharp contrast with the highway and water modes, there is a continuing need for system coordination.

Commercial Aviation

From an organizational perspective, commercial aviation lies somewhere between rail and the highway and water modes. Under the Soviet system, civil aviation was more underpriced, relative to world prices, than even bread. Demand, accordingly, was stimulated far beyond what a market economy would sustain. Air travel in Russia dropped by 60 to 70 percent from 1990 to 1993, as the price of jet fuel rose (though slowly) toward world levels and the successor companies to Aeroflot raised fares to generate funds to replace their aging and fuel-inefficient aircraft. Continued increases in the real price of air travel are expected and a further shrinking of traffic may occur. The most likely forecast would be that it will take until the next century for air traffic volumes to regain levels of the late 1980s.

Aeroflot has devolved into many locally based, vertically integrated aviation enterprises, which combine an airline, the home airport, and air traffic operations. Extreme confusion reigns over the rights and responsibilities of central, regional and city governments and their respective local "chosen instrument" airlines. The extreme fragmentation of Aeroflot into more than 200 airlines is almost certainly counterproductive.

The proliferation of air carriers, though, is not without some benefits. Many aviation enterprises in Russia and the other former Soviet republics have launched direct international services to Europe and Asia, breaking the Soviet mold which required almost all international travel to transit through Moscow. Such international traffic is expected to grow, with important potential implications for airport and air navigation needs.

Although the airline industry has many competitive characteristics, aviation infrastructure is characterized by many of the scale and network characteristics found in rail. Accordingly, governmental or some central responsibility for air safety and air traffic control must be restored. Centralized air reservation and navigation systems are warranted, as they constitute essential infrastructure for a competitive air sector and will generate hard currency from growing international traffic. The opening up of polar routes and other shortcuts between Western Europe and the Far East – already a reality by the end of 1992 – promises considerable savings to international airlines, part of which can be captured by the new republics through overflight fees.

As with the other modes, vertical divestment is required. There is no need for individual airlines to own or operate their local airports and airways. Indeed, the airways are almost surely better operated on a centralized, even multi-republic, basis. Airlines are also naturally competitive but not to the same extent as highway and water operations. The former Soviet Union does not need one hundred or more airlines, but probably can sustain ten or so airlines quite efficiently and competitively. Accordingly, some reconsolidation is in order. Furthermore, airlines, like railroads, need integrated payment and reservation systems so as to better coordinate and improve service. These systems logically might be cooperatively owned joint ventures of the various airlines. Many CIS cities want to upgrade their airports. However, the most worthwhile projects are those that have a sound institutional framework and a credible business plan based on realistic traffic forecasts and cost-recovery mechanisms. In most instances, this policy will require relatively modest incremental investments to improve existing facilities.

Summary: Policy Options and the Role of Government

The modal surveys, summarized in chapters 4 through 7, comprise an initial diagnostic review of the transport situation and prospects in the former Soviet Union. These opportunities represent a major challenge for governments (everywhere, but especially in the former Soviet Union given its history) and for multilateral institutions: a shift from a direct, primary provider role to a marshaling, managing, and monitoring function. Whether this transition can be achieved by these organizations remains an open question, but much hinges on their success.

Above all else, a successful transition to a market economy requires that market and legal fundamentals be in place. Government can help fill the void by creating a better framework for development of market institutions – by defining legal rights, reducing social welfare burdens on enterprises, deregulating tariffs and factor prices (particularly for energy), and providing some residual regulation wherever it still might be needed. Bankruptcy laws should be introduced so that failing companies can transfer operating assets to other firms. Transport companies that remain in the public sector must be managed in a more commercial manner, with greater accountability.

Financial institutions, both foreign and domestic, can be helpful by providing support for key initiatives, particularly those aimed at organizational restructuring and infrastructure. The experience of other nations suggests that substantial benefits in construction and operating efficiency, financing, and capacity management may be possible by developing a larger role for the private sector in road infrastructure. The development of toll or other user-cost funding mechanisms should encourage limited or nonrecourse lending structures, thereby preserving government resources for more general purposes. Also, it should not be assumed that if sovereign finance is required initially, it will continue to be needed over the longer term. As an economy stabilizes and demand patterns become apparent, project or user financing becomes more feasible. This might be done either by converting full-recourse to a limited-recourse basis at some point, or by fully substituting private finance for the sovereign issue when possible. The strategy should be to think of sovereign finance not as a long-term commitment but rather as "seed" or "bridge" capital to get projects up and running during the riskiest early phases.

The role of government in transport does not disappear with the transition from a command to a market economy. It is not even obvious that the total scope or scale of government activities is diminished by such a transition, at least by many measures. What is clear is that the nature or character of the government role changes with the transition. Specifically, in a market economy, the government's roles as auditor, regulator, contractor, jurist, overseer, rule-maker, and monitor all appear to increase, while government becomes less involved in the management and operation of most sectors, including transport.

In essence, the critical distinction may not be so much how much government there should be, but rather what kind of government should be established. This perspective requires defining the frontier between the public and private sectors, based on what each sector can do best. The creation of such an environment will not be easy, especially in the increasingly complex world of international finance, with its proliferation of forms, instruments, and institutions. However, that same proliferation also creates opportunities of great potential, enhancing possibilities for managing a variety of policy problems in the transition economies.

Notes

1   "Company towns" have been characteristic of market economies for centuries, if not millennia.

2   See R. Frydman and A. Rapaczynski, "Evolution and Design in the East European Tradition," C. V. Starr Center for Applied Economics Economic Research Report 91–3, New York University (September 1991); EBRD, IMF, OECD, and the World Bank, *Joint Study of the Soviet Economy* (OECD: Paris, 1991); World Bank, *Russian Economic Reform: Crossing the Threshold of Structural Change* (Washington, DC: World Bank, 1992), ch. 6; J. Kornai, "The Soft Budget Constraint," *Kyklos* 39 (1986): 3–30; J. Kornai, *The Socialist System: The Political Economy of Communism* (Princeton, NJ: Princeton University Press, 1992); Kornai, "The Postsocialist Transition and the State," *American Economic Review* 82, 2 (May 1992): 1–21; E. Hewett, *Reforming the Soviet Economy* (Washington, DC: Brookings Institution, 1988).

3   See O. Williamson, *Markets and Hierarchies: Analysis and Antitrust Implications* (New York: Free Press, 1975); O. Williamson, *The Economic Institutions of Capitalism* (New York: Free Press, 1985).

4   These "ties that bind" are likely to induce aggressive opportunism from each party attempting to extract rents from the bilateral relation. This situation is worsened in the presence of readily available inter-enterprise credits and the soft budget constraint. These credits create impediments to separating these activities, while giving rise to contentious issues over which partner contributed more to the relationship.

5   See J. A. Goméz-Ibañéz and J. R. Meyer, *Going Private: The International Experience with Transport Privatization* (Washington: Brookings Institution, 1993), chap. 11.

6   See W. Baumol, "On the Perils of Privatization," C. V. Starr Center for Applied Economics, Economic Research Report 93–22, New York University (May 1993).

7   See L. Lowenstein, *Sense and Nonsense in Corporate Finance* (Reading, MA.: Addison-Wesley, 1991); J. C. Coffee, Jr., L. Lowenstein, and S. Rose-Ackerman, *Knights, Raiders, and Targets: The Impact of the Hostile Takeover* (New York: Oxford University Press, 1988); A. Shleifer and L. Summers, "Breach of Trust in Hostile Takeovers," in A. Auerbach, ed., *Corporate Takeovers: Causes and Consequences* (Chicago: University of Chicago Press, 1988), 33–56.

8   See J-J. Laffont, "The New Economics of Regulation: Ten Years After," *Econometrica* 62, 3 (May 1994): 507–537; C. D. Foster, *Privatization, Public Ownership, and the Regulation of Natural Monopoly* (Oxford: Blackwell, 1992).

9   See J. A. Goméz-Ibañéz and J. R. Meyer, *Going Private: The International Experience with Transport Privatization*, chaps. 2–4.

Bibliography

Moses Abramowitz, "Catching Up, Forging Ahead, and Falling Behind," *Journal of Economic History*, Vol. 46, No. 2, June 1986.

Aerodev Consultants Ltd., *Aviation Surveys of Russia, Belarus, Ukraine, and Kazakhstan* (London: European Bank for Reconstruction and Development, 1993).

Aerodev Consultants Ltd., *Civil Aviation Sector Survey* (London: European Bank for Reconstruction and Development, 1993).

Abel Aganbegyan, *Moving the Mountain: Inside the Perestroika Revolution* (London: Bantam Press, 1989).

Anders Åslund, *The Post-Soviet Economy: Soviet and Western Perspectives* (London: Pinter, 1992).

Alan Auerbach, ed., *Corporate Takeovers: Causes and Consequences* (Chicago: University of Chicago Press, 1988).

Harvey Averch and Leland Johnson, "Behavior of the Firm Under Regulatory Constraint," *American Economic Review*, Vol. 52, No. 4, December 1962.

Joseph Badaracco, "Changing Forms of the Corporation," chapter 4 in John Meyer and James Gustafson, eds., *The U.S. Business Corporation: An Institution in Transition* (Cambridge, MA: Ballinger, 1988).

Leszek Balcerowicz and Alan Gelb, "Macropolicies in Transition to a Market Economy: A Three-Year Perspective," mimeo, Annual Bank Conference on Development Economics, Washington: World Bank, April 1994.

Nicholas Barr, "Income Transfers and the Social Safety Net in Russia," Studies of Economies in Transition No. 4 (Washington: World Bank, 1992).

Christopher Bartlett and Sumantra Ghoshal, *Managing Across Borders: The Transnational Solution* (Boston: Harvard Business School Press, 1989).

William Baumol, "Productivity Growth, Convergence, and Welfare: What the Long-Run Data Show," *American Economic Review*, Vol. 78, No. 5, December 1986.

William Baumol, "On the Perils of Privatization," C. V. Starr Center for Applied Economics, Economic Research Report #93-22, New York University, May 1993.

William Baumol and David Bradford, "Optimal Departures from Marginal Cost Pricing," *American Economic Review*, Vol. 60, No. 2, 1970.

William Baumol and Alvin Klevorick, "Input Choices and Rate-of-Return Regulation: An Overview of the Discussion," *Bell Journal of Economics*, Vol. 1, No. 2, 1970.

William Baumol, John Panzar, and Robert Willig, *Contestable Markets and the Theory of Industry Structure* (San Diego: Harcourt Brace Jovanovich, 1982).

Abram Bergson, *Planning and Performance in the Socialist Economic System* (London: Routledge, 1986).

Abram Bergson, *Planning and Performance in Socialist Economies: The U.S.S.R. and Eastern Europe* (Boston: Unwin Hyman, 1989).

Joseph Berliner, *The Innovation Decision in Soviet Industry* (Cambridge: MIT Press, 1976).

Oliver Blanchard, Simon Commander, and Fabrizio Coricelli, "Labor Markets in Eastern Europe," mimeo, World Bank, 1993.

Tito Boeri and Mark Kwwaw, "Labour Markets and the Transition in Central and Eastern Europe," *OECD Economic Studies*, No. 18, 1992.

Arnoud Boot and Anjan Thakor, "Security Design," *Journal of Finance*, Vol. 48, No. 4, September 1993.

Booz-Allen & Hamilton and Travers Morgan, *Railway Sector Survey of the Independent States of Russia, Belarus, Ukraine, and Kazakhstan* (London: European Bank for Reconstruction and Development, 1993).

Stijn Claessens, "Alternative Forms of External Finance: A Survey," *World Bank Research Observer*, Vol. 8 No. 1, January 1993.

John Coffee, Jr., Louis Lowenstein, and Susan Rose-Ackerman, *Knights, Raiders, and Targets: The Impact of the Hostile Takeover* (New York: Oxford University Press, 1988).

Commission of the European Communities, Directorate-General for Economic and Financial Affairs, *Stabilization, Liberalization, and Devolution: Assessment of the Economic Situation and Reform Process in the Soviet Union*, No. 45 (Brussels: European Commission, 1990).

Julian Cooper, *The Soviet Defense Industry* (London: Royal Institute of International Affairs, 1991).

Vittorio Corbo, Fabrizio Coricelli, and Jan Bossak, *Reforming Central and Eastern European Economies* (Washington: World Bank, 1991).

COWIconsult-TecnEcon, *Roads and Road Transport in Russia, Ukraine, Belarus, and Kazakhstan* (London: European Bank for Reconstruction and Development, 1993).

Robert Davies, Mark Harrison, and Stephen Wheatcroft, eds., *The Economic Transformation of the Soviet Union, 1913–1945* (New York: Cambridge University Press, 1994).

David Dollar and Edward Wolff, *Competitiveness, Convergence, and International Specialization* (Cambridge: MIT Press, 1993).

John Donahue, *The Privatization Decision: Public Ends, Private Means* (New York: Basic Books, 1989).

Michael Dutta, "Economic Regionalization in Western Europe: Macroeconomic Core, Microeconomic Optimization," *American Economic Review*, Vol. 82, No. 2, May 1992.

W.W. Eason, "The Soviet Population Today," *Foreign Affairs*, Vol. 37, No. 4, July 1959.

William Easterly and Stanley Fischer, *The Soviet Economic Decline*, Policy Research Working Paper No. 1284 (Washington: World Bank, 1994).

European Bank for Reconstruction and Development, *EBRD Economic Review: Annual Economic Outlook* (London: European Bank for Reconstruction and Development, September 1993).

Malcolm Falkus, *Industrialisation of Russia 1700–1914* (London: Macmillan, 1972).

Stanley Fischer, "Privatization in East European Transformation," in Christopher Clague and Gordon Rausser, eds., *The Emergence of Market Economies in Eastern Europe* (Cambridge, MA: Blackwell, 1992).

Stanley Fischer, "Russia and the Soviet Union: Then and Now," Working Paper No. 4077 (Cambridge, MA: National Bureau of Economic Research, May 1992).

Stanley Fischer and Alan Gelb, "Issues in Socialist Economy Reform" PRE Working Paper 565 (Washington: World Bank, December 1990).

Christopher Foster, *Privatization, Public Ownership, and the Regulation of Natural Monopoly* (Oxford: Blackwell, 1992).

Roman Frydman, Andrzej Rapaczynski, John Earle, et al., *The Privatization Process in Central Europe* (two volumes) (Budapest: Central European University Press, 1993).

Dennis Gayle and Jonathan Goodrich, eds., *Privatization and Deregulation in Global Perspective* (New York: Quorum Books, 1990).

José Gómez-Ibañez, "The Political Economy of Highway Pricing and Congestion," *Transportation Quarterly,* Vol. 46, No. 31, July 1992.

José Gómez-Ibañez and John Meyer, *Going Private: The International Experience with Transport Privatization* (Washington: Brookings Institution, 1993).

Cosmo Graham and Tony Prosser, *Privatizing Public Enterprises: Constitutions, the State, and Regulation in Comparative Perspective* (Oxford: Clarendon Press, 1991).

Loren Graham, *The Ghost of the Executed Engineer: Technology and the Fall of the Soviet Union* (Cambridge, MA: Harvard University Press, 1993).

Brigitte Granville, *Price and Currency Reform in Russia and the CIS* (London: Royal Institute of International Affairs, 1992).

Edward Hewett, *Reforming the Soviet Economy* (Washington: Brookings Institution, 1988).

Harold Hotelling, "The General Welfare in Relation to Problems of Taxation and of Railway and Utility Rates," *Econometrica*, Vol. 6, No. 4, December 1937.

Jerry Hough, "The Soviet Attitude Toward Integration in the World Economy," in Gary Bertsch and Steven Elliott-Gower, eds., *The Impact of Governments on East-West Economic Relations* (London: Macmillan, 1991).

Holland Hunter, *Soviet Transport Experience* (Washington: Brookings Institution, 1968).

Holland Hunter, ed., *The Future of the Soviet Economy, 1978–1985* (Boulder: Westview Press, 1978).

Holland Hunter, Peggy Dunn, Vladimir Kontorovich, and Janusz Szyrmer, "Soviet Transport Trends, 1959–1990," *Soviet Economy*, Vol. 1, No. 3, July-September 1985.

Holland Hunter and Janusz Szyrmer, *Faulty Foundations: Soviet Economic Policy 1928–1940* (Princeton: Princeton University Press, 1992).

Barry Ickes and Randi Ryterman, "The Inter-Enterprise Arrears Crisis in Russia," *Post Soviet Affairs* (formerly *Soviet Economy*), October-December 1992.

Ian Jeffries, *Industrial Reform in Socialist Countries: from Restructuring to Revolution* (Aldershot: Edward Elgar, 1992).

Ian Jeffries, *Socialist Economies and the Transition to the Market* (London: Routledge, 1993).

Michael Jensen, "The Modern Industrial Revolution, Exit, and the Failure of Internal Control Systems," *Journal of Finance*, Vol. 48, No. 3, July 1993.

Paul Joskow, Richard Schmalensee, and Natalia Tsukanova, "Competition Policy in Russia during and after Privatization," *Brookings Papers on Economic Activity: Microeconomics 1994*.

Michael Katz and Carl Shapiro, "Network Externalities, Competition, and Compatibility," *American Economic Review* Vol. 75, No. 3, June 1985.

Michael Katz and Carl Shapiro, "Systems Competition and Network Effects," *Journal of Economic Perspectives*, Vol. 8, No. 2, Spring 1994.

John Kay, Colin Mayer, and David Thompson, eds., *Privatization and Regulation: The U.K. Experience* (Oxford: Clarendon Press, 1986).

Sunita Kikeri, John Nellis, and Mary Shirley, *Privatization: The Lessons of Experience* (Washington: World Bank, 1993).

Lawrence Kolbe, William Tye, and Stewart Myers, *Regulatory Risk: Economic Principles and Applications to Natural Gas Pipelines and Other Industries* (Boston: Kluwer, 1991).

Janos Kornai, "The Soft Budget Constraint," *Kyklos*, Vol. 39, No. 1, 1986.

Janos Kornai, "The Postsocialist Transition and the State: Reflections in the Light of Hungarian Fiscal Problems," *American Economic Review*, Vol. 82, No. 2, May 1992.

Janos Kornai, "The Principles of Privatization in Eastern Europe," *The Economist*, Vol. 140, No. 2, 1992.

Janos Kornai, *The Socialist System: The Political Economy of Communism* (Oxford: Oxford University Press, 1992).

Rachel E. Kranton, "Pricing, Cost Recovery, and Production Efficiency in Transport: A Critique," World Bank Working Paper WPS 445 (Washington: World Bank, June 1990).

Jean-Jacques Laffont, "The New Economic of Regulation: Ten Years After," *Econometrica*, Vol. 62, No. 3, May 1994.

Edward Leamer, *Sources of International Comparative Advantage: Theory and Evidence* (Cambridge, MA: MIT Press, 1984).

Jeffrey M. Lenorovitz, "Former Soviet Union Expands Air Safety Ties with West," *Aviation Week and Space Technology*, January 25, 1993.

Stanley Liebowitz and Stephen Margolis, "Network Externalities: An Uncommon Tragedy," *Journal of Economic Perspectives*, Vol. 8, No. 2, Spring 1994.

David Lipton and Jeffrey Sachs, "Creating a Market in Eastern Europe: The Case of Poland," *Brookings Papers on Economic Activity*, No. 1, 1990.

Louis Lowenstein, *Sense and Nonsense in Corporate Finance* (Reading, MA: Addison-Wesley, 1991).

Ronald McKinnon, *The Order of Economic Liberalization: Financial Control in the Transition to a Market Economy* (Baltimore: Johns Hopkins University Press, 1991).

Julian Moxon, "Testing Times," *Flight International*, December 15–21, 1993.

Roger Munting, *The Economic Development of the USSR* (London: Croom Helm, 1982).

Nedeco Consultants, *Waterborne Transport Survey: Russian Federation, Ukraine, Kazakhstan* (London: European Bank for Reconstruction and Development, 1993).

John Nellis, "Contract Plans and Public Enterprise Performance," World Bank Working Paper PPR WPS-118 (Washington: World Bank, October 1988).

Richard Nelson and Sidney Winter, *An Evolutionary Theory of Economic Change* (Cambridge, MA: Harvard University Press, 1982).

Richard Nelson and Gavin Wright, "The Rise and Fall of American Technological Leadership," *Journal of Economic Literature*, Vol. XXX, No. 4, December 1992.

Alec Nove, *An Economic History of the USSR* (London: Penguin Press, 1969).

Clinton Oster, John Strong and C. Kurt Zorn, *Why Airplanes Crash: Aviation Safety in a Changing World* (New York: Oxford University Press, 1992).

Dwight Perkins, "Reforming the Economic Systems of Vietnam and Laos," in *The Challenge of Reform in Indochina*, Börje Ljunggren, ed. (Cambridge, MA: Harvard Institute for International Development, 1993).

Russell Pittman, "Some Critical Provisions in the Antimonopoly Laws of Central and Eastern Europe," *The International Lawyer*, Vol. 26, No. 2, Summer 1992.

Frank Ramsey, "A Contribution to the Theory of Taxation," *Economic Journal*, Vol. 37, No. 1, 1927.

Jeffrey Sachs, "Privatization in Russia: Some Lessons from Eastern Europe," *American Economic Review*, Vol. 80, No. 2, May 1992.

Jeffrey Sachs, "Russia's Struggle with Stabilization: Conceptual Issues and Evidence," mimeo, Annual Bank Conference on Development Economics, Washington: World Bank, April 1994.

Jeffrey Sachs, "Beyond Bretton Woods: A New Blueprint," *The Economist*, Vol. 333, No. 7883, October 1, 1994.

Geoffrey Schroeder, *Soviet Economic Reform Decrees*, United States Congress Joint Economic Committee (Washington: Government Printing Office, 1992).

Geoffrey Schroeder, "The Soviet Industrial Enterprise in the 1980s," in Ian Jeffries, ed., *Industrial Reform in Socialist Countries: from Restructuring to Revolution* (Aldershot: Edward Elgar, 1992).

William Geoffrey Shepherd, "'Contestability' versus Competition," *American Economic Review*, Vol. 74, No. 3, June 1984.

Andrei Shleifer and Lawrence Summers, "Breach of Trust in Hostile Takeovers" in A. Auerbach, ed., *Corporate Takeovers: Causes and Consequences* (Chicago: University of Chicago Press, 1988).

Andrei Shleifer and Robert Vishny, "Reversing the Soviet Economic Collapse," *Brookings Papers on Economic Activity*, No. 2, 1991.

Andrei Shleifer and Robert Vishny, "Corruption," *Quarterly Journal of Economics*, Vol. CVIII, No. 3, August 1993.

Alan Smith, *Russia and the World Economy* (London: Routledge, 1993).

George Stigler, "The Theory of Economic Regulation," *Bell Journal of Economics*, Vol. 2, No. 2, Spring 1971.

William Tye, *The Transition to Deregulation* (New York: Quorum Books, 1991).

Alexander Velovich, "A Safe Place to Fly?" *Flight International*, January 12-18, 1994.

Raymond Vernon, "The Fragile Foundations of East-West Trade," in Raymond Vernon, ed., *Exploring the Global Economy: Emerging Issues in Trade and Investment* (Lanham, MD: University Press of America, 1985).

Raymond Vernon, *The Promise of Privatization: A Challenge for U.S. Policy* (New York: Council on Foreign Relations, 1988).

John S. Vickers and George K. Yarrow, *Privatization: An Economic Analysis* (Cambridge, MA: MIT Press, 1988).

Martin Weitzman, "Soviet Postwar Economic Growth and Capital-Labor Substitution," *American Economic Review*, Vol. 60, No. 5, December 1979.

Oliver Williamson, *Markets and Hierarchies: Analysis and Antitrust Implications* (New York: Free Press, 1975).

Oliver Williamson, *The Economic Institutions of Capitalism* (New York: Free Press, 1985).

Robert Willig, "Public versus Regulated Privated Enterprise," *Proceedings of the World Bank Annual Conference on Development Economics* (Washington: World Bank, 1993).

James Q. Wilson, *The Politics of Regulation* (New York: Basic Books, 1980).

World Bank, *Sector Report: Russian Federation Transport Sector Strategy* (Washington: World Bank, May 1993).

David Zaslow, "Trucking in the Soviet Economy," *Soviet Geography*, Vol. 31, No. 1, March 1990.

Richard Zeckhauser and John Pound, "Are Large Shareholders Effective Monitors?" in R. Glenn Hubbard, ed., *Asymmetric Information, Corporate Finance, and Investment* (Chicago: University of Chicago Press, 1990).

Index